Researching the Middle East

RESEARCH METHODS FOR THE ARTS AND HUMANITIES

Published Titles

Research Methods for Creating and Curating Data in the Digital Humanities
Edited by Matt Hayler and Gabriele Griffin

Research Methods for Reading Digital Data in the Digital Humanities
Edited by Gabriele Griffin and Matt Hayler

Research Methods for Memory Studies
Edited by Emily Keightley and Michael Pickering

Research Methods for English Studies (2nd edition)
Edited by Gabriele Griffin

Research Methods in Theatre and Performance
Edited by Baz Kershaw and Helen Nicholson

Research Methods for History (2nd edition)
Edited by Simon Gunn and Lucy Faire

Practice-led Research, Research-led Practice in the Creative Arts
Edited by Hazel Smith and Roger T. Dean

Research Methods for Cultural Studies
Edited by Michael Pickering

Research Methods for Law (2nd edition)
Edited by Mike McConville and Wing Hong Chui

Researching the Middle East
Edited by Lorraine Charles, Ilan Pappé and Monica Ronchi

edinburghuniversitypress.com/series/rmah

Researching the Middle East

Cultural, Conceptual, Theoretical and Practical Issues

Edited by Lorraine Charles, Ilan Pappé and Monica Ronchi

EDINBURGH
University Press

Edinburgh University Press is one of the leading university presses in the UK. We publish academic books and journals in our selected subject areas across the humanities and social sciences, combining cutting-edge scholarship with high editorial and production values to produce academic works of lasting importance. For more information visit our website: edinburghuniversitypress.com

Edinburgh University Press Ltd
The Tun – Holyrood Road
12 (2f) Jackson's Entry
Edinburgh EH8 8PJ

Typeset in 11/13 Ehrhardt by
Servis Filmsetting Ltd, Stockport, Cheshire

A CIP record for this book is available from the British Library

ISBN 978 1 4744 4030 1 (hardback)
ISBN 978 1 4744 4031 8 (paperback)
ISBN 978 1 4744 4032 5 (webready PDF)
ISBN 978 1 4744 4033 2 (epub)

Contents

Figures

Introduction

Lorraine Charles, Ilan Pappé and Monica Ronchi

In this past decade, it has become quite challenging for Middle Eastern scholars to conduct research inside and on the region. It has never been easy to research an area where archives were either closed or absent altogether and where non-transparent political systems control every aspect of people's socio-political life. More recently, political instability has made research even less feasible and, in some cases, research on the ground has constituted a personal threat for scholars, who have been persistently under the surveillance of suspicious governments and their agencies.

While protracted political instability and conflict in Syria, Iraq and Yemen have made research in these countries almost impossible, countries that are considered 'safe' have also posed physical dangers to researchers of the region. The arrest, imprisonment and subsequent life sentence for alleged spying of PhD student Matthew Hedges in the United Arab Emirates; the brutal murder of PhD student Giulio Regeni in Egypt, possibly at the hands of the Egyptian government; and the gruesome murder of journalist Jamal Khashoggi in the Saudi Embassy in Turkey ordered by the Saudi government, are all examples of the current challenges (and dangers) that researchers (and journalists) face when conducting research in, and writing on, the Middle East.

This was not always the case and may probably change in the future. But, for the present, for scholars engaging with the region this is an acute issue, and this volume is written mainly by such scholars who in their work have confronted this and other predicaments. This publication reflects other principal concerns of new and more veteran researchers working in and on the Middle East and North Africa (MENA). The first issue to face in our exploration is the question of ethics as manifested in constant reference to positionality and full awareness of previous warnings, from as early as the 1960s, of adopting condescending or reductionist orientalist attitudes and practices. In a sense, this volume allows the researcher to share invaluable experiences surrounding the academic work itself.

As the various chapters of this volume show, the personal experience of the researcher within the area plays an important part in addressing the usefulness of conceptual or theoretical frameworks and the employment of methodologies, carved in theory and tested on the ground. This experience is an important constitutive element of research, and just as relevant to understand the process of knowledge production as theory, methodology and data.

This new volume also seeks to question accepted typologies and categorisations in former studies of the area. Some of the old, and misleading framing has returned to the public domain in the wake of the Arab Spring and here we seek to rely again on the more constructive and complex reference to notions such as sectarianism, tribalism, ethnicity and terrorism.

Methodology is one of the central themes visited and re-visited in this publication. Discussions revolving around each scholar's methodology are closely associated with questions of positionality and of the awareness of contextualisation by Western-educated scholars examining data coming from the region. Whether quantitative or qualitative, this data is contextual and dependent on research paradigms, as can be seen from the various chapters in this volume.

The habitat, interests and tastes of scholars are not far removed from those of the younger generation of people from the region that have attempted so drastically and dramatically to change its history. Thus, both the internet and fashion also feature in this volume as indicators of trends within different strata of society, influencing and in turn being influenced by countless generations of men and women.

This also seeks to be a volume made by (and, more importantly, for) researchers safely navigating the question of Middle East exceptionality as a study area. The common theme is that without intending to propagate the narrative of Middle East exceptionalism, this volume explores the necessity of a close familiarity with language, culture and localities in order to fully understand the social, political, economic and historical dynamics that have shaped both space and peoples. This volume provides an exploration of various aspects of Middle East studies as seen through the lens of the individual experiences of researchers and provides insight into a complicated region that still fascinates local and international scholars alike.

The first chapter is designed to introduce the reader to the intricacies of past and present research in the region, setting the thematic path on which reader is set to travel within this volume. To do so, Pappé looks at the methodological and theoretical developments in the field of Middle Eastern Studies in the twenty-first century. While decidedly focusing on developments in the modern history of the region, it also acknowledges the need to investigate similar developments in ancient and early modern historiography, and to revisit historiographical research in search of clarifications and explanations of the new upheaval and uncertainty that is evident in the Middle East today. In this chapter Pappé therefore focuses on new methodologies that have been employed to investigate a number of questions at the core of Middle East and Islamic studies: the role of Islam and the Left in modern times; the validity of the post-World War I diplomatic arrangements; the role of imperialism and settler colonialism in the Middle East; political culture and its development; the impact of Zionism and finally the political economy of the region.

Moving on to the second chapter, Costantini and Milton bring us closer to a more specific typology of scholarship on the Middle East, evaluating the specificities of conducting research on conflict and post-conflict settings in the Middle East within the context of the Arab Spring. This chapter draws on the real-life experience of the authors, who have conducted research on Iraq and Libya, and identifies the limits that these, as well as similar contexts, could impose on the self-aware researcher. Costantini and Milton's use of social and political categories, as well as geography, is problematised as part of the reading and interpretation of observations. The authors evaluate their role as researchers, their positionality and reflexivity against the role and functions of research in the midst of conflict and violent post-conflict transitions.

The third chapter takes a closer look at our understanding of sectarianism within the region, questioning the sectarian lines in Lebanese politics and society beyond the most visible forms of the sectarian system. Almuedo-Castillo specifically examines those cases where Lebanese do not give way to the tentacles of the sectarian dominance and find their paths of resistance. The author argues that these forms of research, consisting in extended ethnographic work and in-depth case-study research, give real visibility to these quiet actions of resistance, creating a better understanding of the sectarian system and the diverse forms of contention. Through her own reflection upon her time conducting fieldwork in Lebanon, she provides an understanding of a different, lesser known and prone to the spotlight, side of Lebanon. Through ethnographic techniques this chapter allow us to fully understand the process of construction and deconstruction of the Lebanese sectarian system as an 'ideological hegemon'.

In the fourth chapter of this volume, Charles moves on to exploring the challenges in conducting research on livelihoods in protectionist labour markets in Jordan, Lebanon and Turkey, focusing specifically on the context of the Syrian refugee crisis. In her work, she explores how conventional narratives need to be reconsidered when carrying out research on livelihoods in such protectionist environments. In particular, the author highlights how research around livelihoods for refugees require focus on alternative and innovative interventions that bypass the legal restrictions imposed by governments. The chapter, therefore, not only looks at the challenges in conducting research, but also at the opportunities that have evolved through the examination of this very difficult topic, and that have helped influence broader scholarship in the region.

Opening our reflections on identity and positionality in Middle East Studies and moving closer to the Gulf Region, Chapter 5 focuses on conducting ethnographic research in the United Arab Emirates among the Emirati population. This subject is often overlooked within the field, particularly due to the issue of access. Hoping to help overcome this age-old obstacle to Gulf Studies research, this chapter examines the ways in which young Emirati nationals who come from diverse tribal, ethnic and racial origins and legal statuses articulate and experience their national identity. Akinci's ethnographic fieldwork on such a difficult topic was made possible due to her own experience living in the country prior to her fieldwork and teaching at an Emirati university while conducting her research. The chapter discusses the methodological challenges encountered in the field, unique to the topic, and the obstacles of accessing and convincing informants to take part in this research, highlighting practical ways in which they were eventually overcome. She also describes how her positionality (particularly her role as part of an institution of higher education) and her nationality (Turkish), made it possible to conduct what would otherwise be highly difficult fieldwork.

The sixth chapter explores the methodological limitations affecting the contemporary study of 'terrorism', particularly focusing on addressing how and why the researcher – and academia as a whole – has been unable or unwilling to adequately address long-standing academic issues. McNeil-Willson suggests that the researcher has become both an accomplice and a hostage to mechanisms of governmental power, becoming thus implicated in, and acting to perpetuate, processes of societal securitisation. Moreover, the author argues that critical terrorism paradigms are in fact limited by their theoretical entanglements, methodological paucity, and their ultimate inability to adequately dislodge the current security paradigm. He concludes that such problems ultimately risk entrenching the impasse in the already impoverished contemporary research of so-called 'terrorist' groups. The chapter weaves a general and critical methodological discussion with particular reference to its application to the Middle East. Indeed, one cannot, and should not exceptionalise the discussion on terrorism in the region. On the other hand, one should recognise that problematising the question of terrorism in the Middle East is most relevant to the general question of how to research terrorism. As this chapter clearly shows, in our century most cases associated with terrorism are in or from the area, hence their analysis cannot be dissociated from the general discussion on this problem.

The following chapter remains within the geographical scope of the Arab Gulf to once again discuss issues of positionality and access as key challenges for conducting quantitative research in the area, using academic research on women in politics in the Gulf, particularly examples from Qatar, to offer practical advice for researchers seeking to collect and examine data from the region. In particular, Shockley argues that bridging the divide between qualitative and quantitative methods in the Arab Gulf is only possible when researchers share a common concern for data quality and cultural relevance, and that collecting and analysing high quality quantitative data requires cross-cultural coordination to overcome the challenges of positionality and access often faced by researchers. What is unique in this particular chapter is the wish, quite typical to a new generation of scholars, to extend the ethical discussion also to the dry collection of quantitative data – it is a neutral act of scholarship. While it seems natural that qualitative research is done within a subjective context, this is rarely assumed to be the case for quantitative analysis. It may seem a mundane issue, but quantitative scholars need to partner with firms for conducting their research. The choice of partners is both professional and ethical. Ethically, issues of gender, class and politics can affect the partnership and should be taken into consideration. Protecting the anonymity of the partners themselves should be considered, as well as the limitations of joint publishing.

Moving away from the Gulf region, which had been at the core of research discussed in previous chapters, we reach contested regions such as Palestine and Kurdistan, which are placed at the centre of Richter-Devroe and Buffon's reflections on what feminist research practice means in the context of conducting ethnographic work in politically-charged settings. Relying on their long-term experience in the Kurdish region of South-West Turkey and in Palestine, the authors attempt to uncover and account for ordinary women's subjective and experience-based knowledge of everyday life. They challenge Western hegemonic, modernist, elite-based and/or male-dominated knowledge claims in fields ranging from politics and history to medicine and healing and ultimately argue that that 'gender is everywhere', i.e. that any research, not only if focused on women, needs to consider gender in its intersection with race, class, sexuality, etc., as a core analytical variable influencing dynamics in the region.

Moving from the exploration of the self to that of the 'other' is integral to ethnographic research, and in Chapter 9 Mahoudeau and Mirman examine methodologies and ethics related to working with interpreters in qualitative research. In their work, they show how being bilingual in scholarly research can provide the opportunity to observe relations with interpreters as a practice of research, instead of rendering it taboo. Moreover, they explore how this relationship manifested as a useful tool in their own fieldwork, and how they were able to integrate, understand and describe the local social dynamics, managing potential conflicts by integrating the interpreters themselves into the research. They argue that in this context, interpreters became 'third men' in the fieldwork, an integral yet external factor in their own ethnographic research in the Middle East.

Continuing on from Mahoudeau and Mirman's evaluation of language as a tool for the evaluation of social dynamics, Giorgia Ferrari explores the specific challenges related to conducting research on the Arabic language itself. As Arabic is characterised by different language varieties coexisting within the same speech community, conducting research in the Arab-speaking world requires linguistic competence in at least two varieties of Arabic, namely Standard Arabic and one local or regional Colloquial Arabic. Ferrari explores how the language choices that native speakers make in both intra- and inter-cultural communication provide an elaborated source of sociolinguistic and metalinguistic information, in turn aiding or hindering the Middle East Studies scholar. It shows why particular language varieties are permeated with meaning and power, and why metalinguistic competence is crucial to conduct in-depth research. The author goes as far as suggesting a new methodology for Arabic language acquisition, one that would equip the researcher with tools to acquire two language varieties simultaneously and effectively prepare him or her for scholarly work in the region.

Still focusing on the difficulties related to research through text, the eleventh chapter explores an issue that has long plagued the study of Arabic literature in the West. Deuchar explores the potential pitfalls of applying Western theory to Arabic texts, discussing the temptation that many 'Western' students of Arabic literature may have to read such texts as foreshadowings, permutations, or imitations of dominant Western forms. In particular, she bases this analysis on the recent scholarship of the Lebanese author Fāris al-Shidyāq, discussing his texts as tools to examine the various approaches to this broader 'problem': how to square a theoretical apparatus drawn largely from the study of Western texts and contexts, with texts from the Arabic tradition.

Moving from text to visual discourse, Schmitt draws on his research in East Jerusalem and the Al-Aqsa Mosque, to explore how YouTube can become a powerful tool for ethnographic researchers, particularly in instances where access and safety are an issue. He argues that while YouTube has opened new and expansive horizons for social science research, the implications for this new avenue of exploration are not well defined or understood. The chapter explores the opportunities and benefits, complications and limits that ethnographers encounter by including YouTube videos in their methodological toolkit when they conduct research in conflict zones. In particular, Schmitt argues that since people's social interactions are both online and offline, ethnographers have little choice but to include both. The use of online content for researching Middle Eastern conflict zones allows research-ers to gain access to otherwise restricted locations and circumvent personal risk. The videos therefore reconfigure temporal and spatial limits, allowing researchers access to past events and to be present virtually in multiple sites simultaneously.

Finally, in the chapter that concludes our journey through the challenges and opportunities presented by research in this particular field, Hecker explores symbolism and discourse in Turkey, in particular investigating modest fashion in Turkey through a semiotic lens and adopting Hebdige's methodological approach. The author's approach achieves two main objectives. First and foremost, Hecker wishes to explore ideological dimensions of modest fashion as represented in fashion and lifestyle magazines, advertisements, and fashion shows in Turkey. Moreover, this particular method allows him to demonstrate the breakdown of consensus among pious Muslims in contemporary Turkish society and their changing perception of fashion. Through his work, Hecker therefore provides us with an insightful analysis of how shared meanings can become contested ground, debated through the language of symbolism and visual culture.

Before letting our readers embark on the path detailed in this introduction, we should mention our own journey in creating and curating this volume. This publication is a result of a Research Conference titled 'Researching the Middle East: Fieldwork, Archives, Issues and Ethics' held at the University of Exeter in June 2015. Here, upcoming and established scholars from around the world gathered to share their own experience navigating the field of Middle East and Islamic Studies, and worked towards gaining a better understanding of how to continue our efforts as self-aware researchers in a fast-changing academic environment. This is the core mission of this volume, to help and support the growth of both new and established scholars looking to expand their own research down different and possibly challenging avenues, navigating issues that relate to positionality, ethics and ethnocentric biases.

We do not believe we have gathered all the answers, and in fact it is our opinion that much work has to be done to truly support researchers in their efforts to contribute to such a vast and diverse field. However, we hope this volume will be a starting point for any scholar seeking advice from their peers, as the experience of those who have come before may be a comfort and guide for researchers yet to conduct their own investigations.

Researching Political Dynamics in the Middle East

CHAPTER I

The Past is Here: Reflections on Modern Middle Eastern Historiography

Ilan Pappé

The late Albert Hourani called his last opus magnum *A History of the Arab Peoples* and not *The History* as he believed that there is always more than one version of history and there is never a definitive history (Hourani 1991). A chapter on the history of the historiography of the Middle East is not only one possible version of history, it also, inevitably, will be somewhat idiosyncratic as its scope requires a certain focus that leaves out areas of inquiries, themes and interests that would occupy a central place in someone else's survey. As one of the editors of this book, I was fortunate enough to have access to other contributions and thus knew in advance which historiographical major developments have already been covered by other chapters and I have therefore attempted to highlight those which were of less interest to the other authors of this collection.

I chose two different approaches while reviewing the trajectory of modern Middle Eastern historiography since the 1950s. The first approach traces the fortunes of the meta theory that informed much of Middle Eastern modern historiography: the theory of modernisation. This theory served as the principal prism for analysing the modern history of the region and was employed by historians, knowingly and unknowingly, in their research. This is thus a short history of the modernisation theories in the regional historiography.

The second approach follows the developments in the historiography of the region through some of the major debates that haunted the community of orientalists in the modern era. The most recent debate was the one generated by the the Arab Spring. I hope that such a reprisal will help to identify more clearly patterns of continuity and change in the histography of the region.

A MODERN TRAJECTORY OF HISTORY

Until recently the 'modern' period in the history of the Middle East was defined as that moment in time when the 'traditional' Middle East encountered 'modern' Europe and the West. Europe became modern as a result of an accumulative effect of four revolutions. The Industrial, American, French and Soviet revolutions created a 'modern' Europe within a period of two hundred years that extended to the rest of the world through the twin forces of colonialism and imperialism. The scholarly community in the world engaged in researching the area regards, still today, this encounter as the most significant factor in the lives of the people of the Middle East.

The theoreticians of modernisation assumed that the local society experienced a traumatic moment when the encounter took place: their value system and tradition were challenged by political, moral, economic and social Western notions. This was, according to this view, the moment a non-western society became modern. It was a detectable period of time that involved a sharp break from the non-modern traditional past. It is in essence a rapture with the past that began in Europe and spread throughout the world. The West held the magic wand whose touch enabled allegedly non-Western societies to leave the past behind them (the belief was that with Westernisation came enlightenment and progress).

The 'trauma' according to this analysis produced a mass cognitive dissonance. The reality that had to be protected by, and preserved as, Islamic and in many ways Ottoman values was, in essence, destroyed by the Western invasion. As almost with all cognitive dissonances there were three responses to the dissonance; either adhering to the new dogma, entrenching in the old one, or looking for a golden mean between them. The scholarly research, it should be said, focused mainly on this predicament within the elites. The first response was to be fully Westernised (with all the implications of such a transformation); the second was to retreat into tradition even deeper and reject any innovation that came from the West as 'Bid'a'. The third response was to look for fusion between the two cultures. Secularists, democratic or not, liberals and socialists, followed the first line of reaction; the Salafiyya and other fundamentalist and purist formations the second, and probably most people were in between; notable among them Islamic thinkers, such as Muhammad Abduh, fusing the new and the old into a fresh perception of the changing reality.

The dominant academic response was an elite history of the region. As the 'pre-modern' past was irrelevant, the locals themselves, as long as they were not westernised – were not part of the modern history. To the historian subscribing to classical modernisation theories, natives appear only as receptacles, passive human beings whose lives are changed through the intervention of external dynamic powers that could potentially save them from stagnation.

Modernisation can be traced thorough various phenomena: the industrialisation, urbanisation, hygienisation, secularisation, centralisation, and politicisation of societies. Most of these processes can be quantified by pointing to numbers of factories and hospitals, demographic growth in cities, declining numbers of religious institutions or of religious curricula in schools, new and more centralised administrative units, new representative bodies and new foreign organisations and agents (such as consulates and embassies) and so on. This created the overwhelming impression that modernisation could be articulated and examined in a scientific way.

This conventional view of modernisation enabled theoreticians to construct a pattern of development. Western territorial expansion brought with it technological innovation that triggered social, economic, and political structural changes in non-Western societies, which generated a more stable and successful stage of modernisation. The further adoption of Western political institutions and organisations then helped to reshape local societies 'in the image of the West', on both macro and micro levels. In other words, a society solidified its modernity when certain conditions were met. First, the local people were reorganised in modern social forms: they moved from *Gemeinschaft* (membership in 'intimate' communities) to *Gesellschaft* (membership in a 'nonintimate' society) or from the organic familiar society to the expanded impersonal one. Thus, for instance, the traditional clan was broken down into several more 'functional' Western-style core families, and professional elites were chosen according to their qualifications vis-à-vis the new system and no longer because of their network of connections (which in any case was a very optimistic and unfounded assumption about any modern human society).

The process was seen as inevitable, but nonetheless could be encouraged by Westernised educational systems, secularised political institutions, and reforming policies aimed at capitalising agrarian societies, settling nomads and centralising loose communities.

Per this view, these structural changes were further cemented with the mortar of European political and moral thought. First came ideas that transcended geographical barriers in that they could be applied anywhere – democracy, liberalism, and above all nationalism. Then, at a later stage, perceptions lying behind these ideas were absorbed bringing the process to a successful closure.

Until the 1980s, the theoreticians and orientalists concurred that modernisation was a positive process that would benefit the region as a whole; they disagreed about the chances of success. The optimists among them, such as Albert Hourani, believed not only that this would be a successful process, but that it would be also a profound one. Like his hero Abduh, Hourani believed the internal dynamics of modernisation, and not superficial echoing of external models, would transform the Middle East for the better (Hourani

1993). Pessimists, such as Eli Kedouri and to a certain extent Bernard Lewis (although he excluded Turkey from his pessimistic outlook), doubted the success of such processes of change (Kedourie 1980). Politically this second school of thought provided scholarly scaffolding for an invasive and aggressive Western, and particularly American, policy towards the Middle East. At its worst, this academic view suggested viewing the region as an arena in which the West could rely only on Israel, should bribe autocratic regimes to retain their allegiance, and topple by all means possible those who sided with the Eastern Bloc or did not succumb to Western interests.

Intellectually, the optimist viewpoint resurfaced after the fall of the Soviet Union into even a more simplistic, be it Hegelian, form when scholars such as Francis Fukuyama articulated the modernisation trajectory as leading to his famous 'end of history'; while the pessimist posture found its own successor in the form of a 'clash of civilisations' propagated by Samuel Huntington (Huntington 2005).

In recent years, historians of the Middle East have been making a conscious effort to distance themselves from traditional modernisationist approaches to the area's history. A new generation of historians of the region, inside and outside of it, have adopted a more complex view on this momentous encounter between East and West. Taken together, these historians already form an impressive reformist, and at times, revisionist school; in many ways deconstructing previous Western scholarship on Middle Eastern history. They brought to the fore a far more critical assessment of modernisation as a process and depicted it as a more complex development of change and continuity, benefiting the few at the expense of the many. The destruction and disappearance of past and traditional structures were not always welcomed and in some cases their absence was catastrophic, rather than a blessing. The interests of those pushing forward modernisation and westernisation were exposed quite often as cynical and manipulative; be they insiders or outsiders. This was a more nuanced examination – unearthing the positive impact alongside the more disastrous aspects of the encounter with the West.

This century brought to the fore a more complex study of the processes of change that affected the region. In many ways, like the area itself, scholars were also busy navigating this new paradigm. This is the navigation between modern secularism and features that were deemed by modernisation theories as obsolete and obstacles to progress in the future but turned out to be formidable and resistant residues of the past. Tradition, religion, faith and sectarian identities are not relics of the past that disappeared with the advent of modernisation and westernisation. They adapted to changing realities and remained a vital part of people's lives. They gained resonance when it transpired how disappointing the process of modernisation was for huge sections of the local society. It failed to satisfy the most basic needs of many in the modern Middle East.

It was wrong to essentialise the Middle East, or the Arab World and Islam for that matter, as an object that was modernised successfully or disastrously, just as it is wrong to essentialise the West. The West is a construct as much as the East is – in it live as many victims of modernisation as in the Middle East. It is not a historical coincidence that two failed popular buds of revolutions wilted the moment they began: a social anti neo-liberal protest movement in 2008 in Europe and the USA, which has been silenced and tamed, and the 2011 Arab Spring that turned sour everywhere. The whole globe is now charted in a similar way to the map of the modernised Middle East. Changes of pace take place in Europe as much as they do in the Middle East. The inner cities of the USA, and the slums of South American capitals are as immune to the benefits of modernisation as the Middle Eastern countryside or refugee camps.

So maybe we have returned in a way to the 1950s, when secular left organisations did not single out the Middle East as a unique culture or area, but just another arena for the struggle for social and economic justice. But can they again disregard the powerful message of the other two potent actors on the ground claiming to work for change on behalf of the victims of modernisation: political Islam and nationalism (be it sectarian, ethnic or religious)?

There are various political Islamic groups who perceive Islam as a panacea for the ills of society. Neither in the 1950s, nor today, has it been possible to fuse the two impulses – the universal critique of modernisation and the Islamic one – into a transformation of reality that could survive without a post-revolutionary eternal war between secular and religious forces.

And can the impulse to universally change society be reconciled with the strong wish of ethnic, cultural and religious groups to maintain their autonomy and special characteristics in a changing world? I have no scope here to deal with the issue of gender but obviously testing a universal position on gender with those offered by various political Islamic and ethnic groups illuminate best the challenges ahead (and they are engaged with in other chapters in this book).

In an attempt to provide some answers to these questions, recent scholarship has connected to post-colonial and cultural studies. From there it drew the insight that any dialectical situation (in this case between religion and sectarian affiliation on the one hand, and the impact of modernisation, on the other) means that at the heart of any chance of avoiding a bloody conflict is a dialogue. Not a dialogue that is a war in other means to defeat a rival or a competing point of view, but rather one that transpires as a way of life in a new reality and not as a means of changing it. It is a tough dialogue that does not hide past discriminations and exposes deep moral disagreements. It is not the false dialogue of multiculturalism that is based on amnesia or the existence of parallel worlds with little communication between them. It is the tough terrain charted so well by S. P. Mohanty in his discussion with Cornel West about multiculturalism:

> How do we negotiate between my history and yours? How would it be possible for us to recover our commonality, not the ambiguous imperial-humanist myth of our shared human attributes, which are supposed to distinguish us from animals, but, more significantly, the imbrication of our various pasts and presents, the ineluctable relationships of shared and contested meanings, values, and material resources? It is necessary to assert our dense particularities, our lived and imagined differences; but could we afford to leave untheorized the question of how our differences are intertwined and, indeed, hierarchically organised? Could we, in other words, afford to have entirely different histories, to see ourselves as living – and having lived –in entirely heterogeneous and discrete spaces? (Mohanty 1989)

Mohanty refers of course to an abstract deliberation about these dialogical realties, but they can easily be applied to real life and politics. What they mean in essence is that the dialogical modern and future Middle East nation states will weaken and will have to respect smaller autonomous formations of ethnicity, culture and religiosity in return for keeping the state free from the economic and political domination of one group over others. The history of the region since 2011 has unfolded a different kind of dialogue. The area is engulfed in bloody conflicts where both regimes and the opposition to them have abused basic human and civil rights in their struggle for dominance. And thus, the most relevant scholarship for understanding the origins of this recent calamity is the one that has offered original insights on political Islam on the one hand, and on sectarianism and anti-sectarianism, on the other. The former is a rather a veteran field of Middle Eastern studies and the latter is just emerging.

The new approach to political Islam provides tools for looking at each case study as one possible manifestation of modern adaptation of Islam that is different from one place to another. The scope revealed indicates the multitude options for Islamic groups to engage with political issues that ensure the survival of this point of view for many years to come.

As for sectarianism, which became a popular framework for certain groups of orientalists as a key and a code that explains the present violence in the region (see Chapter 3 in this book), this has been challenged on two levels. The first was to point to the huge impact external intervention has had on the eruption of the present wave of violence, destabilising the political system and at times delicate equilibriums. The second challenge was based on a new reading of the history of various sects that showed that many other options were attempted in reconciling internal solidarity with a more common good, be it social or national.

DEFINING MOMENTS FOR SCHOLARSHIP

We are yet to digest the unfolding dramatic events coined the Arab Spring in the area of which we claim to be academic experts on. This is particularly difficult if we are historians by profession. Very few disciplines can offer caution and measurability at times of dynamic change as history can and should do. The historian's impulse is to wait for a perspective of time, availability of sources and a comprehension of wider contexts. Yet many were the historians who were invited to comment on the present dramatic realities in the Arab world due to their expertise in the history of the area as a whole or a particular country. We were there before when many of us were asked to comment instantly on the 9/11 events. In both cases, long before the haze of uncertainty disappeared, 'experts' of the area in the West, knew they were facing a defining moment in their ability to understand, explain and predict the region's past and present developments.

This transitional period is enigmatic in two major ways. First, one does not know how long this could take and second, we do not possess a clear vision of what is it leading to – in concrete and definable terms. The potential power of these events is strongly felt nonetheless, and even our cautious colleagues and veteran members of our community of scholars concede they are watching history in the making and are even willing to call it a defining moment in the history of the region.

Since there are so many question marks about the significance of recent events for the region's future, it seems a good idea to divert attention to those, like us, who are 'experts' on the area. It seems even more appropriate to call what has become known as the Arab Spring a defining moment for our historiography before concluding if the same is true about the area itself.

The first indication that a regional event is indeed a 'defining moment' is when it seems to take by surprise most experts and scholars engaged in the history and current affairs of that particular region. Surprise of this magnitude beset the orientalist community twice in the past: first when a secular revolutionary wave brought an end to European colonialism in the region in the 1950s and 1960s, and then when a religious one toppled the Shah's regime in Iran in 1979.

An overwhelming sense of inadequacy due to the unpredictable nature of one's field of inquiry is not unique to Middle Eastern Studies. Think about the collapse of the Soviet Union and Sovietologists, and the financial crisis and economists – two out of many examples. The abundance of case studies raises the suspicion that this is a general deficiency of academia that tries to provide goods for its society that it is incapable of delivering.

These inadequacies fed three famous historiographical debates in the field of Middle Eastern studies. Revisiting them is another possible way to appreciate properly the trajectory of Middle Eastern historiography. These were moments of uncertainty that remind us of our present debate in the wake of the Arab Spring.

REAPPRAISAL AND DISSENT: PAST DEBATES

There were three major debates among professional orientalists about their area of inquiry, an uncommon and uncomfortable instance in the life of any academic community. It was when the very essence of what this community of scholars were doing was discussed, either in a very general way or in reference to a particular topic. Quite often, these debates were not triggered by a momentous event but rather, as is so often the case in academia, by a new publication: a new journal in the first two instances and a book in the third.

The first publication was *The Review of Middle East Studies* (RMES), which has attempted since it was published (1972) to redefine the scholarly effort and promote more profound theorisation and conceptualisation in the field so as to overcome western biases and in places to improve what was deemed as poor scholarship. Inevitably this included severe criticism of the mainstream orientalist establishment. *The Review* felt that most research at its time was motivated by a political agenda that blinded it to certain sources, sections of the society and more progressive theorisation. Within the United Kingdom other scholars, such as Albert Hourani, felt too that a more objective scholarship was needed, and a much-expanded interdisciplinary and theoretical acumen was required so that a fuller and a better picture of the past could be presented. While the first assumption – on objectivity – has lost some of its validity, the second one still seems very relevant.

On the other side of the Atlantic, others in the field were pushing forward a similar agenda. Leonard Binder too, in 1976, felt something was missing and wrote that Middle East Studies were 'beset by subjective projections, displacement of affect, ideological distortion, romantic mystification and religious bias' (Binder 1976). In the words of one of the leading members of this group, Talal Asad, these critical voices were looking to distance themselves from their peers' representation of the Middle East as a 'static integral cultural whole' or as essential entity in the words of Edward Said (Asad and Owen 1980).

The first challenge was made by Roger Owen, who confronted head-on one of the basic textbooks of the time on the Ottoman Empire and modern Muslim history in general and offered an alternative way for viewing in particular the period its authors, Gibb and Bowen, described as the decline of the Ottoman Empire (Owen 1975). It has relevance to our present case study, as it was a debate about both the causes for, and consequences of, the fundamental changes in the Middle East. The new focus suggested looking closer at internal, rather than external and Western, dynamics of change. Hence, decline was in the eyes of the Western beholder, not necessarily the reality on the ground.

Owen and the RMES were involved also in the second debate, which was in the late 1970s. One of the leading orientalists of the day, Clement Dodd, stood on the other side of the debate while Owen was joined by Talal Asad. This time the topic was even more relevant to our present predicament: what is the nature of popular revolutions in Arab and Muslim history? In articles in the Review of Middle East Studies (RMES) and in the British Society for Middle Eastern Studies (BRISMES) bulletin, Talal Asad revived an old idea of Marshal Hodgson of a global village (who, alas, died long before this debate granted fresh legitimacy to his views) while challenging Clement Dodd's analysis of popular revolutions in Islamic history. Dodd chose to describe them as 'disorders' and saw uprisings in Muslim history as indicative of disorder as well as constituting it. Talal Asad disagreed and claimed that these uprisings were expressions of a popular resentment to oppression (a notion supported by the social anthropologists of the day such as Evan Pritchard and others) (Asad and Owen 1980).

It may seem absurd today, but there was a need to grant the same universal empathy and admiration to anti-oppression revolutions that were common in the West to similar eruptions in the history of the East. But these were, in both cases, revolts that had a leader or leaders and always had an organisation behind them. And in those instances when these were missing, the events and the people behind them were not counted. Analysing the leaders of revolutions and not the people who make them did not prepare us for the leaderless revolutions of 2011.

This debate was, in many ways, a very late response to the 1950s revolutions in the Arab world. But at the end of the day, Middle Eastern scholarship benefitted enormously from it, since scholars were able to leave behind fossilised notions of what the area was and how it should be studied. The mid-twentieth-century revolutionary age was thus analysed in a more universal, rather than orientalist, way. Now that we are witnessing the attempt to liberate the people from the 1950s revolutions that liberated the lands (but not the people), it may have been too optimistic to see those past revolts in such a universalist light but sticking to the universal and humane approach is even more desirable today than it was then.

So 'Arabs' can revolt, even Muslims, something that the British media, let alone the American media, find bewildering and almost unimaginable. But can revolt be pushed forward without organisation and institutions? It seems that on this Asad and Dodd agreed: populist revolts cannot be substitutes for participatory institutions. So far it seems that their assertion is vindicated by developments on the ground and may offer some learning process for those attempting revolutions without institutions.

The third debate was triggered by Edward Said's *Orientalism* (Said 2000). It was a bitter debate when conducted at the American Middle Eastern Studies Association (MESA) (Bernard Lewis and Leon Wieseltier vs Edward Said and Christopher Hitchens (2018)). Said's severe criticism of scholarly orientalist work was countered from two directions. The first was from Western Middle Eastern scholars, who spent most of their academic time, sometimes even their entire lives, in the Arab world, and needless to say knew the relevant languages well and felt they represented their subjects of inquiry with empathy and solidarity.

The second challenge came from the social scientists, especially those with strong Marxist leanings, who felt that both their ideological preferences and their theoretical expertise made them immune from the kind of misrepresenta-tion the book *Orientalism* exposed and moreover felt that their history from below and their political economic challenges to the hegemonic orientalist scholarship were somewhat sidelined by Said's stress on cultural deconstruc-tion of the orientalist discourse.

Ten years later (1993), in a much calmer tone, Fred Halliday in front of the annual BRISMES meeting debated Said's criticism from this particular angle: Halliday claimed that the pitfalls Said has detected were less dramatic or prevalent in the 1980s due to the powerful entry of social scientists to a field dominated by historians, theologians and linguists. The new contingent pro-vided a unique opportunity to expand the borders of the inquiry and versify its tools. The hybrid of social sciences with history produced an impressive yield of social history books as it provided a deeper and far-sighted sociological and anthropological view of the region's history and current affairs (Halliday 1993)

These and other criticisms were valid and in later editions of his book and on other occasions Said took some of them on board. Halliday and others, with time, gave space to Said's ideas. Said proposed that analysis of the area should be widened with the help of cultural or post-colonial studies, through the disciplines of literary critique and hermeneutics, and via these disciplines he made his own significant contribution to the vast study of every aspect of life in the past and present Middle East.

The legacy of these debates, and those that followed, was that first and foremost internal criticism is constructive and essential. The need for a more universal and interdisciplinary study was now fully recognised and applied. Moreover, as in other human sciences, here too a reflective response to events was finally legitimised as an essential factor impacting and at the time trans-forming scholarly research.

This new approach included an analysis of the people and the emotions that are so prominent in the present upheaval in the Arab world. In fact, they were mentioned again and again, and yet they did not occupy the place that would have allowed most of us to be sufficiently attentive to their importance and urgency. Hence our total surprise today. The people of the revolutions were not there even in the best of the academic work and the emotions that propelled them were even less present. It was the Arab Spring, and not scholarly energy, that brought the missing voices to the fore.

Maybe the reason is that the ordinary people of the Middle East appear mainly in discussions about our profession, but not in concrete studies produced by our profession. The people and their emotions were recognised by the meta historical debates, some of the best of which were conducted during events such as the Arab Spring.

THE REGIONAL EXPERT'S SEARCH FOR UNIVERSALISM

We have wide and steady shoulders on which to stand when we consider our future research agenda. One of the most important legacies left us is a well-charted map for how to navigate between regional and universal expertise in the study of the Middle East. We were cautioned earlier to adopt a universalist approach on the one hand, but also to redefine universalism on the other, so that it does not become a condescending tool for depreciating non-Western societies. We still need this map today, as never before.

This meta historical debate on universalism versus particularism needs to continue. Experts in this area are still rightly convinced that they possess knowledge that is peculiar to the area they study; one which cannot be sidelined in the name of interdisciplinarity or universalism.

The objective features of the area – language, religion, shared regional history and internal voices insisting on it being a cohesive geopolitical space – justify the requirement of an area studies' expertise. This expertise will be needed in the future; even if the events in Tunis and Cairo in 2011 and 2012 required a universal understanding of human being, rather than a peculiar orientalist one.

Yet, justification for expertise can dim the need to maintain a universal perspective that requires a safe navigation between mastering the peculiarities of a given society or culture and recognising its location in the general human experience. Theoretically and methodologically this means that there is not, and never was, a particular tool kit that was needed for studying Islam, the Arab world or the Middle East. There was always a need for perpetual improvement of the kit to help explain human behaviour and reality.

There is no better example to illustrate this point than the effect of both feminist critiques and political economy on the way Middle Eastern History has been re-written. Feminist scholars writing the history of Arab women applied successfully universal methodologies and theories to case studies that required what traditionally can be called orientalist expertise. This kind of literature explains the role young women played in those, so far botched, revolutions and the role that they may play in the future. Similarly, political economists understood that the integration of the area to the world economy is a fertile ground for oppression but were quite wrong in explaining where the resistance to that oppression would come from (due to somewhat religious adherence to a Marxist analysis). They never imagined that the counter revolution would emerge from among the young middle classes. However, many of their contributions are still relevant today. But we still have to go back to the works written under the influence of scholars such as Samir Amin and Immanuel Wallerstein, who restudied the concept of global economy and offered fresh and new interpretations for the relationship between capitalist and non-capitalist societies. We have to return to these debates and extract some relevant input for today's reality if we are to remain relevant as students and observers of the internal dynamics of change and not just advisors for our own society's future relations with the region.

The point I am making here is that despite all the achievements of the past recent events have exposed a certain deficiency: we fail to fully comprehend contemporary and modern undercurrents mainly because we engage with an inconclusive chapter of history. The last person warning that this indeed is still a structural problem in Middle East Studies, be it in a brusquer and uncompromising way, was James Bill in an article published *in The Middle East Journal* in 1996 (and which was delivered as a speech to MESA that year). He wrote how disappointed he was that the 'Political systems in the Middle East remain as resistant to Western comprehension today as they did half a century ago'. The systems in fact were quite decipherable; the resistance to it was either ignored or misunderstood (Bill 1996).

Like Talal Asad and Roger Owen before him, Bill claimed that the problem in the field was the search in vain for Western political systems, concepts and structures in Middle Eastern history. In short he pointed to the failure of both the anti- and pro-disciples of the modernisation theories. Owen and Talal suggested not using these Western concepts as paradigm for analysing success or development; Bill, on the other hand, just noted how fifty years of research was unable to find out whether they were applicable or not and in addition failed to offer something more appropriate in their stead.

Bill had perfectly defined what was wrong. The failed attempt to understand 'Middle East power and authority relations, as they form, reform and transform themselves in the face of a rapidly-changing world'. The closest in his view that we arrived at anything tangible was by imposing the term 'civil society' on this question; but even that he thought was useless. Ironically, it is this particular term – 'civil society' – that is an entry point for many who have looked at recent developments in the area, proving that a constant dialectical relationship between general conceptualisation and concrete regional expertise is still valid and useful (Bill 1996). It seems that whatever tools we use, western theories, or whether we adapt them and their methodologies to non-western realities, we are still in greater need of engaging with the societies at large, when analysing pivotal moments such as the Arab Spring

With the benefit of hindsight, we should go back to these debates and jux-tapose them against the scenes at Maydan al-Tahrir, the influence and role of Facebook, the demands for democracy, for Suqut al-Nizam (regime change), the objections to *fasad* (corruption), and the unorganised nature and magni-tude, not to mention the power, of leaderless committed young global and local (perhaps 'glocal') groups of people to topple regimes. As we should ponder once more the failure of all these movements and the grim reality in recent years of bloodshed and suffering on a momentous scale, not seen in the region for many years.

When we embark on such a journey we should remember Said once more, who in the context of our area studies insisted that the inquirer, the orientalist, is not outside the inquired area, the orient or an unbiased assessor of the reality in the Middle East. Therefore, the orientalist research itself is yet one more additional aspect of that encounter.

Said in fact went further than just commenting on the historian's subjectiv-ity in writing about the Middle East. Said was openly talking about the moral commitment of historians. Said injected optimism, activism and agency into any historical, sociological and economic analysis. These qualities and charac-teristics are still regarded as drawbacks if integrated into scholarly work.

'If those are the facts' he wrote, referring to the pessimism and desperation in face of the imbalance on the ground accompanying some of Palestine's best friends' analysis in the wake of the 1982 Israel attack on Lebanon, 'then so much the worse for the facts' (Said 1984). Nothing in that particular struggle, the Palestinian one, and nothing in the struggle elsewhere in the Arab world against oppression, colonisation and tyranny is over even if the 'facts' are on the side of pessimists. An analysis invigorated by such hopes and optimism sometimes has more resonance than the pedantic pessimist representation of the reality as it were or as it is. This optimism is a form of solidarity that Said, admittedly in a too generalised and sometimes in an unfair manner, felt was missing even from the best of the orientalist approach in general and towards Palestine in particular.

Said's following words still sound like heresy to many of us today:

But what are facts if not embedded in history, and then reconstituted and recovered by human agents stirred by some perceived or desired or hoped-for historical narrative whose future aim is to restore justice to the dispossessed? (Said 1984)

Said of course referred to the way Palestine's immediate and almost current history was narrated and debated, but the dispossessed Palestinians can easily be replaced with the oppressed Egyptians and Tunisians.

He further suggested that:

> ... what is needed is a theory of *intellectual activity* (rather than merely collecting and collating facts), and an epistemological account of ideological structures as they pertain to specific problems as well as to concrete historical and geographical circumstances. None of these are in the capacity of a solitary individual to produce; and none is possible without some sense of communal or collective commitment to assign them more than personal validity. (Said 1984)

Scholars thus are not islands unto themselves. They need to interact, something historians are quite often reluctant to do, in order to face challenging events such as the Arab Spring. They are also far more hybrid these days than they were at the time that oriental studies was male and white. Indeed, as Said and others noted, in hindsight, we realise that the encounter with the West that created 'The Modern Middle East' can also be viewed positively. It can be seen as an encounter that produced, and continues to produce, hybrid human culture when it is allowed to develop naturally, namely without coercion and manipulation (Said 2000). For various reasons, humanity still dreads hybridity and prefers homogeneity – be it national, ethnic or religious. The craving for homogeneity, however, after two hundred years of interaction requires harsh acts of purification and cleansing as we can see around us today. The encounter still goes on and therefore any definitive historical conclusions about it are useless. The tendency to correctly assess trends, whether it was the inevitable secularisation before the Iranian revolution and total Islamisation after it, was bound to fail. The same is true for the momentous earthquake that continues to shake the region since 2011.

BIBLIOGRAPHY

Asad, Talal and Roger Owen, 'A Critique of Orientalism: A Reply to Professor Dodd', *Bulletin of the British Society for Middle Eastern Studies*, vol. 7, no. 1 (1980), p. 35.

Bernard Lewis and Leon Wieseltier vs Edward Said and Christopher Hitchens, YouTube video (2018), added by Terron Poole [online], available at: https://www.youtube.com/watch?v=PE0q3PZKEQs (last accessed 20 May, 2019).

Bill, James A., 'The Study of the Middle East Politics, 1946–1996: A

Stocktaking', *The Middle East Journal*, vol. 50, no. 4 (Autumn 1996), p. 501.

Binder, Leonard, 'Area Studies – A Critical Assessment' in L. Binder (ed), *The Study of the Middle East* (New York: Wiley and Sons, 1976), p. 16.

Fukuyama, Francis, *The End of History and the Last Man* (New York: Free Press, 2006).

Halliday, Fred, '"Orientalism" and its Critics', *British Journal of Middle Eastern Studies*, vol. 20, no. 2 (1993), pp. 145–63.

Hourani, Albert, *A History of the Arab Peoples* (Cambridge, MA: The Belknap Press of Harvard University Press, 1991).

Hourani, Albert, *Arabic Thought in the Liberal Age, 1798–1939* (Cambridge: Cambridge University Press, 1993).

Huntington, Samuel, *The Clash of Civilizations and the Remaking of World Order* (New York: Simon and Schuster, 2005).

Kedourie, Eli, *Islam in the Modern World and Other Studies* (London: Frank Cass, 1980).

Mohanty, S. P., 'Us and Them: On the Philosophical Bases of Political Criticism', *Yale Journal of Criticism* (Spring 1989), p. 13.

Owen, Roger 'The Middle East in the Eighteenth Century: An Islamic Society in Decline; A Critique of Gibb and Bowen's Islamic Society and the West', *Review of Middle Eastern Studies*, vol. 1 (1975), pp. 101–12.

Said, Edward, 'Permission to Narrate', *Journal of Palestine Studies*, vol. 13, no. 3 (Spring 1984), p. 45.

Said, Edward, *Orientalism* (Cambridge: Vintage Books, 2000).

CHAPTER 2

Doing Research in Conflict and Post-conflict Contexts

Irene Costantini and Sansom Milton

With the demise of the Cold War, the wave of wars that plagued the 1990s ushered in a new epoch of international engagement in conflict and post-conflict settings. As a consequence, the challenge of finding appropriate means to promote peace and prevent a relapse into conflict has informed the work of a growing number of researchers. Either motivated by the need to critically understand conflict and post-conflict dynamics or by the need to solve practical problems, a vast array of scholarship has contributed to the emergence of a research field with a sizeable body of literature that cuts across various disciplines.[1] Mapping this vibrant and lively field of knowledge is an arduous task since conflict dynamics and post-conflict reconstruction have been addressed from a vast range of perspectives, such as the economic, social, political, psychological, and humanitarian, to mention just a few.

Despite its multidisciplinary and multi-thematic nature, scholarship focusing on conflict and post-conflict reconstruction is bonded by a common problématique: conflict-affected contexts impair the possibility of conducting 'research as usual' and require a context-specific analysis, the elaboration of which starts with a reflection on the methodological challenges of researching conflict and post-conflict countries. Calls for a contextual analysis span from the practitioner to the academic literature, yet in many cases no more than lip service is paid to this commitment. When researching conflict-affected settings we should start by recognising that they are characterised by 'varying forms of fluidity, uncertainty, volatility, risk, and insecurity' (Bush and Duggan 2013: 7). These characteristics mark both conflict and post-conflict settings, often making this distinction analytically void. Incorporating fluidity, uncertainty, volatility, risk, and insecurity in research design and methodology is a major challenge for researchers working in this field.

The authors' research examined respectively the emerging forms of economic governance in post-conflict transitions and the role of higher education systems in post-war recovery through the case studies of Iraq and Libya.[2] Despite dealing with very different topics, we encountered similar challenges when approaching Iraq and Libya as case studies for in-depth qualitative research. These challenges are ultimately related to the ways in which different conflict contexts affect the way we plan, design and conduct research. In the process of questioning how the highly volatile and insecure contexts of Iraq and Libya affected our research we encounter another similarly challenging question: to what extent does the conduct of research in conflict-affected countries contribute to the structures and processes of peace or conflict? By bridging a reflection on the role and function of research in conflict-affected contexts and on the methodological challenges we faced in our research, the present contribution is not intended to provide a blueprint for researchers. Rather, it aims at encouraging a debate on research, which can contribute to a more conscious production and use of research in, on and around conflict.

ARE IRAQ AND LIBYA UNIQUE CASES OF CONFLICT-AFFECTED CONTEXTS?

Even prior to the armed campaign and consequent conquest by the Islamic State of large swathes of territory across Iraq and Syria, Iraq witnessed high levels of violence and insecurity: in 2013 alone the total number of casualties reached 7,818 killed and 17,981 injured (UN Iraq 2014). Previous trends followed the ups and downs of the post-2003 transition, with very high levels of violence during the 2005–8 period, after which security improved relative to this period but with levels of violence that remained alarming by international standards. While Libya did not descend into immediate insecurity following the ousting of Muammar Qadhafi, the country has witnessed a downturn of spiralling violence with targeted assassinations and violent clashes, and since the 2014 battle between 'Operation Karamah' (dignity) and 'Fajr Libya' (Libya Dawn) open conflict in the country. Violence is the tip of the iceberg of broader insecurity that manifests in the everyday life of conflict-affected societies: language of violent incitement (i.e. intimidation and threats) and physical barriers (i.e. checkpoints, kidnappings, and separation walls) often radicalise post-conflict environments, by preventing the articulation of more moderate discourses.

In Iraq and Libya, security-related issues are aggravated by the fact that a distinction between the conflict and the post-conflict phases has been always difficult to draw. On the one hand, Iraq and Libya are similar to most post-conflict countries as nearly all face difficult and chaotic transitions from war to peace. On the other hand, Iraq and Libya are specific cases, which fall in the 'regime-change' category, as neither country went through a peace agreement but rather experienced a complete overthrow of previous regimes. Therefore, the post-conflict momentum is deeply related to the sustainable reconstruction of their respective polities. Within the MENA region, Iraq and Libya add to the list of civil conflicts (Syria and Yemen), and to recent and ongoing changes in the socio-political orders of some Arab countries (Egypt and Tunisia). Iraq and Libya are instances of a changing landscape in the region: understanding conflict and post-conflict dynamics has become an important part of the broader debate on continuities and changes in the MENA region after the 2011 uprisings.[3]

Conflict is not a new trait in the historical development of the countries in the region. After the decolonisation period the inter-state and intra-state dimensions of conflicts have often interlaced contributing to the eruption and continuation of conflicts. What is new is that more than a decade into the twenty-first century MENA region is witnessing a growing contestation within its state borders (Khalidi 2013), sustained by a more particularistic construction of identities that calls into question two key dimensions of the state: its representative function and its forms of intervention in society (Jessop 1991). This trend does not however stop at the state's borders: the new fault-lines in the region form a complex context where particularistic sub-national claims are instrumentally tied to macro-regional dynamics, including a struggle over hegemony in the region, which is defined in both ideological and material terms.

Are conflict and post-conflict settings in the MENA region unique? The answer to this question is certainly negative. Despite each conflict-affected setting having its own specificities, patterns and commonalities are found across regions and countries. Varying forms of fluidity, uncertainty, volatility, risk, and insecurity characterise Iraq and Libya but also Syria, Yemen, the Palestinian Territories, and some areas within other states, including the Sinai Peninsula, and the north of Lebanon. At the same time, similar patterns are also found in other regions of the world where violence in its different forms – militarised, social or criminal – is distinctly part of social, political, and economic processes. While the *uniqueness* of the region is rejected, there are peculiarities that make these contexts difficult to research. This chapter focuses precisely on the conditions under which inquiry is conducted in Iraq and Libya and on the obstacles we encountered while doing research. Among the most compelling issues we identified, among others, is the controversial relationship between the region and Western countries. This controversial relationship is the result of a Western foreign policy that cannot decide between the political imperatives of security and stability, on one hand, and supporting authentic political transformation on the other hand (Delacoura 2005; Ottaway and Carothers 2004). As a consequence, researchers need to negotiate their positionality in the midst of this ambiguity and, at times, of dif-fused anti-Western sentiments. This and the fluid, uncertain contexts in Iraq and Libya impose the necessity of considering the *why* and *how* of conducting research during and after conflict.

THE ROLE AND FUNCTION OF RESEARCH BETWEEN AREA STUDIES AND PEACE AND CONFLICT STUDIES

Why do we conduct research in conflict-affected countries where there are evident limits to data collection? Why do we treat the MENA region as a field of knowledge where there exist important differences between and within its countries? The genealogy of both fields of knowledge deeply problematises the subject and object of research and their political relationship. In short, the colonial root of area studies and the concerns for what are misleadingly interpreted as *ungoverned societies* frame at least the origin of area studies and peace and conflict studies. The relationship between knowledge and power is certainly not novel in the social sciences; yet, the increased standardisation and technicalities in research methods and design often leave little space for reflect-ing upon this relationship. What is the relationship between research and the politics of conflict-affected countries? What are the intended and unintended consequences of conducting research in/on conflict-affected countries? And what are the specificities when the MENA region is added to the equation? A better understanding not only of conflict dynamics but also of how conflicts have been studied in the MENA region would certainly contribute towards answering these questions.

The implications of conducting research in these and similar contexts are well explained by the following example. In parallel with the invasion of Iraq in 2003 and the military and civil occupation that followed, counting war-related casualties became a highly politicised exercise that involved government as well as independent institutions and renowned journals (Hoyt 2007; Steele and Goldenberg 2008). What should have been a basic and objective counting transformed into a harsh debate about methodological choices, survey samples, and sources. Research became the battlefield for justifying or criticising the intervention in Iraq. While 'researchers tend to overestimate the impact of their research ... [and] policy makers ... to underestimate it' (Smyth and Darby 2001: 34) there is no doubt that research (including the lack of it) can have an impact. In the research-policy nexus then, both researchers and policy-makers face institutional and procedural constraints, which undermine their capacity to respectively influence policy-making or absorb research findings.

Research is usually classified as having two major uses: a conceptual use that aims at producing 'changes in level of understanding, knowledge and attitude' and an instrumental use that aims at producing 'changes in practice and policy making' (Walter et al. 2003: 11). Despite researchers being usually motivated by either of the two uses, a neat distinction between the conceptual and instrumental use of research is difficult to establish. Changes in understanding social, political, and economic dynamics can produce changes in the design and application of political responses. The concept of the 'fragile state', which emerged over the last decade, has certainly produced a different understanding of the international system, one in which states are qualitatively different from one another. This understanding, in turn, has been used to justify a more deeply interventionist foreign policy that reaches beyond 'wartorn' or 'failed states' to manage the domestic affairs of so-called 'fragile states'. Another example can be drawn from the framing of the authoritarian regimes in the MENA region as forms of 'strong states' and the influence that this had on the reading of Arab societies, at least until the events of the so-called Arab Spring. Both the conceptual and instrumental uses of research are tightly tied to policy-making. In conflict-affected countries, where multiple actors (international, national and local) have competing political agendas, the purpose of research becomes a sensitive issue in itself.

The political aspects of conducting research are not only confined to the purpose or the audience of research in terms of the process of research uptake by policy-makers, but extend also to the way in which research is conducted.[4] How do we transform empirical evidence into narratives for research? And how responsible are these narratives? In an interview conducted by one of the authors, a young man from Kirkuk described pre-2003 Iraq under Saddam Hussein as a much better place to live in comparison with the post-2003 environment.[5] The dire security situation in Kirkuk can certainly justify the comment. However, the author was struck by the fact that the comment was made by a person who identified himself as a Kurd and previously contextualised his personal experience as part of the collective experience of the Kurdish people. His voice cautioned the researcher to question prevailing narratives either within or outside the country and to responsibly account for a diversity of perspectives, without however falling into pure relativism. The example suggests that the transformation of empirical facts into research narratives matures in a context in which there exist dominant narratives that need to be continuously questioned and sometimes challenged.

The example above introduces another relevant issue when researching conflict-affected contexts. The use and application of categories is a basic procedure in elaborating parsimonious explanations for understanding complex processes. But the choice of categories is not always a neutral exercise. The comparison between Iraq and Libya is, in this regard, telling. Since the ousting of Saddam Hussein, Iraq has been described as a highly divided society stratified across ethno-religious categories (Dodge 2010). Framing the understanding of Iraqi society around an ethno-religious primordial template has not only disregarded the effects of the invasion and the struggle for authority in the country, but has also contributed to framing the solution to the Iraqi quagmire around the idea of separating the country into three constituent communities (Gelb 2003; Galbraith 2004; Biden and Gelb 2006). In contrast, after the ousting of Muammar Qadhafi in 2011, the initial enthusiasm for a rapid and peaceful transition was largely justified by the notion that Libya, in contrast with Iraq, was a homogeneous society due to the fact that its population is 97% Sunni Muslim (St John 2013). This simplified view presents the same pitfall of describing Iraqi society as formed by three primordial communities. It is similar in that it interprets communalistic identity in perennial, cultural, and static terms, and does not consider the contingent and political formation of communalistic structures. While the question concerning what makes a society highly-divided[6] remains unanswered, the risk of a simplified use of categories is not only to misleadingly interpret social and political phenomena, but also, and most importantly to 'contribute to producing what they apparently describe or designate' (Bourdieu 1991: 220). But then, how can we make sense of the reality? And, how much of the complexity of the cleavages do we perceive and do we account for?

METHODOLOGICAL AND LOGISTICAL ASPECTS: HOW TO INTEGRATE UNPREDICTABILITY AND LONG-TERM DYNAMICS IN RESEARCH DESIGN?

In Iraq and Libya access to data is severely restricted. Official (government and international organisations) data are often scarce, widely scattered, undisclosed, or simply absent. Collecting data either for quantitative or qualitative analyses is similarly difficult. Data scarcity not only characterises the two cases of post-2003 Iraq and post-2011 Libya: data manipulation and non-disclosure by the regime of Saddam Hussein and Muammar Qadhafi added to restrictions on foreign and domestic researchers, with the consequence that many aspects of the respective countries are under-researched. In Iraq, the looting and destruction of state institutions in 2003 led to the loss of significant amounts of data while also crippling the data collection capacity of many national institutions – both in terms of infrastructural capacity and the loss of expertise due to the exodus of an estimated 40% of the professional class in the post-2003 period. While the same did not occur in post-war Libya, a Professor of Mathematics at Tripoli University held that the Qadhafi regime intentionally weakened statistical training in the national education system so that Libyans would be deprived of the ability to offer empirically-grounded critiques of social conditions in the country.[7] In some cases, the poor data landscape may become functional to shaping post-conflict transitions: for instance, in Iraq the still unresolved issue concerning the so-called contested areas between Baghdad and the Kurdistan Regional Government is intimately related to the unwillingness to understand the realities of these territories, illustrated clearly in the political infeasibility of carrying out a national census.

However, the difficulty of accessing data should be thought of in relation to the specificities of research methodologies in conflict-affected countries. Methods are the procedures that link a research question to the type of data collection and analysis, and the scientific nature of the findings. In conflict-affected contexts it must be asked, how can research methodology guarantee reliability, replication, and validity in the midst of fluidity, uncertainty, volatility, risk and insecurity? To answer this question 'we must begin with a fundamental shift in how methodology is defined – not as a rigid or fixed framework for the research but, rather, as an elastic, incorporative, integrative, and malleable practice. It should be informed by the shifting social complexities unique to unstable field sites and should depend on a level of investigative flexibility' (Kovats-Bernat 2002: 210). For instance, flexibility becomes essential in light of the prevalence of informal repertoires (institutions and practices at various levels and in various areas – political, economic, and social). Researchers should then cast their analytical net wide enough to capture dynamics often obscured by a rigid search for criteria or thresholds at which conflict or post-conflict reconstruction processes are evaluated as either successes or failures. At the same time, fluidity and volatility frustrate the research task of attributing values (or consequences) to processes or relations, thus making it difficult to distinguish causal or non-causal relationships from intervening factors.

In logistical terms, fluidity, uncertainty, volatility, risk and insecurity influence the decisions on when, where and how to conduct fieldwork in conflicted-affected countries: the difficult location and the unpredictability of crisis are among the primary challenges identified for conducting research (Belousov et al. 2007). Personal security remains, ultimately, the distinctive element determining the (im)possibility of conducting fieldwork in certain settings. While concerns for personal security are factored into the researcher's decision to conduct fieldwork, university risk restrictions and insurance policies are often insurmountable obstacles. The case of Iraq well illustrates this point. Until 2014, obtaining university permission or insurance coverage to conduct fieldwork in Iraq outside the Kurdistan region has proven difficult for the authors. The result is that fieldwork has often been possible only in certain areas within a country or in neighbouring countries, with important consequences for the elaboration and interpretation of the findings beyond the particularistic reality to which we had access.

In the case of Iraq, the authors identified as locations to conduct fieldwork the Kurdistan region of Iraq and Amman, Jordan. The Kurdistan region has since the beginning of the 2003 invasion experienced a much higher level of security than the rest of the country – being described as an 'oasis of stability and tranquillity while much of the rest of Iraq burns' (Krieger 2007). The September 2013 suicide attacks against the headquarters of the intelligence service was the first attack in Erbil, the regional capital, since 2007. The Kurdistan region has successfully promoted Erbil as the gateway to Iraq, especially for conducting business in the country. Access to the Kurdistan region is, therefore, the result of growing economic ties between the region, its neighbours of Iran and Turkey, and Western countries. Amman, on the other hand, has represented a 'refugee heaven' for the Iraqi population (Chatelard 2010; al-Ali 2006). Jordan's migration policies – foremost, the fact that it is not part of the 1951 Geneva Conventions for refugees and asylum seekers – highly modified the composition of the Iraqi community in Jordan that the government has estimated at around 500,000 people since 2007. This community is largely formed by educated middle class and professional Iraqis, of which a great number have gained residency permits as investors. A similarly important number of Iraqis commute from Amman to Iraq.

Conducting fieldwork in Amman or the Kurdistan region provides access to primary sources, either for interviews or for other types of data collection. But what are the implications for research? The special status granted to the Kurdistan region by the 2005 Iraqi Constitution has favoured a progressive process of parallel state formation, which has often been described as a 'quasi-state' (Natali 2010). The risk therefore is that having access only to some areas in the country could produce a biased analysis by 'taking the part for the whole'. A similar dynamic occurred in Libya during the period 2011–14 in which many researchers could access Tripoli but not the East and South of the country, which contributed to a failure to grasp the scale of the post-war challenges. This risk of perceptual bias was even held by Libyan officials from Misrata, a city at the heart of the country's post-war troubles, to afflict policy-makers based in Tripoli who were 'blind' to the severity of the impact of conflict outside the relatively unscathed capital.[8] The second risk is to privilege a certain narrative over others when access is limited to certain types of interlocutor. While Iraqis of all backgrounds are living in Amman, Jordan hosted a higher proportion of Iraqi Sunni Arabs which can lead to forms of sectarian bias when relying on displaced Iraqis as a sample population. The prevalent presence of educated middle class and professional Iraqis can furthermore lead to forms of socio-economic bias in analysis. These risks push the researcher to continuously question the implications of their choices. Mitigation strategies are therefore useful as long as their inner implications are constantly reflected upon and are then integrated in the research.

Lastly, the unpredictability of crisis imposes a reflection on the timing of research. In the span of a few months one author was able to conduct fieldwork in Libya while the second was prevented from doing so by the rapid deterioration in the political and security situation in 2014. The unpredictable eruption of crisis urges researchers to constantly evaluate their research strategy against the changing reality on the ground without, however, falling into the trap of 'presentism'. A reflection on timing should also consider how timing is incorporated in the research narrative. The rapid and unpredictable unfolding of events can easily translate into a research narrative that offers a mere snapshot of a phenomena at a particular moment in time or a description of events as they are unfolding. Contextualisation in space and time remains a crucial aspect that needs to be incorporated into the design, data collection, and analysis. As Smyth (2001: 7) argues, 'the embedding of conceptualisations of conflict or its consequences in their local contexts is essential to the robustness of the analysis'. In our view, the embedding of conceptualisations of conflict or its consequences in time is similarly essential to the robustness of the analysis. This means placing events in their historical course but also pushing the analysis to grasp long-term impacts and consequences.

CONCLUSION: THE ETHICS OF RESEARCHING CONFLICT AND POST-CONFLICT CONTEXTS

The difficulty of conducting 'research as usual' in conflict-affected settings is also due to the fact that ethical issues cannot be separated from the logistical, methodological, and political aspects of research. Research ethics informs (or should inform) the entire process of research. In relation to the logistics of conducting research, ethical considerations become important when defining the limits of research, foremost in locations that cannot be accessed. In relation to the methodologies for conducting research, ethical considerations inform the use of data and the procedures to link empirical evidence and theory. In relation to the politics of conducting research, ethical considerations are essential in guiding our use of culture, history, and socio-political categories. In addition, ethical considerations also inform which intellectual lines cannot be crossed: when research is precisely aimed at understanding conflict and post-conflict dynamics, it inevitably engages with a range of sensitive topics. Understanding which lines cannot be crossed is certainly part of the researcher's responsibility, which extends to the people involved in the research, including informants, interviewees, and translators. When other people are involved in conducting research, their personal experience as well as their role in society cannot be neglected.

The inter-connections between ethics, volatility and the temporal dimension of conflict can be illustrated by the issue of informed consent in conflict-affected and post-conflict contexts. Procedures for guaranteeing informed consent from research participants are in most research projects developed prior to fieldwork and pertain to a consideration of the conflict context at a particular moment in time. However, due to the volatility of post-conflict contexts the ethical imperative to do no harm to research participants must be cognizant of the potential for the risks inherent in any context to shift over time. For instance, during the immediate post-Qadhafi situation in Libya, there was widespread optimism over the prospects of transformational social change. In this particular research environment many interviewees were open to providing consent for their views to be attributed to them, including on controversial issues such as the role of militias in post-war Libyan society. The breakdown in security experienced in Libya since then constitutes a very different and much more dangerous context. This volatility over time necessitates a higher standard for ethical considerations in research in conflict-affected contexts.

Ethical considerations caution researchers to continuously interrogate their position vis-à-vis the subject of research. Reflexivity as a methodological stance can strike a balance between distance from and empathy – as an effort to fully understand other's positions and conveying them – with the subject of research, avoiding the perpetuation of dominant discourses of which researchers, disciplines, and cultural frameworks are all parts. The ethics of researching conflict-affected settings starts with a reflection of the self in order to avoid 'the risk of reading our own agendas into our observations' (Kappler 2013: 130) as the researcher's exclusion from power relations is an assumption that needs to be challenged; it develops as a continuous interrogation of the relationship between the self and the subject of research to 'acknowledge the multiple roles, identities, and positions that researchers and research participants bring to the research process' (Milner IV 2007: 395); and it concludes by positioning this relationship within the wider context.

By extending a practitioner perspective into the academic world, research can be conducted on conflict (when conflict dynamics are the research subject), in conflict (when conflict dynamics represent a research variable), or around conflict (when conflict is the context where a phenomenon is researched). In all three cases, termination of human suffering is most likely a common concern for most researchers. This and similar concerns channel research towards the realm of politics to the point that the paradigm of action-research tears down the distinction between research and politics. Arguments for or against this paradigm have first to deal with the similarly problematic question of the neutrality or impartiality of research: is research neutrality really achievable in conflict-affected contexts? While we do not have an answer to this question, our reflection cautions against the risk of falling into the trap of normative thinking as it tends to perpetuate the identification of post-conflict societies as an object of research instead of recognising the agency of individuals in post-conflict societies and their capabilities to participate in, inform, conduct and critique research. In conducting research it is vital to acknowledge the multiple roles, identities, and positions that researchers and research subjects bring to the research process. In Iraq and Libya, as in other conflict-affected settings, conducting research is also acknowledging those roles, identities, and positions that due to their controversial, radical, or marginalised status in relation to the dynamics of conflict are hardly accessed and remain mostly outside of the research process.

NOTES

1. Cox's (1981) distinction between critical and problem-solving approaches to research is widely used to review the literature on conflict and post-conflict reconstruction and to identify commonalities and divergences between approaches.
2. The initial version of this chapter was written in Spring 2015. The authors' research mentioned in the chapter refers to the work they have conducted previous to this date.
3. See for instance the special issue 'Continuity and change before and after the uprising in Tunisia, Egypt and Morocco: regime reconfiguration and policy making in North Africa', *British Journal of Middle Eastern Studies*, vol. 42, no. 1.
4. A thorough reflection on the purposes and audiences of research should also problematise the role of funding agencies as agenda-setting entrepreneurs.
5. Author's interview, Erbil, Iraq, November 2013.
6. A divided society is defined as 'a polity in which ethnic, religious, racial, regional and allied cleavages are so fundamental that most political relations, especially involving competition for power and scarce resources hinge on these differences' (Osaghae 2001: 16).
7. Author's interview, Tripoli, October 2012.
8. Author's interviews, Tripoli, Libya, 2012.

BIBLIOGRAPHY

Al-Ali, Nadje Sadig, *Iraqi Women: Untold Stories from 1948 to the Present* (London: Zed Books, 2006).
Belousov, Konstantine, et al., 'Any Port in a Storm: Fieldwork Difficulties in Dangerous and Crisis-ridden Settings', *Qualitative Research*, vol. 7, no. 2 (2007), pp. 155–75.

Biden, Joseph R. and Leslie H. Gelb, 'Unity Through Autonomy in Iraq', *The New York Times*, May 2006, available at http://www.nytimes.com/2006/05/01/opinion/01biden.html?pagewanted=all&_r=0 (last accessed 1 June 2015).

Bourdieu, Pierre, 'Identity and Representation: Elements for a Critical Reflection on the Idea of Region', in *Language and symbolic power*, Bordieu, Pierre (Cambridge: Cambridge University Press, 1991).

Bush, Kenneth and Coleen Duggan, 'Evaluation in Conflict Zones: Methodological and Ethical Challenges' *Journal of Peacebuilding and Development*, vol. 8, no. 2 (2013), pp. 5–25.

Bush, Kenneth and Coleen Duggan, 'How can Research Contribute to Peacebuilding?', *Peacebuilding*, vol. 2 no. 3 (2013), pp. 303–21.

Chatelard, Géraldine, 'Jordan: A Refugee Heaven', *Migration Policy* (2010).

Cox, Robert, 'Social Forces, States and World Orders: Beyond International Relations Theory', *Millennium: Journal of International Studies*, vol. 10, no. 2 (1981), pp. 126–55.

Dodge, Toby, 'State collapse and the rise of identity politics in Iraq', in *The Ethnicity Reader: Nationalism, Multiculturalism and Migration*, Montserrat Guibernau and Rex John, Second Edition (Cambridge: Cambridge University Press, 2010).

Galbraith, Peter W., 'How to get out of Iraq', *New York Review of Books*, 13 May (2004), available at http://www.nybooks.com/articles/archives/2004/may/13/how-to-get-out-of-iraq/ (last accessed 1 June 2015).

Gelb, Leslie H., 'The Three State Solution', *The New York Times*, 25 November (2006), available at http://www.nytimes.com/2003/11/25/opinion/25GELB.html (last accessed 1 June 2015).

Hoyt, Clark, 'The reality in Iraq? Depends on who's counting', *The New York Times*, 7 October (2007), available at http://www.nytimes.com/2007/10/07/opinion/07pubed.html?pagewanted=all&_r=0 (last accessed 1 June 2015).

Jessop, Bob, *State Theory: Putting the Capitalist State in its Place* (Philadelphia: Pennsylvania State University Press, 1991).

Kappler, Stefanie, 'Coping with research: local tactics of resistance against (mis-)representation in academia', *Peacebuilding* 1:1 (2013), pp. 125–40.

Khalidi, Ahmad Samih, Palestine, peoples and borders in the new Middle East map, *Open Democracy* 29 May (2013).

Krieger, Zvika, 'Oasis in Iraq: Universities flourish in Kurdistan', *The Chronicle of Higher Education* 17 August (2007), available at http://chronicle.com/article/Oasis-in-Iraq-Universities/32091 (last accessed 1 June 2015).

Kovats-Bernat, Christopher, 'Negotiating Dangerous Fields: pragmatic strategies for fieldwork amid violence and terror', *American Anthropologist*, vol. 104, no.1 (2002), pp. 208–22.

Milner IV, H. Richard, 'Race, Culture, and Researcher Positionality: Working through Dangers Seen, Unseen, and Unforeseen', *Educational Researcher*, vol. 36, no. 7 (2007), pp. 388–400.

Natali, Denise, *The Kurdish Quasi-state: Development and Dependency in Post-Gulf War Iraq* (Syracuse: Syracuse University Press, 2010).

Osaghae, Eghosa E., 'The Role and Function of Research in Divided Societies: The Case of Africa', in *Researching Violently Divided Societies*, Marie Smyth and Gillian Robinson (eds) (Tokyo, New York and Paris: United Nations University Press and London: Pluto Press, 2001).

Smyth, Marie, 'Introduction' in *Researching Violently Divided Societies*, Marie Smyth and Gillian Robinson (eds) (Tokyo, New York and Paris: United Nations University Press and London: Pluto Press, 2001).

Smyth, Marie and John Darby, 'Does Research Make any Difference? The Case of Northern Ireland' in *Researching Violently Divided Societies*, Marie Smyth and Gillian Robinson (eds) (Tokyo, New York and Paris: United Nations University Press and London, Pluto Press, 2001).

Steele, Jonathan and Suzanne Goldenberg, 'What is the real death toll in Iraq?', *The Guardian* (2008), http://www.theguardian.com/world/2008/mar/19/iraq (last accessed 1 June 2015).

St John, Ronald Bruce, 'The Post-Qadhafi Economy' Chapter Three in *The 2011 Libyan Uprisings and the Struggle for the Post-Qadhafi Future*, Pack, Jason (ed.) (London: Palgrave Macmillan, 2013).

UN Iraq, 'UN casualty figures for December 2013 deadliest since 2008 in Iraq', United Nations Iraq website (2014), available at http://www.uniraq.org/index.php?option=com_k2&view=item&id=1499:un-casualty-figures-for-december-2013-deadliest-since-2008-in-iraq&Itemid=633&lang=en (last accessed 1 June 2015).

Walter, Isabel, Sandra Nutley and Huw Davies, *Research Impact: A cross sector review, literature review*, Research Unit for Research Utilisation, St Andrews University (2003).

CHAPTER 3

Researching (and Deconstructing) Sectarianism in Lebanon and Beyond

Ana Almuedo-Castillo

There is no shortage of views on sectarianism in Lebanon. Media, academia and popular discourses have contributed to the over-study (and perhaps even the reification) of sect as the primordial social category in Lebanese politics and society. This body of literature tends to see sectarianism as an outcome; as essentialised identities that are inevitably salient. By featuring sectarian identities as fixed categories, violent conflict is interpreted within this school of thought as an inevitable outcome when two sectarian groups interact.

Contrary to this body of literature, this chapter aims at contributing to the scholarly work of authors that contest the notion of sectarian identities as something primordial and unchanging. Sectarian identities are perceived as unitary and immutable only in their appearance. Rather than as an outcome, this body of literature sees sectarianism as a dynamic process that is continuously produced, reproduced, performed, while similarly permanently contested and resisted. Sect and sectarian identities are constantly constructed through networks, institutions and provision of services that have developed particular understandings of sect and sectarian affiliation.

I believe critically studying the concept of sectarianism is especially crucial at the present crossroads in which conflicts are increasingly following sectarian explanations in the Middle East, from Syria (Phillips 2015) to Iraq (Haddad 2011) and sectarian discourses are becoming hegemonic in explaining both domestic and geopolitical dynamics. Neither Lebanon nor any other Arab country has been driven exclusively by sectarian calculations.

In December 2010 a wave of popular uprisings sparked from Tunisia across the entire Arab world. From Morocco to Oman Arab citizens have challenged in their countries the political establishments in their own way and with varied outcomes. What commenced as peaceful uprisings mutated into regime-manufactured sectarian conflicts in countries such as Syria, Bahrain or Yemen, where authoritarian regimes advanced sectarian calculations to construct lines of violent confrontation and divert domestic pressures, or even to advance their geopolitical objectives abroad (Matthiesen 2013; Salloukh 2013).

This overlapping use of sectarianism was particularly striking in Syria. The traditional discourse of 'cultural harmony' manufactured by the Syrian regime turned into sectarian disharmony and violent manipulation of sectarian discourse and practices. As Kastrinou (2016: 232) explains it: 'Disharmony is the inevitable outcome of cultural efforts to manufacture harmony; it is the self-fulfilling prophecy'. Sectarianism is constructed and reproduced as a modern event, the consequences of which are always political. Sectarianism represents the political manipulation of social identities and as such, it corresponds to a long-term instrumentalisation of sectarian political identities by the Syrian state. Something both recent Syrian and Lebanese history shows is that reproduction of sectarian identities and kin endogamy might be reinforced in times of war, even though sectarian ideology predated war manipulations.

What is more, the sectarian use of political identities and mobilisation in the wave of Arab uprisings shows the instrumentalisation and malleability of sectarian identities. Against primordial assumptions of unitary and cohesive communal groups based on immutable and ahistorical emotions, sectarian identities are, like any other vertical cleavage, historically constructed identities, the intensity, relevance or salience of which depends on political, geographic, economic and social contexts. Like any other vertical cleavage, sectarian identities overlap with other cleavages. As historical constructions, their salience depends on how these cleavages become relevant in a time when domestic and regional dynamics in the Arab world suddenly seem to be exclusively driven by sectarian calculations. First and foremost, sectarian cleavages overlap with other social cleavages, and as this chapter will show, it is sometimes even reinforced or constructed by other systems of power that are external to the sectarian dynamics. Thus, far from being natural groups, Fawwaz Traboulsi (2007: vii) argues that sects serve as 'enlarged clientelist networks designed to resist the inequalities of the market and compete for its benefits and for the appropriation of social wealth and service of the state'. Anthropologist Suad Joseph researched first how sectarian cleavages are intimately related to class structures (Joseph, 1983), but she also has remarkably contributed to the study of sectarianism as concomitant of kinship and the patriarchal system (Joseph 1975, 1993, 1999, 2000, 2005, 2011).

An entire ensemble of networks, institutions and spatial relations develop particular understandings of sect and sectarian affiliation, which constantly delimits the meaning of this concept. As defined by Nucho (2017: 6), 'in Lebanon, the relationship between infrastructures in urban spaces and sectarianism is dialogic – many urban infrastructures and services are produced by sectarian political and religious organizations at the same time that they are the channels through which sectarian belonging and exclusion are experienced, produced, and recalibrated'.

Not only authoritarian regimes began to mobilise sectarian political identities for their own benefit, but also sectarian narratives became hegemonic in academia, the media and other pieces of literature to explain the Arab uprisings and violent conflicts in the Middle East. As Haugbolle contends, '[a]mong the many things the war did was to establish sectarianism as *the* central feature of Lebanon in academic studies of the country' (Haugbolle 2013: 435). Certainly, the same could be said about Syria, Yemen, Bahrain or many other Middle Eastern countries nowadays.

Paradoxically, while in the early stages of protests and mobilisations Arab citizens took to the streets to ask for freedom, dignity and the end of authoritarian regimes, Lebanon had no one long-term ruling leader to overrun, but rather several of them. The Arab uprisings sparked in Lebanon a wave of popular mobilisations protesting against the pervasiveness of sectarianism and the confessional political system in their country. With banners of 'The dictatorship of the eighteen' (referring to the eighteen officially recognised religions in Lebanon), 8,000 Lebanese took to the streets of Beirut on 6 March 2011. Among their different demands, the second edition of the 'Lebanese Laique Pride' or '*La al-Taiffyia*' (No to Sectarianism) called for the unification of a Civil Code for Personal Status Law and 'an end to the country's deep-rooted sectarian system'.[1] According to their Facebook page, the group consider the sectarian system responsible for hindering economic development, engendering corruption and empowering and entrenching long-standing kins of political leaders.

When the Arab uprisings spilled over into Lebanon, its citizens took to the streets to protest against the pervasive consequences of the confessional system and the post-war politics of sectarianism; in the meantime, the incipient Arab revolts in countries such as Syria, Yemen or Bahrain have been hijacked by these very sectarian dynamics that the Lebanese mobilised against. Authoritarian regimes and other geopolitical actors have used and manipulated sectarian discourses in order to deter popular revolts in these countries.

This chapter will first briefly define sectarianism in the context of Lebanon; second, it will provide a historical overview of how sectarianism has been constructed in Lebanon (and Mount Lebanon), and third, it will provide a glimpse of the attempt to deconstruct the sectarian paradigm. Firstly, arguing that other political and social practices that are not sectarian or not interpreted as such, also contribute to the reification and reinforcement of the sect and sectarian identities. Secondly, I will briefly present the case of civil marriage, an example of how Lebanese resist and challenge, daily and quietly, sectarian practices.

A BRIEF DEFINITION OF SECTARIANISM

Part of the difficult endeavour of defining sectarianism is that the same concept connotes different realities. In opposition to work in which sectarianism is conceived as biologically inherited, primordial or tribal, this chapter understands sectarianism as a modern political, social and economic dynamic process, rather than a simple outcome. Sectarianism can refer to the *institutionalised confessional system of governance*, for example, in which electoral laws divide parliamentary seats based on sectarian quotas, and personal status laws determine citizens based on fifteen different juridical systems (Baydoun 1999). Sectarianism is also defined as a *political discourse*. In that sense, sectarianism occupies a hegemonic position with regards to the history, politics, society, economy, culture and even the past and future of the Lebanese state and is read from the lens and system of the 'truth' of sectarianism (Mikdashi 2011). Sectarianism has also been defined as 'a way of being in the world that depends upon a set of *cultural markers* and *social practices*' [emphasis added] (Weiss 2010: 13). Sectarianism is not a religious or theological concept, but it is rather a marker or an important means of *differentiation* in terms of identity and membership of the in-group or the out-group (Joseph 2008).

The uses and descriptions of sectarianism are in line with the understanding that Ussama Makdisi (2000b) developed of sectarianism as a modern phenomenon that resulted from the 1860 Maronite–Druze conflict. With his masterpiece, Makdisi followed the emergence in time and history of sectarianism as a definer for social groups. This chapter will follow his definition of sectarianism as both a *practice* and a *discourse*:

> ... a *practice* that developed out of, and must be understood in the context of, nineteenth-century Ottoman reform. Second, it is a *discourse* that is scripted as the Other to various competing Ottoman, European, and Lebanese narratives of modernization [...] a discourse – as the set of assumptions and writing that described this changing subjectivity within a narrative of Ottoman, European and Lebanese modernization. [emphasis added] (Makdisi, 2000b: 5–6)

Sect and sectarian categories are only immutable in appearance. This thesis intends to contribute to the work of authors that contest the notion of sectarian identities as something primordial and unchanging. It is through the networks, institutions and provision of services that particular understandings have developed and reified notions of sect and sectarian affiliation (see: Abu-Rish 2014; Cammett 2014; Kingston 2013; Mikdashi 2014; Nucho 2017; Picard 1994; Rivoal 2014; Salloukh et al. 2015; Weiss 2010).

It is within these historical constructions of political practices and ideological discourses that sectarianism appears. This representation of individuals is the result of a set of historical circumstances that created an 'imagined community' (Anderson 1983) with political legitimacy in 1860 on Mount Lebanon (Makdisi 2000b). Not only these historical, social, political and cultural dynamics contribute to the (re)production of sectarian identities, but also sects have been formed in Lebanon through other social and political practices that are not exclusively sectarian. These non-sectarian practices contribute to the demarcation and differentiation between sectarian groups, and sometimes they may even be interpreted as sectarian, even if they correspond to radically different systems of power. That is, for example, geography segregation (Deeb and Harb 2013; Harb 2007; Humphreys 2015; Nagel 2002), socio-economic classes ('Amel 2005 [1980]; Joseph 1983), patriarchy (Joseph 1993, 1999, 2000) or others such as infrastructures (Nucho 2017).

THE ROOTS OF SECTARIANISM: THE HISTORICAL MAKING OF SECTARIANISM IN OTTOMAN MOUNT LEBANON

Thorough work by historians has traced the mobilisation of religious minorities to their penetration of European powers such as France, Britain or Russia and their interventionist policies in the Ottoman Empire. The work of Saba Mahmood, on religious minorities and freedom in Middle Eastern politics, traces the development of human rights discourses and religious freedom as a strategy of fragmenting the religious groups under the Ottoman Empire. The European powers emerged as the protectors and advocates of these religious minorities, in need of a patron to guarantee their 'religious freedom'. This *modern* concept of freedom cannot be detached, as Mahmood (2012: 419) explains, from 'how the national and the international regulation and protection of religious minorities makes specific notions of freedom and unfreedom possible and unimaginable'.

These discourses on human rights and religious freedom were complemented with broader concepts of 'self-determination', which were the basis on which the boundaries of ethno-religious groups started operating. Timothy Mitchell highlights the benefits associated with this concept for the expansionist and colonialist purposes of European powers; 'since no population was ethnically homogeneous, this created the possibility of identifying or shaping groups as "minorities". The imperial powers could then claim the duty to protect them as an endangered fragment of the population' (Mitchell 2011: 99). This is not to say that European powers operated on non-existent groups or religions in the Middle East. Religious communities already existed in the Middle East, but they were neither politically salient, nor clustered in geographical boundaries where they could easily claim 'sovereignty'. Thus, the violence that erupted between 1858–61 in Mount Lebanon was of a local nature and:

> … it is imperative to dispel any illusion that sectarianism is simply or exclusively a native malignancy or a foreign conspiracy. Sectarianism can be narrated only by continually acknowledging and referring to both indigenous and imperial histories, which interacted – both collided and collaborated – to produce a new historical imagination. Sectarianism is a modern story, and for those intimately involved in its unfolding, it is *the* modern story – a story that has and that continues to define and dominate their lives. [emphasis in the original] (Makdisi 2000b: 2–3)

Historian Leila Fawaz has also contributed to the study of the social, political and economic transformation of Mount Lebanon in the nineteenth century, and its definition of being mainly marked by the local transformation triggered by the Egyptian occupation under Muhammad Ali, the European intervention, the Ottoman defeat (Fawaz 1994), as well as economic profits harvested by the Maronites from the French investment in the silk industry that operated through their networks (Khatter 2001). Pre-1860 Ottoman society in Mount Lebanon was characterised by 'a network of alliances among its leading Druze and Maronite [Christian] families based on a chain of clan loyalties that cut across sectarian lines and took precedence over loyalty to village, district, or church' (Fawaz 1994: 17).

1858 Shahin's revolt: from Jumhur upheaval to 'inevitable' Druze-Maronite hatred

Mount Lebanon region was composed of a Christian population, mainly Maronites, and Druze. Life, for the *ahali* (people), but not the *a'yan* (nobility), revolved around the agricultural cycle and cultural practices which were common among the Druze and Maronite *ahali* (Makdisi 2000b: 30). Religion played a role in their lives, even though the categorisation of the society is not defined by religion, but by a division between the *ahali*, the population majority, the peasants, and the *a'yan*, with alliances that cut across Druze and Maronite divisions. What is more, even if not a predominant practice, interfaith marriages among members of noble families was not unknown in historical Mount Lebanon, a practice that was completely unthinkable between a noble and a peasant, even from the same faith, although it did require the lord's permission. Trespassing the line between the nobles and the *ahali* meant cutting the line of *ta'ifa*, that is the social and family rank, which was the meaning of *ta'ifa* prior to the mid-nineteenth century, rather than 'sectarianism' as it signifies nowadays (Makdisi 2000b: 35–7).

Between 1858 and 1861 the uprising led by peasant revolutionary Tanyus Shahin constituted a great challenge to the politics and monopoly of power and knowledge of the *a'yan*. It also signified a turning point for the transformation of the *ahali* into *jumhur* (the general population) through their organisation into popular committees and claims of political representation. Shahin successfully organised peasant revolts in the region of Kesarwan that succeeded in evicting the Christian lords who were oppressing Christian peasants and seized power through organised popular committees. The initial revolt, with class struggle connotations, took on a sectarian character when Shahin and his comrades were also invited to 'liberate' other peasants in mixed villages in Mount Lebanon, where the peasants were Christians and the Druze were the lords. Beyond interpretations on how a revolutionary struggle tragically turned into sectarian violence, Makdisi (2000a: 207) adds another layer of understanding to this episode. He argues that Shahin's rebellion 'belonged to the modern world' because it reflected the new sectarian society, echoing global 'discourse of freedom, representation, and equality', in line with the theories by Mahmood (2012) and Mitchell (2011), by which discourses on human rights and freedom were extant at the onset of the political salience of religious minorities. Here is how Makdisi has articulated the argument:

> Shahin and his rebels carved out a role for ordinary Maronite Christians in formal politics and anticipated the politics of nationalism. Shahin also deployed a discourse of freedom for Christians that was inherently limiting and exclusionary, for it allowed no space for [...] the Druze and Shi'a inhabitants of Mount Lebanon. (2000a: 207)

Shahin was defeated in 1861 by a Lebanese notable backed by Ottoman forces, the Maronite Church and the European powers, forcing him to surrender. After 1861 the historical traces of Shahin Tanyus are almost impossible to follow (Makdisi 2000a). The events of 1860 became known as the Druze-Maronite massacre, with French and Ottoman officials actively constructing an interpretation of the events as 'inevitable' sectarian hatred, and triggered governance reforms based on political and spatial understandings of 'ethnic hatred' (Makdisi 2000b). The Ottoman government, alongside France, Britain, Russia, Austria and Prussia drew a new division and political autonomy for Mount Lebanon through the approval of the *Règlement Organique* and the adoption of the *Mustarrafiyya* (Fawaz 1994). The political architecture arranged new 'sectarian geographies', as well as social, political and legal divisions of the individuals according to their sectarian affiliation. This fresh socio-political order 'replace[d] a non-sectarian elitist culture with a sectarian one since one's sect defined one's involvement in the public sphere and ability to be appointed to office, to govern, to collect taxes, to punish, even to live and exist as a loyal subject' (Makdisi 2000b: 162). Beirut and its port became a hub in which French investments shifted social and class divisions (Hanssen 2005).

Besides emerging political discourses on 'sectarian violence' and incipient legal and political divisions, Shahin's revolt should be examined as a rupture and transformation of the peasants from *ahali* to political subjects. Not just Ottoman and European intervention in the conflict, but popular demands for 'global' discourses on freedom, equality and representation concealed exclusionary and constructed religious groups (Makdisi 2000b). Not only did agency shift from the hands of the nobility, the *a'yan*, to the *ahali*, but also elite control over class and social divisions, power and knowledge, was broken and with it a new social contract emerged in which religious minorities became 'sectarian subjects'.

Everyday non-sectarianism

At the moment, sectarianism in Lebanon has become not only the natural (re) produced social categorisation, but it has also become the hegemonic episte-mological concept through which every social and political act is interpreted. Marxist intellectual Mahdi 'Amel (1979) defined sectarianism as a superstruc-ture that supersedes any other power structure, including class. Within this superstructure there are other structures of power that exist such as patriarchy, space, neoliberalism, etc.

In fact, other systems of power reinforce sectarian powers, which are not necessarily sectarian. One example is post-war spatial segregation, which has advanced the current physical sectarian segregation of Lebanese individu-als. First, neoliberal policies have occupied and privatised traditional public places where different parts of the population used to gather, be it from dif-ferent socio-economic classes or sectarian affiliations (Hanssen and Genberg 2002; Humphreys 2015; Nagel 2002). Second, post-war geographical reality can be described by the territorialisation and confessionalisation of identi-ties driven by massive population shifts. Dislocation of certain groups was accompanied by the reintegration of other people demarcating homogeneous and self-contained spaces. This followed mainly confessional origins, but also socio-economic classes (Nasr 1993).

The second example I will mention here is the patriarchal system. Religious/ sectarian conflict cannot be understood without looking at sexual and gen-dered dimensions. Even though this intertwining of religion and sexuality applies indistinctively to the West as well as the non-West, in societies such as Lebanon it takes a particular form in the institutionalisation of religion/ sectarian-based personal status law. Any attempt to reform family laws and introduce civil marriage regulations have been interpreted by the religious leaders as a violation of their collective right to religious liberty and of their sovereignty over a domain in which they understand to have jurisdiction. Through sectarian family laws, categorisation of citizens goes beyond sectarian identities. The law also produces different citizens depending on the category of 'male' or 'female'. Men and women have a different status in divorce, with regard to the custody of children, and inheritance or spousal maintenance between each other, which overlaps with the differentiation that the law makes between the male/female citizen according to their ascribed sect. To quote Maya Mikdashi (2014: 284), 'The interstitial nature of personal status and civil laws makes possible one of the main functions of the nation-state: to produce a body of people that, although differentiated by sex and sect, are unified under the overarching category of Lebanese citizenship'.

Civil marriage: non-sectarian reproduction

Sectarianism operates in Lebanese society by virtue of a structure of power that operates in political and civil society at the same time. First by coercive means (personal status laws), Lebanese citizens are not allowed to wed in their country but religiously. The cultural hegemony of sectarianism in Lebanon is further achieved by consensual diffusion, that is, the reproduction of sectarian habits (Gramsci 2000).

Kinship, endogamy and same-sect marriages reinforce the reproduction of everyday sectarian habits and people's belief in sectarianism. An ensemble of cultural, social and political practices determines the 'appropriate match' according to written and unwritten rules in Lebanon (Rivoal 2014). Couples succumb to these hegemonic practices and marry through religious ceremony, complying with religious family laws and their families' wishes. Some other couples, however, subvert this power and seek to marry under civil law, which is not availablein their country.

The struggle for civil marriage subscribes to the absence of a non-sectarian alternative to the personal status and family laws (*Qanun al-Ahwal al-Shakhsiya*). The personal status legal system denies the fundamental right of Lebanese citizens to opt out of their patrilineal inherited sectarian ascription, while obliging them to participate within certain sectarian and religious affiliations (Azzi 2007). Intersectarian or non-religious marriages are, of course, not available in this legal custom. In the absence of a civil law, Lebanese couples able to afford it travel abroad, mainly to neighbouring Cyprus, to conduct a civil wedding. These civil engagements are automatically registered in Lebanon and the foreign civil law where the marriage took place applied by the Lebanese judge in civil court in case of divorce, with some exceptions (El-Zein 2010: 213). The paradox of civil marriage in Lebanon is that, although illegal, it has become common and an increasing practice in the country, although it is a right restricted to those who can afford to pay for the cost of a civil wedding in Cyprus, which is at least the equivalent of US$1,000, in a country [Lebanon] where the minimum monthly wage has been only recently increased to the equivalent of US$450.[2]

Civilly married Lebanese spouses have many different intentions as well as different geographical, social, economic, cultural and educational backgrounds. Some of them may follow an activist and militant rationale for deciding to travel abroad and defy religious and sectarian family laws. Some others, however, may not get married due to an activist belief, but for economic reasons or simply because it represents the only choice to get married with the person they would like to form a family with. The latter civilly married Lebanese spouse may not be advocate of the 'civil marriage cause' and may not have joined any movement for the right of Lebanese to have civil marriage in their country. For the many diverse reasons that these couples decide to marry in this way, and even if it is not intended as a form of contestation against the imposition of religious marriage, the act of civil marriage creates a group of Lebanese people who have decided not to live with the sectarian system and the laws that define marriage and family exclusively intrasectarian.

In conclusion, the practice of civil marriage groups many different individuals who resist in a daily and quiet way not only the coercive laws in favour of sectarian marriage, but the accepted social practice of endogamic sectarian marriages.

CONCLUSION

In conclusion, this chapter aims to analyse the ensemble of cultural and social practices, as well as the political discourses that are constantly modelling and reinforcing sectarianism as the dominant social norm. I intended to briefly analyse not only how sectarian social norms are produced and reiterated in Lebanon, but also how they are challenged every day, confronted, contested and resisted. As social scientists we cannot afford not to enquire what purpose lies behind the networks and institutions reproducing sectarian ideology.

Throughout this chapter, sectarianism has been described as having been originated by Ottoman and European powers that imposed a single identity on the diverse inhabitants of Mount Lebanon; this was done as a means of defining Lebanese roles and interactions with the public sphere. This imposition stuck, was followed, and has made sectarianism sustainable for all these decades within an ensemble of institutional, clientelist and ideological hegemony of sectarian discourse and practices (Salloukh 2013). However, as this chapter argues, the term 'sectarianism' is at the same time constantly used while seldom uniquely defined. This is partly because the term 'sectarianism' applies to a wide spectrum of issues related to sectarian identities, but that may not necessarily pertain to that area. That is, when attempting to analyse every social arena through the sectarian lens, the analytical focus might divert from other social issues, such as economic, regional, social class, gender or other local factors.

As the case of civil marriage demonstrates, Lebanese subjects are currently contesting their relationship with their public sphere as sectarian citizens. Their resistance comes from the many different perspectives of citizens who by being secular, non-sectarian and non-patriarchal decide to live by non-sectarian family law, which the state of Lebanon does not provide for them. Non-sectarian and cross-sectarian acts happen every day and contest the pervasiveness of popular mobilisation around sectarian identity markers. In these times of war and devastation in the Middle East we need to unravel, on the one hand, the negativity and on the other hand the indefinability of the term 'sectarianism', critically deconstructing the practices and ideologies that uphold the pervasive beasts of sectarianism.

NOTES

1. Facebook group page 'Lebanese Laique Pride' where the group started to organise itself and the mobilisations: https://www.facebook.com/laique pride
2. 'The Minimum Wage In Lebanon Compared To Others From Around The World', *Blog Baladi*, 11 May, 2015 [online]. Available from: http://blogbaladi.com/the-minimum-wage-in-lebanon-compared-to-others-from-around-the-world/ [last accessed 11 July, 2017].

BIBLIOGRAPHY

'Amel, Mehdi, *Bahth fi asbab al-harb al-ahliya fi lubnan* (Beirut: Dar al-Farabi, 1979).

'Amel, Mehdi, *Madkhal ila ́naqḍ al-fikr al-ṭā'ifi : al-qad̄iyah al-Filasṭīnīyah fi īdyuūlūjīyat al-burjūwāzīyah al-lubnānīyah* (Bayrūt: Dār al-Fārābī, 2005 [1980])

Abu-Rish, Ziad, *Conflict and Institution Building in Lebanon, 1946–1955* (University of California Los Angeles: PhD Thesis, 2014).

Anderson, Bennedict, *Imagined Communities: Reflections on the Origin and Spread of Nationalism* (London: Verso, 1983).

Azzi, John, *Al-Zawaj al-Madani: Al-Qadi al-Lubnani fi Muwajahat Qawanin al-'Alam* (Beirut: n.p. 2007).

Baydoun, Ahmad, *Tis'a 'ashara firqa najiya: al-lubnaniyoun fi ma'arakat al-zawaj al-madany* (Beirut: Dar al-Nahar lil-Nashr, 1999).

Cammett, Melani, *Compassionate Communalism. Welfare and Sectarianism in Lebanon* (Ithaca and London: Cornell University Press, 2014).

Deeb, Lara and Mona Harb, *Leisurely Islam: Negotiating Geography and Morality in Shi'ite South Beirut* (Princeton: Princeton University Press, 2013).

El-Zein, Aref Zayd, *Qawanin wa Qararat al-Ahwal al-Shakhsiya lil-Tawa'if al-Masahiya fi Lubnan* (Beirut: Al-Halabi Legal Publications, 2010).

Fawaz, Leila Tarazi, *An Occassion for War: Civil Conflict in Lebanon and Damascus in 1860* (London: I. B. Tauris, 1994).

Gramsci, Antonio, *The Gramsci Reader: Selected Writings 1916–1935* (New York: New York University Press, 2000).

Haddad, Fanar, *Sectrianism in Iraq: Antagonistic Visions of Unity* (London: Hurst, 2011).

Hanssen, J. P. and D. Genberg, 'Beirut in Memoriam: A Kaleidoscopic Space out of Focus', in *Crisis and Memory: Dimensions of Their Relationship in Islam and Adjacent Cultures*, A. Pflitisch and A. Neuwirth (eds) (Beirut: Orient Institute, 2002).

Hanssen, Jens, *Fin de Siècle Beirut: The Making of an Ottoman Provincial Capital* (New York: Oxford University Press, 2005).

Harb, Mona, 'Faith-Based Organizations as Effective Development Partners? Hezbollah and Post-War Reconstruction in Lebanon', in *Development, Civil Society and Faith-based Organizations: Bridging the sacred and the secular*, Michael Jennings and Gerard Clarke (eds) (London: Palgrave Macmillan, 2007).

Haugbolle, Sune, 'Social Boundaries and Secularism in the Lebanese Left', in: *Mediterranean Politics*. 18 (2013), pp. 427–43.

Humphreys, David, 'The Reconstruction of the Beirut Central District: An urban geography of war and peace', in *Spaces and Flows: An International Journal of Urban and ExtraUrban Studies*, 6 (2015), pp. 1–14.

Joseph, Suad, *The Politicization of Religious Sects in Borj Hammoud, Lebanon* (Columbia University: PhD Thesis, 1975).

Joseph, Suad, 'Working-Class Women's Networks in a Sectarian State: A Political Paradox', in *American Ethnologist*, 10 (1983), pp. 1–22.

Joseph, Suad, 'Connectivity and Patriarchy among Urban Working-Class Arab Families in Lebanon', in *Ethos*, 21 (1993), pp. 452–84.

Joseph, Suad, 'Descent of the Nation: Kinship and Citizenship in Lebanon', in *Citizenship Studies*, 3 (1999), pp. 295–318.

Joseph, Suad (ed.), *Gender and Citizenship in the Middle East* (Syracuse: Syracuse University Press, 2000).

Joseph, Suad, 'The kin contract and citizenship in the Middle East', in *Women and citizenship, Studies in Feminist Philosophy*, Marilyn Friedman (ed.) (Oxford, New York: Oxford University Press, 2005).

Joseph, Suad, 'Sectarianism as Imagined Sociological Concept and as Imagined Social Formation', in *International Journal of Middle East Studies*, 40 (2008).

Joseph, Suad, 'Political Familism in Lebanon', in *ANNALS, AAPSS*, 636 (2011), pp. 150–63.

Kastrinou, Maria A., *Power, Sect and State in Syria: The Politics of Marriage and Identity amongst the Druze* (London: I. B. Tauris, 2016).

Khatter, Akram Fouad, *Inventing Home: Emigration, Gender, and the Middle Class in Lebanon, 1870–1920* (Berkeley: University of California Press, 2001).

Kingston, Paul W. T., *Reproducing Sectarianism: Advocacy Networks and the Politics of Civil Society in Postwar Lebanon* (New York: State University of New York Press, 2013).

Mahmood, Saba, 'Religious Freedom, the Minority Question, and Geopolitics in the Middle East', in *Comparative Studies in Society and History*, 54 (2012), pp. 418–46.

Makdisi, Ussama, 'Corrupting the Sublime Sultanate: The Revolt of Tanyus Shahin in Nineteenth-Century Ottoman Lebanon', in: *Comparative Studies in Society and History*, 42 (2000a), pp. 180–208.

Makdisi, Ussama, *The Culture of Sectarianism: Community, History, and Violence in Nineteenth-Century Ottoman Lebanon* (Los Angeles: University of California Press, 2000b).

Matthiesen, Tobias, *Sectarian Gulf: Bahrain, Saudi Arabia, and the Arab Spring That Wasn't* (Palo Alto: Stanford University Press, 2013).

Mikdashi, Maya, 'What is Political Sectarianism?', in *Jaddaliyya* (2011).

Mikdashi, Maya, 'Sex and Sectarianism: The Architecture of Lebanese Citizenship', in *Comparative Studies of South Asia, Africa and the Middle East*, 34 (2014), pp. 279–93.

Mitchell, Timothy, *Carbon Democracy: Political Power in the Age of Oil* (London: Verso, 2011).

Nagel, Carol, Reconstructing Space, Ee-creating Memory: Sectarian Politics and Urban Development in Post-war Beirut, in *Political Geography*, 21 (2002), pp. 717–25.

Nasr, Salim', New Social Realities and Postwar Lebanon', in *Recovering Beirut*, Samir Khalaf and Philip S. Khoury (eds) (Leiden: Brill, 1993).

Nucho, Joanna Randa, *Everyday Sectarianism in Urban Lebanon Infrastructures, Public Services, and Power* (Princeton: Princeton University Press, 2017).

Phillips, Christopher, 'Sectarianism and conflict in Syria', in *Third World Quarterly*, 36 (2015), pp. 357–76.

Picard, Elizabeth, 'Les habits neufs du communautarisme', in *Culture et conflits* (1994), pp. 49–70.

Rivoal, Isabelle, 'Intimate Politics: The Art of the Political Relationship in Lebanon', in *Anthropology of the Middle East*, 9 (2014), pp. 1–17.

Salloukh, Bassel F., 'The Arab Uprisings and the Geopolitics of the Middle East', in *The International Spectator*, 48 (2013), pp. 32–46.

Salloukh, Bassel F., Rabie Barakat, Jinan S. Al-Habbal, Lara W. Khattab and Shoghig Mikaelian, *The Politics of Sectarianism in Postwar Lebanon* (London: Pluto Press, 2015).

Traboulsi, Fawwaz, *A History of Modern Lebanon* (London: Pluto Press, 2007).

Weiss, Max, *In the Shadow of Sectarianism: Law, Shiism, and the Making of Modern Lebanon* (Cambirdge, MA: Harvard University Press, 2010).

CHAPTER 4

Researching Livelihoods for Syrian Refugees in Protectionist Labour Markets: The Cases of Jordan, Lebanon and Turkey

Lorraine Charles

The protracted Syrian conflict in the Middle East created the worst refugee crisis since the Second World War and has placed host governments under significant pressure to accommodate the needs of individuals who have sought refuge in their countries. By the end of 2020, the crisis had created over 6.6 million registered refugees (31% of the world's refugee population), hosted in countries bordering Syria and further afield (UNHCR 2020a). The number of refugees hosted in the Middle East and North Africa (MENA) region has reached an unparalleled level. Turkey hosts the largest number of Syrians and the world's greatest refugee population, with 3.65 million registered refugees (UNHCR 2020a) and between 300,000 and 400,000 unregistered Syrians (Crisis Group 2018). This comprises 65% of the global Syrian refugee population. Jordan hosts approximately 700,000 registered Syrian refugees (UNHCR 2020b) and, according to the Jordanian government, nearly an equal number are unregistered (Ghazal 2018). Lebanon, which hosts nearly 1 million registered Syrians refugees (UNHCR 2020b), has the largest refugee population per capita, with refugees comprising approximately 25% of its population. As global financial pressures, shrinking economies and rising unemployment plague many Middle East refugee-hosting countries, the presence of these large refugee populations has created an additional burden.

The year 2016 was a turning point for the Middle East refugee-hosting governments and the international community. They began to acknowledge that the Syrian refugee situation was less temporary than expected. The international community and host governments realised that those who had fled violence in Syria were likely to remain in their communities for many years, with many never returning home. At the same time, host countries began to recognise that the current situation was unsustainable from an economic and political perspective.

The extent of the problem compelled governments to change their response to the crisis, from purely humanitarian and temporary solutions-based, toward approaches that were more developmental and (semi-) permanent in nature. The 2016 Supporting Syria and the Region Conference (National Archives 2018) held in London marked a turning point and forced governments to develop a new framework to address the consequences, particularly economic, of the protracted war in Syria and the subsequent displacement of large numbers of Syrians. For the first time, the issue of livelihoods and employment surfaced on political agendas, as host countries realised some sort of local integration, even if only economic, had become necessary.

The adoption of the New York Declaration for Refugees and Migrants (UNHCR 2019a) in September 2016 by the Member States of the United Nations gave shape to new approaches for states to reconceptualise the way that refugees would be managed, and a renewed focus on refugee resilience and self-reliance. It made a range of commitments to enhance the manner in which the international community addressed issues of human mobility, including steps toward a more sustainable system for providing refugee protection as well as responses to the needs of host countries and communities. As part of the New York Declaration, UNHCR was mandated to develop and initiate the application of the Comprehensive Refugee Response Framework {CRRF} (UNHCR 2016a). Two of the four objectives of the CRRF are to ease pressure on the host countries and to enhance refugee self-reliance (UNHCR 2019b). Moreover, the New York Declaration, amended at the end of 2018, also resulted in the adoption of a 'Global Compact on Refugees'. The Compact places a distinct focus on livelihoods for refugees. According to Article 70 of the Global Compact, 'states and relevant stakeholders will contribute resources and expertise to promote economic opportunities, decent work, job creation and entrepreneurship programmes for host community members and refugees' (United Nations 2018a).

Yet, as international attention became focused on viable options for livelihoods for refugees, stressed host economies in the Middle East were struggling to provide employment even for their native populations, making employment for refugee populations extremely challenging and politically unpopular. This brought attention to the protectionist labour market regulations that many Middle Eastern governments were enforcing, with some policies pre-existing and others in reaction to the Syrian refugee crisis.

Due to the legal restrictions preventing refugees from formal access to labour markets and the political sensitivities surrounding refugee employment, conducting research on livelihoods in this context has meant that conventional narratives on employment needed to be reconsidered. Despite the protectionist government policies, refugee employment is a reality. This has meant that research around livelihoods for refugees requires a focus on alternative and innovative interventions that bypass the legal restrictions imposed by governments. Many organisations that run programmes facilitating employment for refugees, particularly in Jordan and Lebanon, act in legislative grey areas in order to facilitate employment opportunities for refugees. This makes researching livelihoods among the Syrian refugee population in the Middle East challenging. The legislative grey area in which many employment-focused initiatives exist as well as the perceived dangers to displaced communities should attention be drawn to their activities could potentially place them at risk. In order to conduct research in this context, I had to think beyond the realms of research convention, beyond merely understanding the context, toward envisioning what potential solutions would look like, and this allowed for the identification of interventions that existed beyond the conventional, in the grey areas.

This chapter looks at how conventional narratives were overcome when conducting research on livelihoods for the Syrian refugee population in protectionist contexts. It will examine how the perspective of the researcher changed to accommodate the legal barriers that prevent refugees from free access to labour markets, and how a paradigm shift in the understanding of the nature of work was necessary to conduct this research. More importantly, this chapter highlights how a solution-based approach to the research was necessary because of the challenges that refugees face, and the potentially precarious situations of refugees who seek livelihood opportunities. Moreover, it not only looks at the challenges in conducting research but also at the opportunities that have evolved through the examination of this very difficult and politically-charged topic.

LOCAL INTEGRATION OF REFUGEES: THE NEED FOR DIGNIFIED LIVELIHOODS

With resettlement an option for very few refugees – only 1% of refugees globally are resettled – and repatriation elusive due to protracted conflict in Syria, local integration has become the most viable option for the majority of Syrian refugees. Yet host countries in the Middle East have been reluctant to integrate refugees due to political, economic and social pressures, instead implementing measures that often make it difficult for refugees to work legally. Without the ability to work formally and often without adequate access to education and services, self-reliance has become almost impossible for the vast majority of Syrian refugees in the Middle East, thus making local integration difficult.

From a socio-economic perspective, local integration occurs when refugees are no longer in physical danger and not at risk of *refoulement*.[1] It also occurs when refugees have freedom of movement and are not confined to camps and settlements. Local integration also implies that refugees have basic socio-economic rights; they are allowed free access to the labour market so that they are able to sustain themselves and their families. It also means access to education and other services and being socially networked in their host community. In other words, local integration occurs when refugees 'have overcome their specific vulnerabilities to the point that they and their hosts show little difference in access to opportunities' (World Bank 2017).

Livelihood activities are perhaps the central component of local integration. They facilitate the creation and maintenance of social and economic interdependence within and between communities and can thus build functioning social networks based on mutually beneficial exchange of labour, assets and food (Jacobsen 2002). With the provision of livelihood opportunities, refugees are able to gain access to resources, have freedom of movement and can work alongside their hosts to pursue productive lives. Local integration also means that refugees are better able to overcome the sources of tension and conflict in their host communities, as they are part of rather than in competition with the host community.

Essentially, livelihoods provide the opportunity for refugees to become self-reliant. When refugees have access to livelihoods, it reduces the burden on the host country by decreasing refugees' dependence on public assistance. This can also contribute positively to the economy of the host community. More importantly, it enhances the wellbeing of refugees by boosting their dignity and confidence and by providing a sense of control over their lives. When refugees are allowed and encouraged to work, they can retain their current skills or develop new ones. This also helps refugees in the long term, improving their future prospects. In contrast, when refugees spend prolonged periods without work, it is often difficult for them to quickly become self-reliant once more.

Yet many refugee-hosting countries have developed policies that prevent refugees from being able to pursue livelihoods. These policies include restrictions on freedom of movement and settlement (including encampment), restrictions on employment, poor standards of protection and physical security for refugees (including a non-guarantee of *refoulement*), and host governments' desire that refugees are temporary not permanent residents (Jacobsen 2002). These policies have had negative consequences for both refugee and host communities.

Countries that have provided refugees free access to the labour market have seen increased economic growth, job creation and an overall positive impact on the local population, where both groups are able to access employment equally. For example, in Uganda, where refugees have access to the labour market, they make a positive contribution to the economy. These contributions are exemplified by the significant exchange of services and goods between refugees and the host community, and refugees' creation of employment opportunities for Ugandan nationals (Betts et al. 2014). Policies such as those implemented by Uganda not only provide the opportunity for dignified livelihoods, and thus productive lives, but also promote social cohesion. Malaysia also presents a counter-example. If refugees in Malaysia, where they are currently not allowed to work, had access to the labour market, the country's GDP would increase by USD 750 million a year through higher spending alone, with potentially larger economic impact (Todd et al. 2019).

Local integration, with the provision of access to dignified livelihoods, provides benefits for refugees, who become self-reliant, which in turn benefits the local economy and host population. Yet, in the Middle East, refugees are not able to truly integrate into host economies because of protectionist labour market restrictions imposed by host governments. These restrictions can be structural, in terms of explicit legal mechanisms that make it impossible to work legally, or can be political, where governments have theoretically allowed legal access yet have made the application process so cumbersome that few work permits are issued to facilitate legal employment.

These protectionist policies impact the way that I conducted research on refugee livelihoods. The majority of refugees, despite the legal restrictions placed on them, find employment in the informal (and unregulated) sector. This means that researching livelihoods for refugees required a paradigm shift in thinking. Therefore I, as a researcher, needed to focus on alternative and innovative interventions that bypass the legal restrictions imposed by governments.

LEGAL RESTRICTIONS TO ACCESS LIVELIHOODS IN JORDAN, LEBANON AND TURKEY

There is wide international and domestic recognition that livelihoods are a priority for refugees to be self-reliant, regain their independence and not depend on assistance from the host government. The Global Compact for Refugees emphasises the importance of self-reliance and increased economic opportunities for refugees. Yet, Middle East refugee host countries have not only been reluctant to integrate refugees into their economies but have placed restrictions on their legal access to employment. This has meant that refugees face significant challenges accessing formal employment.

Though the contexts and the level of labour market protectionism vary across refugee-hosting countries in the Middle East, Syrian refugees face significant restrictions in each country that hinder them from accessing formal employment. It is these labour market protectionist policies imposed in each host country that pose a challenge to conducting research on refugee livelihoods.

Lebanon

Lebanon is not a signatory to the 1951 UN Convention Relating to the Status of Refugees or its 1967 Protocol (UNHCR 2015). It is, however, bound by the customary law principle of *non-refoulement* and by obligations to the UN human rights treaties that it has signed, and which are incorporated in its Constitution. This means that Lebanon is obliged to ensure the safe admission of refugees, to protect them against *refoulement* and to respect their basic human rights.

Historically, Lebanon had a freedom of movement policy with Syria. The 1993 bilateral agreement between Lebanon and Syria for Economic and Social Cooperation and Coordination maintained that nationals of both countries would have the freedom of employment and practice of economic activity in both countries. In fact, at the beginning of the Syrian crisis, Lebanon maintained this 'open border' policy so that registered Syrian refugees were able to work legally in Lebanon in all professions. It had also been lenient to those who had not regulated their stay and to those who were working without permits, as well as tolerant of the opening and operating of unlicensed businesses (ILO 2013). However, as the number of Syrians refugees in Lebanon increased, the initial 'open door' policy and lenience was gradually abandoned, and the government adopted more protectionist measures.

By early 2015, the government had begun to restrict the entry of Syrians into Lebanon, directing UNHCR to stop registering new arrivals from Syria, as well as limiting the renewal of residency permits, thereby making it more difficult for Syrians to remain in the country legally. The government also began to control and restrict access to the job market, only allowing Syrians to work in certain sectors – agriculture, construction and other labour-intensive sectors – where they would not be in direct competition with Lebanese workers (European Parliament 2017). The Lebanon Crisis Response Plan made a clear distinction between creating permanent jobs for Lebanese workers and temporary jobs for Syrians (Government of Lebanon and United Nations 2017).

These protectionist measures are based on the premise that the presence of refugees from Syria is only 'temporary' (European Parliament 2017), and Lebanon is 'not an ultimate destination for refugees, an asylum country, or a resettlement country'. Lebanon regards all individuals who have fled Syria as 'displaced' (United Nations 2014) and is openly resistant to local integration.

Due to these protectionist policies, conventional livelihood interventions for Syrian refugees are scarce in Lebanon. This led me to search for organisations whose interventions were less directly focused on job preparation for the Lebanese economy and provided a solution to skirt around the legal barriers. The interventions that were examined trained refugees to work in the technology sector and then provided employment on a contract basis, with them working remotely and paid in cash. While these interventions existed in legislative grey areas, they allowed access to dignified work.

Jordan

As with Lebanon, Jordan is not a signatory of the 1951 Refugee Convention and its 1967 Protocol. Yet, despite this, the Jordanian government refers to Syrians as refugees and provides appropriate protection including *non-refoulement* and the right to education and healthcare. However, it did not initially provide the right to work.

At the 2016 Supporting Syria and the Region Conference, Jordan announced that Syrians would be allowed to work legally in specified sectors such as agriculture, construction, manufacturing, retail and food services, as well as in designated Special Economic Zones (Betts and Collier 2016). This agreement, known as the Jordan Compact, set out 'a new holistic approach between the Hashemite Kingdom of Jordan and the international community to deal with the Syrian refugee crisis'. The rationale behind its drafting was that 'a new paradigm is necessary, promoting economic development and opportunities in Jordan to the benefit of Jordanians and Syrian refugees' (Government of Jordan 2016). As part of the Compact, Jordan pledged to provide 200,000 work permits to Syrian refugees, in low-skilled professions, so they could contribute to the Jordanian economy without competing with Jordanians for jobs. In exchange for this concession, Jordan would be eligible for humanitarian and development funding through multi-year grants and concessional loans, with pledges of US$700 million in grants annually for three years and concessional loans of US$1.9 billion (Barbelet et al. 2018) to improve the investment climate, attract investors, reform the country's labour market, and grant access to the Syrian labour force (World Bank 2016), which included a US$100 million interest-free loan (Malka 2016).

The Jordan Response Plan (JRP), established to mitigate the effects of the Syrian crisis on Syrian refugees and the Jordanian population, and led by the Ministry of Planning and International Cooperation, set out a comprehensive refugee resilience-strengthening and development response to the impact of the Syria crisis on Jordan. It ensured that all humanitarian measures and medium-term interventions were integrated, sequenced and complemented (Government of Jordan 2019). The 2017–19 Jordan Response Plan included, for the first time, a separate chapter on livelihoods, stressing the importance of job creation and support for entrepreneurs, and the desire to support legal employment for Syrians.

Prior to the signing of the Compact, Syrian refugees had to apply for the same work permits as labour migrants, which meant high fees and administration, including official documentation that most Syrian refugees often did not have. Under these conditions, very few Syrians were issued work permits. As part of the policy shift towards labour market integration through the signing of the Jordan Compact, the government simplified the application process making it easier for Syrians to obtain work permits. Yet the signing of the Compact has not had the impact it could have had due to significant bureaucratic obstacles to formalising employment.

Other key reasons for the slow formalisation of employment have been a lack of financial incentives for employers, a lack of understanding of the implications of formalisation and the still cumbersome or non-optimal bureaucratic procedures and regulations, including application for work permits. Formalising employment means more transparency in wages, benefits and working conditions of employees. This means the employer needs to provide a contract with at least the minimum wage as a stated salary and apply for the work permit on behalf of the employee. It was also the responsibility of the employer to pay for the work permit, though in practice, fees are often passed on to the employee. For many employers, informal employment is more cost-effective, and many Syrians remain in the informal economy (Charles and Van Gunteng 2017).

These obstacles proved a significant challenge for refugees attempting to enter into formal employment. While there had been some success in the provision of legal employment for Syrians, the lofty promises of the Compact had not become a reality, with the numbers of work permits issued falling short of what was promised. By November 2018, approximately 125,400 work permits had been issued (Government of Jordan 2018). Yet, according to UNHCR, as of October 2018, just over 50,000 refugees had active work permits (UNHCR 2018a). According to one report, the number of permits issued support mobility and protection as opposed to work opportunities (Leghtas 2018). Still, the majority of Syrians, an estimated 300,000 (Ibáñez 2018) – like many Jordanians – are still overwhelmingly employed in Jordan's large informal sector.

While Jordan provided access to the labour market for refugees, it was limited to low skilled employment. My research highlighted that many Syrians were unwilling to work in these low skilled jobs, many instead preferring to become self-employed (Charles and Van Gunteng 2017). Many organisations implemented skill-training interventions (often in technical fields) without directly focusing on employment as the final objective. Many of these interventions have been criticised for providing skills training for sectors that were closed for Syrians. Yet training in certain technical skills could provide the opportunity for Syrians to work remotely.

In 2017, the Jordanian government brought into effect a law that allowed individuals (Jordanians and non-Jordanians) to establish home-based businesses (UNHCR 2016b). This law has the potential to provide a measure of protection for Syrians working remotely. However, the lack of clarity in the law means that this still remains a legislative grey area. One organisation discovered a legal loophole for employment in local businesses. If Syrians were employed as contractors, as opposed to employees for local (tech) companies, then laws preventing Syrians from being employed in these sectors (Syrians are not allowed to work in the technology sector) seem not to apply. Again, this places employment in a legislative grey area. These issues present challenges for research in the Jordanian context.

Turkey

Turkey is a signatory to the 1951 Refugee Convention, but it maintains geographical limitations, with restrictions on asylum applications from outside Europe. Thus only Europeans can be automatically classified as refugees. The Turkish government did not formally recognise individuals fleeing Syria as refugees, only recognising them as 'guests', maintaining that they hold residence permits which allowed freedom of movement. A Law on Foreigners and International Protection came into force in April 2014, allowing protection and assistance to displaced populations, regardless of their country of origin. This allowed Syrians what was called subsidiary protection. Thus, Turkey would offer 'temporary' protection, with no time limit, but the status of Syrians would not be normalised. Syrians were provided the right to education, healthcare and employment (upon obtaining a work permit). This protection provided Syrians with a 'humanitarian ID', making them refugees in all but name.

Under the current laws, Syrians could be employed legally, in any sector, six months after they registered as a protected person under the 2014 Law on Foreigners and International Protection. To ensure that employers would not favour Syrian workers over Turkish workers, the law stipulated that the number of refugees employed in one workplace must not surpass 10% of the number of Turkish employees in that same workplace (Turkish Labour Law 2017) and employers must prove that there is no Turkish person who could do the job. In order to support the formal employment of Syrians, in the three months following the Supporting Syria and the Region Conference, Ankara also committed to formally appointing Syrian teachers and health professionals (Gov.UK 2016). Turkey also established a National Employment Strategy (2014–23), with a clear focus on combatting unregistered employment, and thus attempting to formalise the informal economy for both the Turkish and refugee populations (Government of Turkey 2014).

As in Jordan, in Turkey, the employer must apply for a work permit on behalf of any potential Syrian employee and must demonstrate that he or she could not find a Turkish citizen to fulfil the job. The employer must also pay a work permit fee, submit tax reports, commit to paying at least the minimum wage, as well as pay the employee's social security benefits. These requirements and fees were a disincentive for employers to hire Syrians formally, instead preferring them to work informally without work permits. Additionally, there are reports that many Turkish employers have refused to apply for work permits because of increased tax costs (UNHCR 2018b). Though numbers are difficult to ascertain, it is estimated that as few as 20,900 (Multeciler 2018) work permits have been issued to Syrians since 2016.

The challenge for research in this context lies in the continued informality of employment of Syrians in Turkey, despite laws that allow (nearly) full access to the labour market. While labour informality is also present in Jordan and Lebanon as discussed, the protectionist laws in these two contexts provide a rationale for this. Yet, in Turkey, informality is also prevalent, despite legal access to the Turkish labour market. While many livelihood interventions in Turkey aimed to work within the legal parameters, structural barriers made it difficult to do so. Research in this context required that livelihoods be examined from a much broader perspective, looking beyond the boundaries set by legislation and into the reality faced by individual refugees.

Another barrier to (legal) employment of refugees

Overall, these protectionist labour market policies in Jordan, Lebanon and Turkey have had a negative impact on Syrian refugees. Those who are unable to access legal and formal employment resort to informal, and often precarious, employment. Many Syrians are also under-employed, not being able to find formal (or often informal) employment in their professions. They often earn less than the minimum wage and work long hours in substandard working conditions. Without work permits, they are also exempt from the benefits of social security. This increases their vulnerability, as Syrians working under these conditions are prone to exploitation by unscrupulous employers.

In addition to legal and structural barriers to refugee employment, another major issue is the lack of available jobs in refugee host countries. The Syrian crisis has had a significant impact on the economies of the Middle East. The economies in Jordan and Lebanon have been negatively impacted by the crisis. In Jordan, according to a report by the Ministry of Planning and Interior, the country has witnessed an overall 30% increase in youth unemployment since the start of the Syrian crisis (Government of Jordan 2015). Likewise, in Lebanon, there has also been an increase in unemployment, especially among the young and low-skilled workers. The presence of refugees has also resulted in rising social tensions, particularly in areas where refugees are located. In Turkey, there had initially been economic growth despite the presence of Syrian refugees. Moreover, many Syrians brought businesses, as can be illustrated by the increasing number of Syrian-owned companies registered in

Turkey; by the end of 2018, Syrians had established over 7,900 companies in Turkey (The Union of Chambers and Commodity Exchanges of Turkey 2018), which contributed to economic growth. Yet, economic woes throughout 2018 could result in decreased growth in the future (Yackley 2018).

IMPLICATIONS OF PROTECTIONIST POLICIES FOR REFUGEE LIVELIHOOD RESEARCH

With international recognition that the Syrian refugee crisis would be protracted and refugees would require a long-term solution to their displacement, the international community shifted their focus from humanitarian assistance, which provided for the immediate and urgent needs of refugees – food and shelter – toward a more developmental focus, looking at ways that refugees could be self-reliant, without a negative impact on the communities in which they are hosted.

Yet protectionist labour market policies, as well as structural barriers in the affected nations, contradict this recognition that refugees require a more long-term solution to their displacement. As resettlement is not accessible to the majority of refugees and repatriation not possible because of the unstable situation inside Syria, local integration (which would mean allowing refugees to access employment) is the only path toward self-reliance and a long-term or durable solution.

Working in these protectionist contexts has meant that refugee livelihood interventions, and research of them, have needed to be creative in order to circumvent legal restrictions that prevent refugees from free access to the domestic labour market. Thus, NGOs have been innovative in their approach toward livelihood creation. In Jordan a coding education for employment intervention has gotten around the legal restrictions for refugees working in the technology sector, a profession that is closed to refugees, because refugee graduates work under consultancy contracts,[2] so Syrians are not technically employed. An NGO based in Lebanon uses a similar tactic to overcome the employment restrictions for Syrian refugees. They have established their own business entity to enter into a direct relationship with refugees as freelancers. This way, refugees are not considered employed but rather contracted,[3] also a grey area in Lebanon. In Turkey, although refugees are technically able to get work permits, an education and employment NGO based in Istanbul hires Syrians as freelance contractors to work with their private sector clients. They also encourage their Syrian entrepreneurs to register as businesses-owners, to circumvent some of the legal issues associated with obtaining work permits.[4] This is much easier than the cumbersome process of applying for work permits in Turkey.

Livelihood interventions have also taken advantage of the legislative grey area surrounding remote work (Charles 2017; Charles 2019). While the right to work laws strictly cover employment in the local labour market, remote work, where the employer is offshore, is technically not legislated against. NGOs that facilitate job creation have taken advantage of this loophole. An NGO based in Lebanon expressed that hiring refugees as freelancers to work remotely in the technology industry for companies in Europe seemed to bypass the Lebanese protectionist legislation that prevented Syrian refugees from working in the local labour market.[5] A UK-based NGO that hires refugees in the Middle East for language instruction stated that they hire refugees as freelancers remotely, as opposed to employees, because of the increasing challenge of employing people without being able to formally check their legal status to work.[6] An American NGO that hires refugees based in the Middle East to work remotely for American companies also agrees that remote work allows refugees to circumvent the labour market restrictions, particularly in Jordan and Lebanon.[7]

When refugees work remotely, they are able to have greater control of their lives. The aforementioned American NGO reported that many of their remote refugee freelancers had worked in exploitative conditions prior to joining and that being able to work remotely from their homes or from community centres allowed them to work in safety. It also allowed populations who would not normally have access to employment, such as women and the injured, opportunities to work.[8] Remote work for refugees has the potential to change the employment narrative and provide dignified employment for many refugees.

These protectionist labour market mechanisms, while presenting significant obstacles to refugee (economic) integration into host communities, have meant that innovative solutions to livelihood creation needed to evolve. The increased attention for solutions around employment has created a growing interest in the opportunities presented by the digital economy. Remote work for refugees has gained international attention. The Global Compact for Refugees explicitly expresses that this solution requires further exploration:

> Particular attention will be paid to closing the technology gap and building capacities (particularly of developing and least-developed refugee host countries), including to facilitate online livelihood opportunities. (United Nations 2018b, paragraph 71)

The viability of remote work for refugees has also been given attention by UNDP, whose Migrant Nations[9] project examines the potential for this narrative. Increased private sector engagement is also evident.

Researching in this context has meant that a broader understanding of livelihoods needed to be adopted so that interventions that circumvented the protectionist measures would be considered. Conventional livelihood projects that aligned with the legal requirements of host country labour laws – as they had limited success in terms of translation to actual jobs – were insufficient to research as a sole solution. This has led to research into a much broader definition of livelihoods.

This process of understanding through research the problems that Syrian refugees have been facing, as well as recording these issues, has taken me beyond the purely 'research' or 'academic' paradigm toward what could be considered a solution-based approach. Observing the problems that protectionist labour markets (as well as the lack of economic opportunity) had caused in Jordan, Lebanon and Turkey demanded a new perspective. This has led to the exploration of a new area of research focusing on the opportunities presented by the digital economy for remote work for refugees.

NOTES

1. A state shall not deport or return an individual to a country where his right to life or personal freedom is in danger of being violated because of his race, nationality, religion, social status or political opinions (UNHCR 1977: 4).
2. NGO community in Istanbul, Suriye Gönüllüleri Koordinasyon (SGF) Group, What's App message to author, 29 December 2018.
3. Interview with NGO in Lebanon, June 2018.
4. Interview with NGO in Turkey, June 2018.
5. Interview with NGO in Lebanon, June 2018.
6. Interview with NGO in the UK, June 2018.
7. Interview with NGO in the US, June 2018.
8. Interview with NGO in the US, June 2018.
9. Interview with UNDP representative, May 2019.

BIBLIOGRAPHY

Barbelet, V., J. Hagen-Zanker and D. Mansour-Ille, 'The Jordan Compact: Lessons learnt and implications for future refugee compacts', Overseas Development Institute (2018) [online], available at https://data2.unhcr.org/fr/documents/download/61932 (last accessed December 2018).

Betts, A., P. Collier, 'Jordan's Refugee Experiment: A New Model for Helping the Displaced', *Foreign Affairs*, (2016) [online], available at https://www.foreignaffairs.com/articles/middle-east/2016-04-28/jordans-refugee-experiment (last accessed 19 December 2018).

Betts, A., L. Bloom, J. Kaplan and N. Omata, 'Refugee Economies: Rethinking Popular Assumptions, Refugee Studies Centre', University of Oxford

(2014) [online], available at: https://www.rsc.ox.ac.uk/files/files-1/refug
ee-economies-2014.pdf (last accessed 19 December 2018).

Charles, L., 'An Examination of Remote Work for Refugees', Averroes Academy (2019) [online], available at http://averroes-academy.com/poli cypapers/36 (last accessed 15 May 2019).

Charles, L., 'How remote work could help refugees', World Economic Forum (2019) [online], available at https://www.weforum.org/agenda/2017/11/ remote-work-could-help-refugees/ (last accessed 19 December 2018).

Charles, L., S. Van Gunteng, 'Livelihoods for Syrian Refugees: Transitioning from a Humanitarian to a Developmental Paradigm: Labour Market Integration in Jordan and Turkey', Emirates Diplomatic Academy (2017) [online], available at http://www.eda.ac.ae/docs/default-source/ Publications/livelihoods_for_syrian_refugees_eda_working_paper_full_ version1e36fe38ddfe6fca8ebaff00006646c8.pdf?sfvrsn=2 (last accessed 19 December 2019).

Crisis Group, 'Turkey's Syrian Refugees: Defusing Metropolitan Tensions' (2018) [online], available at https://www.crisisgroup.org/europe-central-asia/western-europemediterranean/turkey/248-turkeys-syrian-refugees-defusing-metropolitan-tensions (last accessed 19 December 2018).

European Parliament, 'Syrian Crisis: Impact on Lebanon' (2017) [online], available at http://www.europarl.europa.eu/RegData/etudes/BRIE/2017 /599379/EPRS_BRI(2017)599379_EN.pdf (last accessed 19 December 2018).

Ghazal, M., 'Syrian refugee population increases slightly last year', *The Jordan Times* (2018) [online], available at http://www.jordantimes.com/news/ local/syrian-refugee-population-increases-slightly-last-year (last accessed 19 December 2018).

Government of Jordan, Jordan Response Platform for the Syria Crisis (2019) [online], available at http://www.jrpsc.org/ (last accessed 5 April 2019).

Government of Jordan, 'Syrian Refugee Unit Work Permit Progress Report November 2018', Ministry of Labour Syrian Refugee Unit (2018) [online], available at https://reliefweb.int/sites/reliefweb.int/files/resources/ 67243.pdf (last accessed 19 December 2018).

Government of Jordan, 'Jordan Response Plan for the Syria Crisis Appeal 2016–2018, Hashemite Kingdom of Jordan, Ministry of Planning and International Cooperation (2015) [online], available at https://reliefweb. int/sites/reliefweb.int/files/resources/JRP16_18_Document-final+draft. pdf (last accessed 19 December 2018).

Government of Jordan, 'Jordan Compact: A New Holistic Approach between the Hashemite Kingdom of Jordan and the International Community to deal with the Syrian Refugee Crisis' (2016) [online], available at https://

reliefweb.int/report/jordan/jordan-compact-new-holistic-approach-bet ween-hashemite-kingdom-jordan-and (last accessed December 2018).

Government of Lebanon and United Nations, 'Lebanon Crisis Response Plan 2017–2020' (2017) [online], available at http://reliefweb.int/sites/ reliefweb.int/files/resources/2017_2020_LCRP_ENG-1.pdf (last accessed 19 December 2018).

Government of Turkey, 'National Employment Strategy (2014–2023)', Ministry of Labour and Social Security General Directorate of Labour (2014) [online], available at http://www.uis.gov.tr/Media/Books/UIS-en. pdf (last accessed 19 December 2018).

Gov.UK, 'Supporting Syria and the Region London 2016 – Turkey Statement' (2016) [online], available at https://www.gov.uk/government/publica tions/supporting-syria-and-the-region-london-2016-turkey-statement (last accessed 19 December 2018).

Ibáñez, A., 'Jordan issues more than 100,000 work permits for Syrians', *The Jordan Times* (2018) [online], available at http://www.jordantimes. com/news/local/jordan-issues-more-100000-work-permits-syrians (last accessed 19 December 2018).

ILO, 'Assessment of the Impact of Syrian Refugees in Lebanon and Their Employment profile', International Labour Organisation (2013) [online], available at http://www.ilo.org/wcmsp5/groups/public/---arabstates/ ---ro-beirut/documents/publication/wcms_240134.pdf (last accessed 19 December 2018).

Jacobsen, K., 'Livelihoods in Conflict: The Pursuit of Livelihoods by Refugees and the Impact on the Human Security of Host Communities', *International Migration*, 40 (5) (2002).

Leghtas, I., 'Out of Reach: Legal work still in accessible to refugees in Jordan', Refugees International (2018) [online], available at https://reliefweb.int/ sites/reliefweb.int/files/resources/Jordan%2BReport%2B2018%2B-% 2B9.10.2018%2B-%2B647%2Bpm.pdf (last accessed 19 December 2018).

Malka, K., '$300m World Bank project for labour market reform 'to be approved in September' (2016) [online], available at http://www.jordan times.com/news/local/300m-world-bank-project-labour-market-reform- be-approved-september%E2%80%99 (last accessed December 2018).

Multeciler, D., 'Number of Syrians in Turkey Granted Work Permits' (2018) [online], available at https://multeciler.org.tr/turkiyede-calisma-izni- verilen-suriyeli-sayisi/ (last accessed 19 December 2018).

National Archives, 'Supporting Syria and the Region London 2016' (2018) [online], available at https://www.supportingsyria2016.com/ (last accessed 19 December 2018).

The Union of Chambers and Commodity Exchanges of Turkey, Press Release of Statistics of Established and Closed Companies (2018) [online], available at http://tobb.org.tr/BilgiErisimMudurlugu/Sayfalar/Eng/KurulanKapananSirketistatistikleri.php (last accessed 19 December 2018).

Todd, L., A. Amirullah and W. Shin, 'The Economic Impact of Granting Refugees in Malaysia the Right to Work', Policy Ideas, no. 60, Institute for Democracy and Economic Affairs (2019) [online], available at https://www.tent.org/wp-content/uploads/2019/08/IDEAS-Malaysia.pdf (last accessed 19 January 2020).

Turkish Labour Law, 'Work Permit Fees of Syrian Nationals Reduced' (2017) [online], available at https://turkishlaborlaw.com/news/business-in-turkey/563-work-permit-fees-of-syrian-nationals-reduced (last accessed 19 December 2018).

UNHCR, 'Figures at a Glance' (2020a) [online], available at http://www.unhcr.org/figures-at-a-glance.html (last accessed 5 April 2019).

UNHCR, 'Operations Portal Refugee Situations' (2020b) [online], available at https://data2.unhcr.org/en/situations/syria (last accessed 28 November 2020).

UNHCR, 'New York Declaration for Refugees and Migrants' (2019a) [online], available at https://www.unhcr.org/new-york-declaration-for-refugees-and-migrants.html (last accessed 28 November 2020).

UNHCR, 'Global Compact on Refugees Platform' (2019b) [online], available at http://www.globalcrrf.org/ (last accessed 5 April 2019).

UNHCR, 'Jordan Fact Sheet' (2018a) [online], available at https://data2.unhcr.org/en/documents/download/66556 (last accessed 19 December 2018).

UNHCR, 'ESSN Task Force Istanbul Minutes' (2018b) [online], available at https://data2.unhcr.org/en/documents/download/66983 (last accessed 19 December 2018).

UNHCR, 'Comprehensive Refugee Response Framework: from the New York Declaration to a global compact on refugees' (2016a) [online], available at https://www.unhcr.org/events/conferences/584687b57/comprehensive-refugee-response-framework-new-york-declaration-global-compact.html (last accessed 5 April 2019).

UNHCR, 'Regulatory Framework for SMEs, Home-based Businesses, Cooperatives and NGOs for Non-Jordanian Nationals' (2016b) [online], available at https://data2.unhcr.org/en/documents/download/49813 (last accessed 19 January 2020).

UNHCR, 'Refugee Response in Lebanon Briefing Documents' (2015) [online], available at http://www.europarl.europa.eu/meetdocs/2014_2019/documents/droi/dv/95_finalbriefingkit_/95_finalbriefingkit_en.pdf (last accessed 19 December 2018).

UNHCR, 'Note on Non-Refoulement' (1977) [online], available at http://www.unhcr.org/afr/excom/scip/3ae68ccd10/note-non-refoulement-submittedhigh-commissioner.html (last accessed 5 April 2019).

United Nations, 'Global Compact on Refugees' (2018a) [online], available at https://www.unhcr.org/5c658aed4 (last accessed 5 April 2019).

United Nations, 'Report of the United Nations High Commissioner for Refugees Part II Global compact on refugees' (2018b) [online], available at https://www.unhcr.org/gcr/GCR_English.pdf (last accessed 19 December 2018).

United Nations, 'Lebanon Crisis Response Plan 2015–2016' (2014) [online], available at http://reliefweb.int/sites/reliefweb.int/files/resources/2015-2016_Lebanon_CRP_EN.pdf (last accessed 19 December 2018).

World Bank, 'Forcibly Displaced: Towards Development Approach to Refugees, the Internally Displaced, and Their Hosts' (2017) [online], available at https://openknowledge.worldbank.org/handle/10986/25016 (last accessed 19 December 2018).

World Bank, '$300 million to Improve Employment Opportunities for Jordanians and Syrian Refugees' (2016) [online], available at http://www.worldbank.org/en/news/press-release/2016/09/27/300-million-to-improve-employment-opportunities-for-jordanians-and-syrian-refugees (last accessed December 2018).

Yackley, A., 'Turkey downsizes economic growth outlook as crisis bites', Al Monitor (2018) [online], available at https://www.al-monitor.com/pulse/originals/2018/09/turkey-economy-plan.html (last accessed 19 December 2018).

Identity and Positionality in Research

Talking to Young People about Being a National: Fieldwork Reflections from Dubai

İdil Akıncı

One of the most dominant understandings of the Arabian Peninsula is that its national population is predominantly Bedouin, Arab and tribal. The exclusion of migrant populations, who outnumber citizens in most of the Gulf States, from accessing citizenship, further consolidate the popular imagination of Gulf nationals as belonging to a homogenous Arab population. In line with this Arab ethno-national project (Samin 2016), ancestral links of some Gulf nationals, including Emiratis, to various parts of the Indian Ocean, Persia, East Africa, Yemen and the wider Arabian Peninsula have been elided with the state narratives of 'nation-ness'. Not surprisingly, immigration to the Gulf, including the United Arab Emirates, is narrated as a post-oil phenomenon, which brought cultural, social, economic and political implications on the 'homogenous native population', leading to the tendency to study these populations through the citizen/migrant distinction (Vora and Koch 2015).

In the last decade a number of interdisciplinary studies pushed for a more nuanced understanding of Gulf societies by attending to the heterogenous demographic reality among nationals. These included histories of pre-oil and pre-nation migrations to the port cities of the Gulf (Al-Rasheed 2005; Onley 2005; Fuccaro 2014; Potter 2014; al-Daliami 2014; Hopper 2014); national culture engineering projects through selective representations of history, heritage and invented traditions (Erskine-Loftus, Hightower and Al-Mulla, 2016; Al-Ragam 2014; Dhaheri 2009; Khalaf 2008); the tensions between the discursive and performed elements of nationhood, arising from ethnic, tribal, linguistic and racial diversities as well as legal statuses among nationals (Nagy 2006; AlMutawa 2016; Akinci 2019b; Akinci 2020; Limbert 2014; Al-Rasheed 2013; Kanna 2011; Kharusi 2013; Gardner and Zakzouk 2014; Holes 2011; Alshawi and Gardner,2013; Dresch 2005; Lori 2019; Jamal 2015).

Framed by theories on everyday nationhood, my ethnographic research in

Dubai contributes to this body of work. I explore historically, and contemporaneously, the migration flows to the area and complexities around competing claims to national belonging as narrated by young Emirati nationals. Some of my participants have parents and/or grandparents who migrated from various parts of the Indian Ocean, Southern Persia, Arabian Peninsula and Africa in the late nineteenth and the mid-twentieth century and since received Emirati citizenship. Engaging with young people's narratives of national and ethnic origins, and their articulation of historical and contemporary migrations to Dubai, my research reconsiders the categories of migrant and citizen in the ways we study Gulf identities, which have been predominantly treated as fixed and unchanging.

In this chapter, I reflect on some of the methodological challenges encountered in my research, unique to the topic investigated, the demographic sample of the study, as well as the positionality of the researcher. Based on my year-long fieldwork in Dubai between 2015 and 2016, I discuss how, in a context where state narratives claim ethnic homogeneity among nationals, this topic might be perceived as socially sensitive. Thus, it may not be always straightforward to discuss with the nationals, especially when the researcher is an outsider. Where presumably national/foreigner divide is a central hierarchy in Gulf societies (Vora and Koch 2015), blurring this divide not only means complicating the state narrative about who Gulf nationals are, but also the social boundaries between migrant and citizen populations, which might become more salient in a research context.I consider the role of my lived experiences in Dubai prior to fieldwork, teaching at a university in Dubai and a perceived cultural proximity by my participants, in navigating some of the issues of establishing rapport, and in producing a nuanced study of Emiratiness.

TALKING ABOUT PRE-OIL AND PRE-NATION MIGRATIONS TO DUBAI WITH YOUNG EMIRATIS

In the pre-oil and pre-nation era, port cities of the Arabian Gulf, such as Dubai, were home to diverse immigrant communities, as a result of trade relations, colonial affairs as well as slavery. As a result of nation-building efforts, which included Arabisation of the national population, some of these culturally and linguistically diverse communities, who have been naturalised as Emirati, are often imagined as a homogenous category. The tendency to treat Gulf societies as a 'sociological exception', due to their perceived 'insular and homogenous make-up' (Alshawi and Gardner 2013: 47), presents itself as a methodological challenge in this context (Kapiszewski 1999: 37).

While it is important to recognise that Gulf societies are not strictly segregated by citizen/migrant divide, the varying degree of social distance between national and migrant groups helps to reproduce widely held beliefs about Gulf national populations as being homogenous. In contrast to the salient distinction between Emiratis and non-Emiratis, internal differences among Emiratis are not easily visible to foreigners across the boundary of nationality (Nagy 2006), and some nationals are discreet about their ancestral origins, depending on their social position and context of the discussion. Since nationality takes priority in social interactions, rarely is there reason to offer further details of one's social identity. Whilst long-term residents who have close relationships with the Emirati community are aware of the 'cosmopolitan' past of this region and the diverse roots of Emiratis, they typically consider these differences as 'unimportant' and instead underline the importance of citizenship and culture that Emiratis share (Akinci 2019a).

Not surprisingly, despite having lived and worked in Dubai for many years prior to this research, it was not until I returned to the city for my fieldwork and started teaching at a university that I understood the extent of diversity among citizens. Students all looked different phenotypically, suggesting the diversity of their heritage, and they also had very diverse, yet Arabised, family names, referencing various parts of Southern Persia, Baluchistan, and South Asia. Whilst my initial PhD project proposed a study of second-generation non-Gulf Arab residents in Dubai and their familial relations to the Emirati community, I soon become intrigued by the ethnic diversity among Emiratis and how this was experienced and narrated by young Emiratis on an everyday basis and implicated on different forms of belonging.

Soon after returning to Dubai for my fieldwork, I shared with an Emirati friend my growing interest in including young Emiratis in my research sample. His initial response was as follows:

> First of all, good luck with finding people willing to open up to you. I am not saying it is impossible but you need a lot of time to sit down and talk to them, to gain their confidence and hopefully they will open up to you ... But many will say who is this Turkish girl wanting to know about our culture and roots?

Accessing participants, especially citizens, is often met with challenges, as there might be a degree of reluctance to take part in any research that can potentially challenge official discourses or produce alternative ones (Kathiravelu 2016). This is particularly relevant to Gulf societies, where official and popular discourses to depict national identity in a binary manner between the supposedly 'homogenous' Emirati citizens versus the 'diverse' migrant population. By side lining ancestral migration trajectories of Emiratis to Dubai, these narratives imply that Emiratis are a timeless community and migration is essentially a post-oil phenomenon. The discreetness of Emiratis about their ancestral origins, especially to an outsider, reflects the potential perception of this topic as socially sensitive. Even though ethnic heterogeneity continues to shape the social organisation of Emiratis, reflected on marriages for example (see Dresch, 2005), acknowledgment of these complexities, and historical migrations, to an outsider might compromise the salient boundaries between migrant and citizen populations.

'PARTICIPANT LIVING' AND THE IMPORTANCE OF EXISTING NETWORKS IN DUBAI

I moved to Dubai from Turkey in 2008. I lived and worked in the city until 2012, when I decided to move to London for postgraduate studies. I was already integrated into the everyday life of the city and had the privilege of extensive knowledge, without theoretical or research concerns. In fact, it was not until after 2014, I have decided to take on an academic career and enrolled on a PhD programme and conduct research in Dubai. This way, I learned the society not through goal-oriented participant observation, but through what Longva calls spontaneous 'participant living' (1997: 13). These stocks of knowledge shaped what type of research I wanted to do, and what type of questions to ask to different groups living in the city. However, it was only when I started my fieldwork in 2015 that I fully appreciated the incomparable advantage of my lived experiences in Dubai, years before I decided to do this research.

As I returned to Dubai, I continued to socialise with my friends over dinners, at weekends at the beach, and on short holidays. My social circles were predominantly second-generation migrants born and raised in Dubai, as well as Emiratis, which meant that in my everyday life I was surrounded by people who 'fitted' my study group. Thus, 'deep hanging out' (Geertz 1998) and immersing oneself in a cultural group or social experience on an informal level was not a method I used deliberately during my fieldwork, but was rather an inevitable consequence of my everyday experience living in Dubai. While I did not use my friends as informants, our day-to-day discussions at times provided me with data that it was not possible to extract from formal interviews. 'Deep hanging out' also helped me to cross-check and discuss some of my findings with my friends and receive feedback. These discussions also paved the way for different venues of exploration that I had not thought about previously.

Knowing my research interest, my Emirati friends took me to neighbourhoods across the city where different Emirati communities historically lived. Thanks to these walking tours, I became aware of Al Rashidiya's Zanzibari community, Al Jafaliya's historical religious minority, different parts of Al Quoz, where *bidoon* (stateless people of the Emirates) lived, Hor Al Anz's past as home to Southern Persian and Baloch migrants who have arrived in Dubai during the first half of the twentieth century, as well as parts of Al Satwa where

Baloch and Yemeni Emiratis lived. If it were not for these visits, which were often followed by invitations to weddings, cultural evenings, *iftar* dinners and social gatherings, I would have never been able to contextualise my fieldwork in the way I did, as well as the narratives I collected. Most importantly, I would never have known the historical significance of these areas for some of the older migrant populations, which are not known to most people living in Dubai, and even some Emirati groups. Moreover, my North African flatmates, with whom I shared a house in an Emirati-dominant part of Jumeirah during my fieldwork, also became an important part of my 'hanging out'. Although they were not within my sampling criteria, since they had not been born and raised in the UAE, their lived experiences in Dubai as non-Gulf Arab residents, and their close relationships with Emirati society, enabled me to locate my study of Emiratiness in the context of the wider Dubai society.

I reached out to potential participants through a network of friends, colleagues and acquaintances. Their large network of friends became my main participant group, people whom I had never met, yet who accepted my invitation to take part in my research, thanks to our common acquaintances. In order to ensure diversity of my sample, avoid possible blockages that could occur during 'snowballing', and eliminate bias-related issues, I identified possible interviewees, not based on their convenience but on their relevancy to my research aims and by bringing in voices that may offer different articulations of nation-ness, citizenship and belonging (Yin 2011).

After demonstrating some 'insider knowledge' (my experiences of living in Dubai, use of colloquial terms, knowledge of urban spaces, and references to urban culture), I felt that I was granted a temporary and partial insider position to these groups (Mullings 1999) and that interviews resembled a conversation about everyday life in Dubai. My attempts to speak Arabic with my participants, at least in colloquial terms, or in the initial interviewing process, also enabled a smooth transition into the interviews.

Having said that, despite the fact that English is the 'unofficial' daily and working language in Dubai, the most challenging component of being an outsider was the fact that I am not a native Arabic speaker. Even though all my participants spoke English and all my interviews were conducted in English, I certainly missed some subtle meanings and insights contained in the words and actions of my participants. While I have some conversational ability, my level of Arabic remained basic at best. I felt the necessity of Arabic mostly when I was surrounded by Emiratis and had the chance to observe their everyday interactions with others, yet I could not do so as they conversed in Arabic among themselves most of the time. I dealt with this challenge, partially, by asking people what particular terms or expressions meant if I did not understand, and by being honest about anything I did not follow in conversation.

Affiliation with a university in Dubai

The difficulties of conducting research in the Gulf States has mainly manifested in the restrictions placed by governments for ethnographic field research, such as difficulties in obtaining visas and permission to conduct research (Kathiravelu 2016: 19; Gardner 2010: 8; Al-Rasheed 2005). This is a particularly relevant issue for researchers who need a visa to enter the UAE and remain on a long-term basis. As a holder of a Turkish passport, in order to reside in Dubai for my year-long fieldwork, I needed an affiliation with a university, which would grant me a visa and permission to conduct research. I also needed to supplement my doctoral stipend by teaching at a university in Dubai, in order to cover expenses such as rent.

I felt that, most importantly, it was my affiliation with a university in Dubai that allowed for successful fieldwork. Working in a campus helped with contextualising my findings and allowed a space to observe interactions among different young people living Dubai on a daily basis. My research being ethically reviewed and approved by a respected and reputable local institution, and my role both as a lecturer and researcher on campus, provided my participants with needed trust and credibility to participate in this research. In this instance, my affiliation with a local university was perceived as more important than my affiliation with my UK institution, as the former institution's legitimisation of my research is what made the study appealing for both Emirati and non-Emirati participants.

The relationships I developed with fellow lecturers and researchers on campus, as well as my everyday observations of students in classrooms, further immersed me. I regularly socialised with faculty members and staff on and off campus, whether these were everyday lunches, departmental drinks or weekly ladies' nights. In these social events, we often shared experiences of teaching and researching in Dubai. The faculty members also helped me to access a number of Emiratis, whom they thought would be particularly interesting for my research. Most of these individuals had an interest in the topics I was investigating, or had done research themselves or planned to do so.

For one year I taught sociology courses to undergraduate students. The relevance of the subjects and related discussions in the classrooms presented a great opportunity to make systematic observations and offered a platform to interact with young people in Dubai. Even though theoretical and conceptual issues were mainly analysed through Western literature and case studies, each class enabled a focus group type of environment. I had approximately twenty students in each class, who were encouraged to reflect on these debates and try to discuss them in relation to their context, whether this was in the form of student presentations, research projects, term papers or classroom discussions.

After classes, just like after each observation or social session, I recorded the (mental) notes I had taken during the discussion. These notes became my fieldwork diary. Having said that, the data I gathered in classrooms was only used to contextualise my research inquiry better and sharpen my interview questions. I did not add this data to the analysis due to the potential ethical and consent issues that could arise.

During these lectures, students often questioned my reason to be in Dubai, which led to discussions about my PhD research. Many students came forward to participate and, in initial stages, it felt that I ended up with a 'convenience' or 'volunteer' sample (Cohen et al. 2007: 113–16). However, as the time progressed, I began to have a more diverse sample. In fact, some of Emiratis who initially identified as Arab, in the course of the interview, shared with me their parents'/ grandparents' migration histories spanning across Southern Persia, other parts of the Arabian Peninsula, Zanzibar or Baluchistan. I also received emails from students I did not know, who heard about the research from their peers and wanted to participate. In the end, I ended up having quite a few participants on-campus, supporting the off-campus Emirati sample.

Moreover, I was often invited by my colleagues as a guest lecturer on topics that were related to my research. Unlike my own classes, these classes provided an environment where students did not feel that they were 'under some tacit obligation to cooperate' (Denscombe and Aubrook 1992: 129) and take part in my research. Seeing me on campus every day familiarised them with my face, while the guest lectures familiarised them with my research topic. Many students approached me after these lectures, interested in taking part in the research.

'Turkish-ness' as an ice-breaker

The nationality of the researcher is an important factor in the UAE, not only because it determines the type of visa and permission required, but also because it defines to a large degree the social proximity that individuals want to establish with each another. Although Turkey's alignment with Qatar, following the Gulf diplomatic crisis in June 2017, impacted severely on Turkey's relationship with the UAE, at the time of this research Turkish nationals were typically well received among both GCC and non-GCC Arabs in the UAE, due to the perceived cultural and political commonalities.

This was mainly a result of the Turkish government's increasingly pro-Islam and Middle Eastern foreign policy, since early 2000s, which made Turkey popular among Arabs, including young Emiratis I spoke to, and the Islamic world. Equally, the popularity of Turkish soap operas in the Middle East, which shape an idealised perception of Turkey being a Muslim yet 'European' country, was another important factor for the favourable reception I had both as a lecturer and a researcher. My Emirati participants often expressed 'how lucky I was to be Turkish' because I came from the country which 'produced all this wonderful culture, food and entertainment'. Many had Turkish actors and actresses on their phone screens or laptops and many of my participants, both Emirati and non-Emirati, knew more about Turkish popular culture than I did. Some of my Emirati students also tried to practise spoken Turkish they had learnt through watching these series.

Turkishness was not received as intimidating or threatening, I was told. Both Emirati and non-Emirati participants told me that they felt more comfortable discussing their opinions with an outsider, as they felt an Emirati might have judged them for their views. Moreover, they often expressed their feelings of cultural proximity to me. Even though my mode of dress and way of talking and presenting myself signalled a sense of 'Western-ness', my Turkish background and my knowledge about the topics I was researching and our common experiences of living in Dubai drew me closer to them. In contrast, they often referred to British people and Europeans as cultural 'outsiders'. In their narratives, there was also a sense of threat and intimidation towards these groups, whose lifestyle, traditions and 'unfair' upper hand in Emirati society were not received well.

METHODS AND PROCESSES OF DATA COLLECTION

While nationhood and nationalism is constructed from above, it

> … cannot be understood unless also analysed from below, that is in terms of the assumptions, hopes, needs, longings and interests as well as perceptions, memories and activities of ordinary people, which are not necessarily national and still less nationalist. (Hobsbawm 1990: 10)

As my aim was to investigate the significance of national identity in the everyday lives of young Emiratis, Hobsbawm's views on adopting a bottom-up approach fitted well with my reasoning. In order to draw a holistic picture of the phenomenon, I utilised inductive reasoning, using qualitative interviews as the primary method of data collection, as well as observations (Goddard and Melville 2004). For this research, as much as it was a methodological preference to take a bottom-up approach, it was also a necessity. The ethnographic research on Gulf citizenry is limited and often depicted through top-down theoretical applications (Alshawi and Gardner 2013; Vora 2013), which may not represent the lived experiences a heterogonous national population.

I conducted fifty-six qualitative interviews, respectively thirty-six of them with Emiratis and twenty with non-Emiratis, aged nineteen to thirty-one. Since the aim was to investigate how Emiratis of different cultural and ethnic origins understood national identity and belonging, the sample was as diverse as possible based on these criteria. Nineteen out of thirty-six participants identified as Arab. What they defined as Arab was however ambiguous, as many also stated to have families across the Indian Ocean, Southern Persia and islands reflecting the complex understanding of Arabness in this geography (Limbert 2014). Others identified as Ajam and/or to have Persian origins, Zanzibari, Balochi, or as having mixed heritage, including a combination of Ajam/Arab, Balochi/Arab. There were also participants with mothers from Philippines, Sri Lanka and India.

While my main aim with using interviews was to understand Emiratiness through the eyes of young nationals, I was also aware of the inherent limitations of this mode of inquiry. Even though my lived experiences in Dubai enabled a degree of proximity to my participants, I do not suggest that these interviews offer 'an authentic gaze into the soul of another' (Atkinson and Silverman 1997: 305). I perceive interviews as a means to explore the discursive strategies deployed by young nationals, indicating what is contextually and socially possible to speak about (Luker 2010: 167). Thus, my analysis of how Emiratis -and non-Emiratis- articulate concepts of national identity, citizenship and belonging also examine what type of articulations were absent from their narratives, and considers the reasons for silences or reluctance to speak about certain issues.

During my initial interviews, when I asked participants whom they saw as being an Emirati, they effectively echoed the official and popular narratives: being Arab, Muslim, speaking Arabic, having ancestral links to the UAE and having citizenship. In fact, these markers were often conflated with each other. These narratives were so recurrent that I found myself thinking that I was perhaps looking for something that had little to no importance for citizens, and that I was imposing my research ideas on them. However, as my interviews progressed, and I further read about the on-going relevance of ethnic and tribal identities among nationals, I established that these repetitive depictions of 'being Emirati' was partially a methodological issue that researchers face when doing research on topics that can emerge as sensitive (Lee 1993). While the definition of a 'sensitive' research topic depends on both context and cultural norms and values, topics that are considered private or prone to cause controversy can create a sensitive research environment (Lee,1993). In the context of my research, ethnic purity, based on Arabness, is an important factor for shaping social hierarchies within the Emirati community (Partrick 2009), thus talking about ancestral origins outside the Arabian Peninsula might be perceived as sensitive for potentially implying 'a lack of Arab purity'.

As I wanted to treat 'identity' as a process that emerges through narration (Anthias 2002: 495), I did not want to impose pre-determined identity categories on participants. For the data to emerge as organically as possible, I started asking participants whom they perceived to be the 'internal others' of their society. The answer was, always, the migrants. This was often followed by *bidoon* and occasionally 'halfies' (a colloquial term to refer to Emiratis with a foreign parent). Thus, explicit in their answer, otherness was solely constructed through citizenship or the lack of it. Considering that these popular narratives were exactly what I tried to dismantle with my research, at times I asked more leading questions, appreciating that both directive and non-directive questioning could produce different kinds of rapport that may be useful at different stages of the inquiry (Hammersley and Atkinson 2007: 120). While I never self-imposed an 'ethnic label' on participants, I asked them how far back they could trace their roots in Dubai, whether they had families living across the Emirates, the Gulf or other parts of the World, whether they had mixed parentage, or whether they spoke languages other than Arabic. The answers to these questions often became the basis of further discussion on internal diversities. The topic of national and ethnic identity were received by most participants as exciting and led to participants talking about their families' migration trajectories and the implications of these on their customs, food, music and clothing, as well as a variety of languages they spoke at home. This way, while I drew the boundaries of conversation, I nevertheless allowed the participants to choose how they wanted to colour it or even move outside these boundaries when needed (Yin 2011).

In order to ensure that the relationship between the participants and myself was non-hierarchical, I often shared personal stories in relation to my research during interviews (Liamputtong and Ezzy 2005). While sharing personal details and motivations behind a specific research may be a conscious part of the rapport-building process (Dickson-Swift et al. 2007), it was, in fact, my personal lived experiences in various multicultural contexts, including Dubai, which shaped this research and I wanted to share it with those who wanted to know. Since participants often presumed that I was referring to migrant populations in terms of ethnic diversity, I explicitly expressed that my research also considered the internal diversities within Emirati citizenry. Whilst my knowledge about the internal differences in their community initially surprised them, it was this reciprocal acknowledgment of diversity that enabled a conversation about these issues.

CONCLUSION

Whilst in the last decades growing ethnographic research on Gulf societies suggest that fieldwork access has become more navigable for some researchers, experiences in the fieldwork remain highly subjective. This is shaped by a variety of factors, including the topic and group of people researched (Lori

2019), the country of fieldwork and shifting political circumstances (Gardner 2010:9; Lori 2019), the race, gender and nationality of the researcher (Vora 2013), as well as the prior connections and lived experiences that researchers may have to the societies in which they conduct research (see Longva 1997). These experiences also determine the degree of comfort and confidence researchers have in disseminating ethnographic material in consideration of their and their participants' safety (see Lori 2019: 243–4).

This chapter has reflected on some of the methodological issues of conducting research among national groups in the Gulf States, based on my ethnographic research in Dubai. I particularly considered a key methodological issue and implication of being an insider/outsider in a context where presumably national/foreigner divide is a central hierarchy in Gulf societies. Having lived and worked in the city, I discussed in this chapter how these experiences enabled a positive experience doing fieldwork, given the social networks and cultural proximity I managed to accumulate. Most importantly, my familiarity with the city and its inhabitants enabled me to locate the study of Emiratiness in the context of the wider Dubai society. I also underlined the importance of affiliating with a university, both in terms of the visa it granted me to conduct research in Dubai and the rapport-building it enabled with young Emiratis. Based on my experiences of living in Dubai, I also considered the role of 'nationality', in my case being from Turkey, and how this facilitated the processes of interacting with and interviewing Emirati nationals. Finally, I discussed the ways in which I manoeuvred the silences and perceived sensitivities during the course of the interviews.

While I acknowledge the various methodological challenges that hinder the processes of conducting research in the Gulf States, especially where the national communities are concerned, I firmly believe that there needs to be more ethnographic research concerning Gulf identities. We know very little about how the top-down process of national identity construction is articulated by a diverse set of citizens, considering the cosmopolitan past of this region, especially the port cities such as Dubai. By attending to the complexities and ethnic diversity of Gulf citizenry, as well as the similarities of processes of national identity construction in the UAE with other societies, such research can break the tendency in academia to treat Gulf societies as exceptional sociological cases, a tendency which often leads to presenting these newly founded, rapidly developed and wealthy states as lacking history and having a 'homogenous' societal structure (Alshawi and Gardner 2013; Vora 2013). In doing so, research on Gulf identities can also complicate some of the naturalised, and taken-for-granted categories, such as Gulf national identities, which are often treated as absolute, and primordial. While the exceptional demographic imbalance and exclusion of migrants from citizenship make migrants in the Gulf States crucial in constructing national identity and reinforcing unity among citizens, more research needs to address how boundaries are similarly created among Gulf citizens and how they are implicated on everyday life. This approach will not only allow the conceptualising of Gulf societies in a more nuanced manner, but also the drawing of connections between the Gulf, and the 'Western' societies, where in both of the contexts, a presumed common culture is increasingly instrumentalised as a justification for the demarcation of national boundaries (Akinci 2019b).

BIBLIOGRAPHY

Akinci, I., 'Culture in the "Politics of Identity": Conceptions of National Identity and Citizenship among Second-generation Non-Gulf Arab Migrants in Dubai', *Journal of Ethnic and Migration Studies* (2019a), pp. 1–17.

Akinci, I,. 'Dressing the Nation? Symbolising Emirati National Identity and Boundaries Through National Dress' *Journal of Ethnic and Racial Studies* (2019b), https://doi.org/10.1080/01419870.2019.1665697.

Akinci, I., 'Language, Nation, Difference: Everyday Language Tactics of Young Emiratis', in *Gulf Cooperation Council Culture and Identities in the New Millennium Resilience, Transformation, (Re)Creation and Diffusion*, M. Karolak and N. Allam (eds) (Singapore: Palgrave Macmillan, 2020).

al-Dailami, A., '"Purity and Confusion": The Hawala between Persians and Arabs in the Contemporary Gulf', in *The Persian Gulf in Modern Times. People, Ports, and History*, 1st edn, L. Potter (ed.) (London: Palgrave Macmillan, 2014).

AlMutawa, R., *Monolithic Representations and Orientalist Credence in the UAE* (Oxford: Oxford Gulf and Arabian Peninsula Studies Forum, 2016).

Al-Ragam, A., 'The Politics of Representation: The Kuwait National Museum and Processes of Cultural Production', *International Journal of Heritage Studies*, 20(6) (2014), pp. 663–74.

Al-Rasheed, M., *Transnational Connections and the Arab Gulf* (New York: Routledge, 2005).

Al-Rasheed, M., 'Transnational Connections and National Identity: Zanzibari Omanis in Muscat', in *Monarchies and Nations: Globalisation and Identity in the Arab States of the Gulf*, P. Dresch and J. Piscatori (eds) (London: I. B. Tauris, 2013).

Alshawi, A. and A. Gardner, 'Tribalism, Identity and Citizenship in Contemporary Qatar', *Anthropology of the Middle East*, 8(2) (2013).

Anthias, F., 'Where do I belong? Narrating collective identity and translocational positionality', *Ethnicities*, 2(4) (2002), pp. 491–514.

Atkinson, P. and D. Silverman, 'Kundera's Immortality: The Interview Society and the Invention of the Self', *Qualitative Inquiry*, 3(3) (1997), pp. 304–25.

Cohen, L., L. Manion and K. Morrison, *Research Methods in Education* (Abingdon: Routledge, 2007), pp. 100–17.

Denscombe, M. and L. Aubrook, 'It's Just Another Piece of Schoolwork: The Ethics of Questionnaire Research on Pupils in Schools', *British Educational Research Journal*, 18(2) (1992), pp. 113–31.

Dhaheri, H. (2009), 'Women and Nation Building: The Case of the United Arab Emirates', *Hawwa*, 7(3), pp. 271–302.

Dickson-Swift, V., E. James, S. Kippen and P. Liamputtong, 'Doing Sensitive Research: What Challenges do Qualitative Researchers Face?', *Qualitative Research*, 7(3) (2007), pp. 327–53.

Dresch, P., 'Debates on Marriage and Nationality in the United Arab Emirates', in *Monarchies and Nations. Globalisation and Identity in the Arab States of the Gulf*, P. Dresch and J. Piscatori (eds) (London and New York: I. B. Tauris, 2005).

Erskine-Loftus, P., Hightower, V. and Al-Mulla, M., *Representing the Nation: Heritage, Museums, National Narratives, and Identity in the Arab Gulf States* (London: Routledge, 2016).

Fucarro, N., 'Rethinking the History of Port Cities in the Gulf', in *The Persian Gulf in Modern Times People, Ports, and History*, L. Potter (ed.) (London: Palgrave Macmillan, 2014).

Gardner, A., *City of Strangers* (Ithaca, NY: Cornell University Press, 2010).

Gardner, A. and Zakzouk, M., 'Cars Culture in Contemporary Qatar', in *Everyday Life in the Muslim Middle East*, 3rd edn, D. Lee Bowen, E. Early and B. Schulthies (eds) (Bloomington and Indianapolis: Indiana University Press, 2014).

Geertz, C., 'Deep Hanging Out', *The New York Review of Books*, 45(16) (1998).

Goddard, W. and S. Melville, *Research Methodology* (Kenwyn, South Africa: Juta Academic, 2004).

Hammersley, M. and P. Atkinson, *Ethnography: Principles in Practice* (London: Routledge, 2007).

Hobsbawm, E., *Nations and Nationalism since 1780* (Cambridge: Cambridge University Press, 1990).

Hopper, M. (2014). The African Presence in Eastern Arabia', in *The Persian Gulf in Modern Times: People, Ports and History*, L. Potter (ed.) (New York: Palgrave Macmillan, 2014).

Jamal, M., 'The "Tiering" of Citizenship and Residency and the "Hierarchization" of Migrant Communities: The United Arab Emirates in Historical Context', *International Migration Review*, 49(3) (2015), pp. 601–32.

Kanna, A., *Dubai, the City as Corporation* (Minneapolis: University of Minnesota Press, 2011).

Kapiszewski, A., *Native Arab Population and Foreign Workers in the Gulf States* (Kraków: Tow, 1999).

Kathiravelu, L., *Migrant Dubai: Low Wage Workers and the Construction of a Global City* (London: Palgrave Macmillan, 2016).

Khalaf, S., 'The Nationalisation of Culture: Kuwait's Invention of a Pearl-Diving Heritage', in *Popular Culture and Political Identity in the Arab Gulf State*, A. Alsharekh and R. Springborg (eds) (London: Saqi Books, 2008).

Kharusi, N., 'Identity and Belonging among Ethnic Return Migrants of Oman', *Nationalism and Ethnic Politics*, 19(4) (2013), pp. 424–46.

Lee, R., *Doing Research on Sensitive Topics* (London: SAGE Publications, 1993).

Liamputtong, P. and D. Ezzy, *Qualitative Research Methods* (Melbourne: Oxford University Press, 2005).

Limbert, M., 'Caste, Ethnicity, and the Politics of Arabness in Southern Arabia', *Comparative Studies of South Asia, Africa and the Middle East*, 34(3) (2014), pp. 590–8.

Longva, A., *Walls Built on Sand* (Boulder: Westview Press, 1997).

Lori, N., *Offshore Citizens: Permanent 'Temporary' Status in the Gulf* (Cambridge: Cambridge University Press, 2019).

Luker, K., *Salsa Dancing into the Social Sciences* (Cambridge, MA: Harvard University Press, 2010).

Mitchell, J. (2016), 'We're all Qataris here: The Nation-building Narrative of the National Museum of Qatar', in *Representing the Nation: Heritage, Museums, National Narratives, and Identity in the Arab Gulf States*, P. Erskine-Loftus, V. Hightower and M. Al-Mulla (eds) (London and New York: Routledge, 2016).

Mullings, B., 'Insider or Outsider, Both or Neither: Some Dilemmas of Interviewing in a Cross-cultural Setting', *Geoforum*, 30(4) (1999), pp. 337–50.

Nagy, S., 'Making Room for Migrants, Making Sense of Difference: Spatial and Ideological Expressions of Social Diversity in Urban Qatar', *Urban Studies*, 43(1) (2006), pp. 119–37.

Onley, J., 'Transnational Merchants in the Nineteenth-century Gulf', in *Transnational Connections and the Arab Gulf*, M. Al-Rasheed (ed.) (London, New York: Routledge, 2005).

Partrick, N., *Nationalism in the Gulf States*, Kuwait Programme on Development, Governance and Globalisation in the Gulf States (London: London School of Economics, Centre for the Study of Global Governance, 2009).

Potter, L., *The Persian Gulf in Modern Times* (New York: Palgrave Macmillan, 2014).

Samin, N., 'Da'wa, Dynasty, and Destiny in the Arab Gulf', *Comparative Studies in Society and History*, 58(4) (2016), pp. 935–54.

Vora, N., *Impossible Citizens* (Durham, NC: Duke University Press, 2013).

Vora, N. and Koch, N., 'Everyday Inclusions: Rethinking Ethnocracy, Kafala, and Belonging in the Arabian Peninsula', *Studies in Ethnicity and Nationalism*, 15(3) (2015), pp. 540–52.

Yin, R., *Qualitative Research from Start to Finish* (New York: Guilford Press, 2011).

CHAPTER 6

'Here be Dragons': Navigating the Problems of Researching 'Terrorism' and Critical Terrorism Studies

Richard McNeil-Willson

Research in the field of 'terrorism studies' has long been criticised as theoretically and methodologically lacking (Schmid and Jongman 1988). Limitations in both academic rigour and self-reflexivity is demonstrated in 'little self-conscious, sophisticated engagement with theoretical developments elsewhere and even less rigorous application of explicitly visible methodologies by the terrorism research community as a whole' (Ranstorp 2009: 24). The limitations within the contemporary field come in a number of different guises: a canonical dearth of empirically grounded research; limits of methodological rigour leading to speculative conclusions; dubious and unethical practices carried out by researchers; and a representative generalisation of the field as comprised of researchers either on short-term projects (and therefore unlikely to stay in the field) or embedded within – and answerable to – governmental (counterterror) power structures (Schulze 2004: 161–7; Ranstorp 2009: 22, 28–30).

These are not new accusations. In 1997, Reid highlighted this lack of rigour, stating that the means by which terrorism studies were conducted constituted a 'feedback loop' as the result of poor methodological practice; a static environment in which 'the same hypotheses, definition and theories continue to be analysed, assimilated, published, cited and eventually retrieved' (Reid 1997). In the period since this indictment, the processes behind this recycling of deficient research material of questionable quality have not been fully addressed and additional problems have become entrenched. As a result, publications within the field have become 'an almost impenetrable mountain of contributions that could be generously characterised as highly speculative in nature and without a high degree of rigorous scientific standard' (Ranstorp 2009: 22). This canon of poor quality works forms a characterisation of a field that is not only deficient in method and theory but lacking in appropriate reflexivity; as Dolnik pertinently stated in 2011, 'while a new book on terrorism comes out roughly every six hours, only three evaluating the state of the field and its future directions have been published in the last ten years' (Dolnik 2011: 3).

This is particularly problematic because of the political context within which this criticism sits. 'Terrorism studies' lies within the growth of a paradigmatic securitisation which has gained traction in Western policy circles following the New York attacks of 11 September 2001 and the Madrid and London bombings of 2004 and 2005, respectively.[1] Since conceptualisations of a 'terrorist threat' entered mainstream governmental and social discourse, it has become one of the main focuses of modern statecraft, re-framed as a unique, unpredictable, irrational and existential threat – a 'different' or 'new' form of violence, 'particularly savage and relentless' in its articulation (Ilardi 2004: 223; Enders and Sandler 2005; Hoffman 1999; Juergensmeyer 2000). Manichaean underpinnings create the conditions for another key feature: that of terrorism as constituting an existential harm to 'every free society' (Brachman 2009: 11; Trent 1980: 12). It is upon this conceptualisation that the paradigm of the long 'War on Terror' rests, actualised in the implementation of sweeping counterterror legislation throughout Western states that have often ensured 'the norms of prosecution and punishment no longer apply' (Buzan 2006; Wintour 2004).

This securitisation process has not gone uncontested and has been accompanied by the far more modest – although increasingly confident – 'critical turn' in terrorism studies, which seeks to illuminate, problematise and destabilise the power dynamics upon which it is founded (Smyth 2009: 210). This school of critical thought has developed amongst scholars from a broad range of academic fields who have begun deconstructing the impact of counterterrorism on society. Such critical theorists posit the construction of 'terrorism' as 'a political tool of immense power, capable of providing a rationale for a range of actions, including war' (Ilardi 2004: 218); it has led to the circumscribing of civil liberties, the stifling of dissent and the diversion of attention away from more entrenched, long-term political problems (Jackson et al. 2011: 105). Such securitisation has not only benefitted established political powers but a host of other organisations, including national and international media, which often act to perpetuate alarmist discourse to their own benefit (Jackson et al. 2011: 53). Academia has been left neither unaffected nor untarnished by this securitisation process; in fact, in many cases it has acted as accomplice, in which 'a triumvirate composed of the media, government and academia has to a great extent proscribed the course of terrorism studies' (Schulze 2004: 163).

In a field dogged by accusations of intellectual poverty, a lack of adequate primary research and methodological shortcomings (Silke 2004: 5–7), contemporary researchers face the dual charges of not only conducting research of dubious quality but of deliberately failing to address these shortcomings through interest-driven adherence to paradigmatic, securitised norms.

This chapter is designed to explore why it is that the contemporary study of terrorism, despite noisy criticism from critical scholars, is either unwilling or unable to address central shortcomings in its approach. It will seek to understand why this reticence to address methodological shortcomings seems not to be diminishing, as well as explore the extent that this can be considered a cycle of complicity so as to determine whether the problem lies in the securitised fortresses of orthodox academia or the ivory towers of critical theorists. This will be carried out by illuminating the power structures within which the social scientist interacts to come to such intentional or unintentional complicity. It will explore the researcher's interactions with structures on the level of the government and media; the level of interaction with academic organisations, peers and ethics; before delving into the researcher's own perceived understanding of risk and good practice on an individual level. This will build a comprehensive relief of how the researcher arrives at the confirmation of their complicity, before considering ways navigate responses to this.

On this basis we can dissect why academia is so heavily implicated in the complicity of the securitisation process and why researchers have acted to perpetuate and advance a paradigm which has ramifications not only in the research community but in government policy, the media, international diplomacy, warfare, civil society and beyond. It will contend that one of the most significant problems with contemporary research is the process by which researchers are encouraged to conceptualise the 'risk of harm' and that by facilitating a shift in this process, we may be able to transcend a proportion of the problems facing the field.

To achieve this, firstly, the chapter will explore current limitations of contemporary social science research on 'terrorism'. Secondly, it will explore how the research generally responds to problems of conducting such research by exploring how the notion of 'harm' is conceptualised by the researcher through a multi-level analysis. Finally, it will begin the priming of an emancipatory process, exploring whether, by altering the researcher's means to evaluate the 'risk of harm' through critical approaches, contemporary scholars studying 'terrorism' can facilitate a reorientation of research barriers and enablers. Finally, this work will conduct a secondary critique of the question, bringing down the edifices of both orthodox and critical scholars, to consider how researchers can best navigate the field in the future.

METHODOLOGY

To explore the securitisation mechanisms that have impacted on and been reproduced by academia in the contemporary study of terrorism, focus is placed on analysing how the concepts of threat and harm are articulated on the levels of the legal/governmental, the ethical/review board and the research/ researcher (Howarth and Stavrakakis 2000: 11). The notion of harm is particularly relevant to terrorism studies, as the contemporary researcher – even with critical aims which look to overcome the suspect legacy of former research heavyweights – faces significant challenges in conducting methodologically rigorous research whilst navigating the ethical maxim of the 'avoidance of harm' (Bresler 1995: 29). This work will draw on work by researchers and 'terrorism' scholars, combining it with elements from the Frankfurt and Copenhagen schools of thought. These will be subjected to a broadly Gramscian process to discern the roots of the hegemonic paradigm of security, before looking for the means of an emancipatory process for both the researcher and wider academia.

As it stands, researchers are caught in a no-man's land, in which the strict adherence to ethical, legal or normative proscriptions can cause the accuracy, legitimacy and credibility of their research to be compromised. It is this work's purpose to destabilise these processes of assessing harm through a multi-level analysis, to gauge whether its present guise leaves the researcher in a position that both favours securitising mechanisms whilst simultaneously causing harm to researchers themselves and the subject of research. For now, 'harm' is a suitable nexus to do this – by unravelling the limitations of concepts of harm, we chart a small area of territory in our understanding of terrorism and contentious politics, offering a guide for future researchers and an alternative to the scrawl of 'here be dragons' that otherwise obscures our view.[2]

MACRO-LEVEL POWER STRUCTURES

The first task of this analysis is to explore how securitisation is developed and reproduced through the macro-level of Western societies, placing the researcher within the maelstrom of activity between the structures of the state and the 'tentacles of terrorism' (Wintour 2004). Since 2001 and the start of the long 'War on Terror', media and governmental mechanisms have acted to create a dichotomy between contentious political actors such as designated 'terrorist' groups – seen as inherently harmful and malign – and the benign rest. In the context of the researcher, this can lead to a set of processes by which researchers themselves can become re-conceptualised as harmful to the liberal-democratic state and its normative values.

Numerous securitising mechanisms can be observed throughout Western media in the years post-2001, with alarmist headlines, reductionist analysis and incendiary reportage ubiquitously evident (Munson 2008: 78). Studies conducted by Grusin highlight some of the dubious practices which media bodies have engaged in, concluding that most outlets are deliberately perpetuating a sense of fear through alarmist discourse as part of a process of 'premediation' – the perpetuation of 'an almost constant, low level of fear or anxiety about another terrorist attack' to support a beleaguered media (Grusin 2010: 2). This alarmist discourse is perhaps unsurprising when seen through a critical lens: the media benefits in numerous ways from dramatic pictures and analysis of terrorist incidents in the form of larger audiences, increased sales, associated revenues – particularly following the growth of online content. This alarmism is particularly clear in the aftermath of the events of 2001 – an attack which 'brought together three sets of circumstances under which journalists can freely abandon their objectivity: tragedy, public danger and threats to national security' (Vultee 2011: 81).

Vultee conceptualises this as a dual process, whereby securitisation is both 'an effect *in* media' and 'an effect *of* media' –driving and responding to securitising mechanisms – with terrorism becoming a 'routine aspect of news framing' (Vultee 2011; Lee 1995: 7). How terrorism is perceived is certainly a product of how the media and the state choose to represent the threat (Wolfendale 2007: 86) and the growth of alarmist frames of extremism, terrorism and radicalisation since 2001 has enabled the conditions for the spread of securitisation rhetoric which conflates security with civil issues of migration and travel, political dissent and democratic engagement (McNeil-Willson 2017). This process has supported, and been supported by, the rise of discourses of terrorism at a governmental level which operate as 'a rather successful macro-securitisation', enforcing the hegemony of state power (Buzan 2006: 1103). This enables the development of premeditative responses to a 'nexus of new threats: rogue states, terrorism, international crime, drug trafficking and the spread of weapons of mass destruction' (Buzan 2006). The raft of subsequent counterterror legislation post-2001 has been framed as protecting civil liberties against the threat of international terrorism, yet critical theorists and activists have raised concerns about the potential and actual impact that such policy has in curtailing human and civil rights to political engagements.

In deconstructing the 'threat' as represented in media and government discourse, Wolfendale states that 'terrorism does not pose a threat sufficient to justify the kinds of counterterrorism legislation currently being enacted' (Wolfendale 2007: 75). What is more, the current counterterrorism practices often pose more of a threat to the individual physical security and well-being of the state's own citizens than the supposed harm emanating from terrorism; as such, she suggests 'we should fear counterterrorism more than we should fear terrorism' (Wolfendale 2007). Anti-terrorism measures have become increasingly normalised within the daily lives of Western citizens as government spending on fighting terrorism – and, increasingly, the 'gateway drug' of extremism – has spiralled (Jackson et al. 2011: 68). As well as a high financial cost, costs to civil liberties have come with the exploitation of fear by politicians as a way of 'ensuring re-election, silencing their critics, controlling dissent, creating a more docile public, distracting the public from more entrenched and difficult social problems', as well as ensuring the creation of a number of other projects not necessarily related to terrorism, such as 'the introduction of identity cards, restriction on immigration, increasing financial regulation and limiting civil liberties' (Jackson et al. 2011: 141). These governmental legislative changes are generally framed as a temporary measure, yet laws made in the name of countering terrorism are rarely, if ever, revoked – as was the case with the anti-terror laws in Northern Ireland and Germany during the 1970s (Wolfendale 2007: 84).

What is particularly problematic about the long 'War on Terror' – in contrast to previous conflict scenarios – is that it is no longer conceptualised as state-against-state but as state-against-'state of mind', in which a 'radical mindset' – rooted in an expansionist and absolutist 'Islamist' doctrine – has become an enemy, in the place of any national or intranational power structures (Hennessy 2008: 15).[3] This is reflected in swathes of governmental discourse warning against an 'aggressive Islamist ethos' constituting a threat that is 'more diffuse, more complicated, more unpredictable' (BBC 2014; Gardner 2013). The nature of this 'ideological threat' has meant that responding legislation has largely been designed as vague in its wording and broad in its scope, leading to its enaction in inappropriate scenarios. These mechanisms of securitisation not only contribute to a sense of anxiety about the threat from terrorism, it also leads to potentially problematic binary in favour of the current power structures – a form of 'hyper-patriotism', under which 'political dissent is seen by society as unpatriotic and/or treasonous', leading to the sidelining of academics who publicly challenge contemporary practice (Vultee 2011: 81).

Many self-professed 'terrorism experts' in the West are linked to high-profile, well-funded counterterror and security institutions and a constellation of other organisations funded and supported through government or government-implicated bodies. In the UK, these include (amongst others) Quilliam, the Centre on Religion and Geopolitics (Tony Blair Faith Foundation) and the Henry Jackson Society, which – despite often openly competing with each other – tend to operate as 'front groups' for governments, part of the strategic communication component of counter-terror policies (Miller and Sabir 2012: 27). By developing recommendations and reports deliberately positioned as in line with government policy, such organisations have been accused of targeting Muslim communities (Dodd 2009, 2010) and aiding the de-politicisation of counter-terrorism (Miller and Sabir 2012). By constructing hegemonic discourse about terrorism in a way which removes not only any counter-narratives to an ideological approach terrorism but overtly supports 'necessary' coercive counterterrorism and counter-extremism tactics, such organisations ultimately act to curtail dissent, reproducing structures of repression. They enable a system which attempts to intimidate sections of the population under the guise of a necessary response to 'terrorism', and become 'essential to the efficacy of coercion and the generation of fear' (Miller and Sabir 2012: 27–8).

Within the context of contemporary academia, a significant issue is their entanglement with university bodies, often engaging with, funding or employing researchers, labs or departments. With a strong alignment and interaction between 'anti-extremism' thinktanks and scholars, orthodox researchers are given 'respectability, and their views are quoted in the popular press and other mainstream outlets' (Smyth 2009: 209). Meanwhile, those who take a more anti-establishment position can face professional penalties such as being barred from accessing high-profile institutions and national media exposure, governmental positions and funding opportunities. As Breen Smyth states, whilst the orthodox 'terrorism' researcher can more readily access professional opportunities, 'the critical scholar, in comparison, ploughs a rather more difficult and lonely furrow' (Smyth 2009). As such, the researcher is strongly incentivised to carry out research that fits with securitised state narratives and is discouraged from taking on the more problematic tasks of conducting critical, primary research that counters the orthodox canon.

MESO-LEVEL POWER STRUCTURES

Researchers are not only disadvantaged in terms of power balance as due to media and government barriers and incentives, but face a problematic power dynamic from current academic ethics procedures (Sleat 2013). The role of the ethics committee began its development in the years following World War II, as revelations about the medical experiments in Nazi concentration camps came to light through the Nuremberg trials which eroded the paradigmatic image of science as 'intrinsically neutral, beneficial and value free' (Bresler 1995: 29). The subsequent Nuremberg Code formed the basis for international biomedical codes of ethics. The development of contemporary ethical research procedures was advanced in the wake of numerous ethnically dubious projects in the second half of the twentieth century – Tuskegee (1932 to 1972), Milgram (1961 and 1963), Zombardo (1973) and Laud Humphrey (Aagaard-Hansen and Johansen 2008; Haggerty 2004). Now, much international ethics is drawn from the Helsinki Declaration, notably the stringent avoidance of harm and the requirement that all research must be conducted to benefit the study group.[4]

Within terrorism studies, ethics has begun to play a more central role as a means of attempting to shore up failing methodological standards. In a field described as one which 'attracts phoneys and amateurs as a candle attracts moths', ethics procedures offer a means of tackling core shortcomings, such as the collection of data through means that are transparent and assessable (Ranstorp 2009: 26). This is particularly important given that researchers have often worked alongside governmental power structures, using closed or classified sources that are impossible to replicate, place within time or location, and may have been obtained under false pretences or duress, such as imprisonment or torture. Such closed source material 'casts a dark cloud over the entire terrorism studies community' as to the general perception of their ethical codes of conduct, and the requirement for researchers to adhere to certain standardised ethics has improved the standard of research and challenged some closed-source analysis (Ranstorp 2009: 28–30).

Current ethics procedures are founded on two central tenets: an overriding moral duty not to do harm throughout the course of the research programme – 'an obligation which "trumps" any other possible concerns' – and; that the risks area research study poses towards individuals who participate are prioritised 'over and above the rights and interests of other individuals including the researcher and society more generally' (Sleat 2013: 15); a process broadly referred to as the Participant Protection Model (PPM). In favouring the subject, PPM opposes more consequential and utilitarian approaches in which benefit is measured against harm, holding respect for the participant sacrosanct. It reflects the roots of contemporary ethics procedures as heavily embedded in biomedical research practices, rebalancing the traditional asymmetry in power between researcher and participant due to their knowledge differentials. As such, contemporary ethics procedures are framed within a context where the researcher has more power to harm than the subject.

The maxim that the research should, 'at the very least, of course, do no harm' to research subjects is the cornerstone of contemporary ethics (Barrett and Cason 1997: 122). To show the ubiquity of this approach, a short study was conducted in which open-source ethics guidelines relevant to social science practice were taken from all major British research ethics institutions and UK Russell Group universities.[5] The language used within these guidelines was examined to assess at which direction harm was conceptualised as occurring. In a study of 26 ethics guidelines, specific discussion on harm occurred in 131 separate occasions or ideas.[6] These ideas were examined and given one of the following designations, depending on how harm was conceptualised:

- *Strong harm to subject:* The idea conceptualised harm as explicitly likely to occur through research to the subject.
- *Weak harm to subject:* The idea conceptualised harm as implicitly or possibly likely to occur through research to the subject or the wider subject community (third-party risks).
- *Neutral:* The idea was either neutral or ambiguous on the direction of harm through research.

- *Weak harm to researcher:* The idea conceptualised harm as implicitly or possibly likely to occur through research to the researcher or the wider academic community (third-party risks).
- *Strong harm to researcher:* The idea conceptualised harm as explicitly likely to occur through research to the researcher.

In examination of this sample, 59 of the 131 total references (45%) of all ideas specifically referenced harm as likely to occur to the subject, rising to 72 of the total 131 if we include ideas implying harm to the subject (13). This means that 55% of ideas conceptualise harm as something that occurs from researcher to subject. References which were either neutral or ambiguous in their discursive conceptualisation of the direction of harm numbered 41 (31.3%), leaving only 18 ideas in which harm was references as potentially directed, at any point during the research process, towards the researcher, both implicitly (11) and explicitly (7), making up only 13.7% of ideas present in the sample.

These findings suggest that, within core British, Anglophone academic ethics, harm is conceptualised as far more likely to occur to the subject than to the researcher. Whilst this supposedly acts to protect the subject, it risks placing the researcher at a structural disadvantage: that the subject is more likely to experience harm often runs against actual power dynamics whereby the researcher is the more vulnerable party. By failing to account for potential power asymmetry that runs the other way, PPM cannot always offer an appropriate ethical foundation for the complex nature of contemporary social science research, particularly when researching armed 'terrorist' groups.[7]

Instances in which the researcher is on the receiving end of power asymmetry include contexts whereby subjects 'have the authority, prestige and capacity to harm the research, either physically (as in the case of more hazardous fieldwork projects) or through harming their interests (e.g. reputations, financial, cutting off future funding or access)' (Sleat 2013: 17). As much of social science research is specifically geared towards assessing and – in many cases – challenging those with significant positions of legitimate (state) or illegitimate (counter-state) power, such subjects are those more likely to be the focus of research, due to greater political capital and 'elite'-level knowledge (Sleat 2013: 16). It would be difficult, furthermore, to assume that a lone researcher, conducting a series of interviews with armed groups, is in the position of power; or a researcher exploring claims of corruption within a state service. Obvious examples of such risks from the security apparatus of a potentially hostile state is that of Giulio Regeni, whose death in 2016 has been extensively linked to the Egyptian police, or arrests of democracy researchers in Russia.

These examples raise other problems of adherence to 'do no harm'. If the power balance can be demonstrated as clearly weighted against the researcher, questions must be raised as to whether and to what extent deception is a legitimate approach to ensure the researcher's safety.[8] For instance, is it more dangerous for a researcher not to actively conceal the truth about their political, cultural and ethnic background or beliefs when conducting research with those that have overtly hostile agendas (such as far-right and National Socialist groups, or authoritarian states)? And is this deception, if carried to out to prevent harm to the researcher, as harmful to the subject as current ethics processes imply? Such situations show PPM as giving implicit preference to the potential harming of the researcher over the subject and may place the researcher in unacceptably dangerous situations.

Another issue is that of consent. In an examination of ethics, Van den Hoonard concludes that, by requiring applicants to seek the permission of persons most likely to be in such direct positions of power over subjects, critical enquiry is being repressed. This places the ethical review board at odds with the critical aims of social scientists, limiting the accuracy of research and risking harm to participants (through the perpetuation of abuse) and the researcher's career.[9] Furthermore, the risk of potential hostility that researchers face when conducting covert data gathering – particularly by those in more junior research positions – can lead to the quick dismissal of projects by academic bodies and funders, the abandonment of the project by researchers and the transformation of important research projects into innocuous enquiry (Katz 2013). The researcher therefore, by default of their research focus, is disadvantaged. The essential nature of research into 'terrorism' means that 'practically no field activity in this area will fall into the category of "low risk research"', leading the researcher to go through the ('dreadful') Institutional Review Board (IRB) or Human Research Ethics Committee (HREC) process before fieldwork (Dolnik 2011: 226). The risk of harm thus becomes ubiquitous with research, in a field that already struggles with accessing primary data. By focusing almost exclusively on the potential for harm to subjects, current Anglophone ethics processes risk overstating the potential for harm, creating a cycle whereby it is impossible to know 'whether fear creates the deviance or deviance the fear'.[10]

This power imbalance is even more obvious when compared to the journalist in their interaction with the research environment. Despite the shared publication interest, the journalist is permitted to carry out actions when gathering data that the social scientist would be condemned for; perhaps then, 'what is sauce for the scientists should be sauce for the journalists and vice versa' (Horowitz and Garn 1979). The current ethics procedures mark the researcher out as a specific threat to the subject, whilst in some cases disenfranchising the subject from making informed decisions about participation in the project and discouraging those that are supportive of their potential involvement by necessitating demonstrable forms of consent.[11] The researcher therefore faces a series of constraints, from disciplining or fines for conducting certain research, to a creeping regulation which 'institutionalises distrust, where researchers are presumed to require an additional level of oversight to ensure that they act ethically' (Haggerty 2004: 392). Whilst ethics procedures should be preventing researchers from using closed sources or unreplicable data sets, it seems to be forcing researchers to either reconsider primary data approaches or avoid certain research completely.

MICRO-LEVEL POWER STRUCTURES

The final level in which securitisation processes impact on the research is on the micro, in terms of day to day preparation, access and implementation of research procedures and localised government counterterror legislation, and here the researcher also faces significant disadvantages through the framing of primary research in the field as threatening. Researchers in contemporary terrorism studies can face a daunting lack of training, provision and care from their institutions when conducting research. Whilst 'creep' from ethics committees mean that researchers are forced accept limitations on conducting research due to the potential harm subjects face, the field researcher themselves are often forced to rely on their own initiative to avoid exposure to danger.

In day to day research practice, the researcher is forced to confront legal barriers which problematise their research practice during field research in both Western Europe and in sites beyond. The expansion of far reaching and internationally-applicable counterterror legislation has greatly challenged the role of the researcher, regardless of their site of research. In British legislation, this includes sections 57, 58 and 58(A) of the UK Terrorism Act 2000, which relate specifically to the possession, collection and publication or eliciting of material likely to be used or to be useful to terrorism and are problematic in their broad conceptualisation of intent (Government 2000: 26–7).

Section 57 of the Terrorism Act 2000 makes it an offence to 'possess an article in circumstances which give rise to a reasonable suspicion that its possession is for a purpose connected with the commission, preparation or instigation of an act of terrorism' (Government 2000: 26). This is not confined to materials that can be used directly in acts of violence, such as arms, chemicals or explosives, but can include a potentially infinite number of more abstract objects. As in the case of Zafar [EWCA Crim 184 (2008) 2 W.L.R. 1013] – in which five individuals were charged for possession of documents, computer discs and drives containing material described as 'radical', 'religious or philosophical' and 'ideological propaganda' – prosecutions were sought based on materials that were 'indirectly' connected to an act of terrorism. This is particularly problematic because of the degree of remoteness the item has to a potential act of terrorism is poorly defined: 'a purpose connected with' an act of terrorism could include a plane ticket to Pakistan, a credit card which was used to book the flight, or even the defendant's passport. Virgo concludes: 'if the lawful possession of such items does fall within section 57, are we not getting perilously close to criminalising thought crimes?' (Virgo 2008: 237–8).

This case raises the issue that the researcher is often left vulnerable to being criminalised for possession of written and electronic materials that could be deemed useful for 'terrorism' or 'terrorists'. Irrespective of whether such prosecution is successful, simply the fact that such a case can be brought to trial should be of concern; even if the researcher is able to 'prove that his possession of the articles was not for a purpose connected with the commission, preparation or instigation' of terrorism, the act of bringing the case to court can have serious ramifications for the anonymity of the researcher and the research subjects. With it possible for research material to be used against both researchers and subjects, scholars are handed a strong disincentive for conducting research into difficult areas of security.

Sections 58 and 58A are perhaps even more problematic, as they confer less importance on the intentionality of accruing information. In section 58, an offence is committed if the individual 'collects or makes a record of information of a kind likely to be useful to a person committing or preparing an act of terrorism' or 'possesses a document or record containing information of that kind' (UK Government 2000). This specifically includes photographic or electronic records. It was these sections, for instance, that were referred to following the killing of US journalist James Foley when UK police states that 'viewing, downloading or disseminating extremist material' such as this 'may constitute offence under terrorism legislation' and 'is a crime' (Halliday 2014). Other problematic sections for the researcher include section 19 of the Terrorism Act 2000, and 21A in the Anti-Terrorism Crime and Security Act 2001, which make it a criminal offence not to disclose information to a constable where a 'person believes or suspects that another person has committed an offence... as soon as is reasonably practical' (UK Government 2000). The expansion of legislation that focuses on countering forms of extremism since 2015 has exacerbated the legal challenges facing researchers. The UK Counter Terrorism and Border Security Bill (2019), for instance, has widened the scope of Section 58 of the 2000 Terrorism Act, lowering the bar of prosecution for viewing extremist material from three clicks to just one, establishing conditions for prosecuting individuals who view online extremist material over another individual's shoulder, broadening what is considered the 'publication' of such material, and stating that UK citizens automatically commit an offence if they travel to certain designated areas (such as areas of Syria and Iraq), under Section 58B. Whilst there is a provision for providing a 'reasonable excuse', researchers still risk questioning or arrest, resulting in the forced relinquishing of sensitive data and the overriding of ethical considerations regarding participant anonymity.

Such laws create potentially impossible conflicts with research practices in this area of study, challenging the bond of confidentiality that is required between a researcher and subject, risking the use of confiscated research material as a meticulously organised and collated set of court evidence, as well as threatening prison for researcher and research subjects and calling into question the ethics of conducting primary research at all if subjects are unable to be shielded from harm.[12] Such laws are also highly racialised, placing minority researchers and interviewees in a more dangerous position because of their being part of a 'suspect community', and are more likely to effect junior or lower-level researchers rather than those who operate at the top of international departments with larger funds and greater reputations.

Beyond Western academic settings, the researcher and subjects face harm due to the legal sensitivity of potential research. Silke identifies two formations of harm facing the field researcher in 'risky' global regions: the ambient and the situational (Silke 2004). Ambient risk is derived 'simply from being in a dangerous setting in order to carry out research' (Silke 2004: 14). In such situations, the researcher's presence has no impact on the level of risk that is faced. However, such risk is difficult to determine. The existence of terrorist and potentially violent actors is often dependent on severe political dissent or instability and, as such, political situations can quickly deteriorate (Barrett and Cason 1997: 98). Research on field anthropologists conducted by Howell found that 22% reported living through political turmoil, such as revolution, war or rioting, 15% being under suspicion of spying, 42% reported criminal interpersonal hazards such as robbery, assault, rape or murder and 2% reported hostage taking incidents during their time in the field (Smyth 2009: 199). The researcher, interacting with potential dangerous subjects, is often required to place themselves within situations that are risky, in areas which operate outside of the law, such as unstable, post-conflict zones or regions of high criminal or military activity.

Situational danger, in contrast, arises 'when the researcher's presence explicitly provokes hostility and aggression from others in the setting' (Silke 2004: 14). This is a particularly significant risk for fieldworkers exploring terrorist groups, as they are required to garner potentially sensitive information from a variety of counter-hegemonic sources that already face a series of threats. This can provoke hostility towards the researcher from numerous actors in situations whereby 'people can and do get killed because of the information they possess' (Barrett and Cason 1997: 98). Any naivety in discerning who to trust or entrust with information could prove fatal. Whilst both kinds of risks can be and are regularly negotiated by researchers, additional factors add greater pressure to the researcher. A lack of training available to researchers lead to an acute reliance on trial and error (Dolnik 2013a: 5). Such a process can yield important findings – teaching the researcher how they best engage in certain forms of research – yet in a field characterised as high-risk, risks immediate, dangerous repercussions. These risks are heightened in an academic environment in which over 90% of research studies are planned, conducted, analysed and written-up by just one person working alone, placing a heavy burden in managing potential harm on the researcher (Silke 2004: 69).

It is impossible to eliminate risk from the day to day activities of the field researcher when violence and instability are at the core the research subject (Dolnik 2013b: 227). But a lack of training provisions, limited support in developing proper fieldwork planning – owing largely to treating fieldwork as an academic 'rite of passage' – and limited access to networks of those who have greater experience all side-line genuine concerns the researcher faces when entering the field. With no formal organisational or association of high-risk field researchers in existence and relatively scant training offered, newcomers to the field are often 'left to their own devices, and this obviously increases the risks unnecessarily' (Taarnby 2013: 218). This risk has led to the researchers curtailing primary research, which becomes framed as either problematic or undesirable, or else suffused by a romanticism that expresses 'the satisfaction of the Great White Hunter who has bravely risked the perils of the [urban] jungle to bring back an exotic specimen' (Lee 1995: 76).

RESPONDING TO POWER IMBALANCES

The researcher is constrained by a tri-level process: on the macro level, the researcher faces a hostile context in which social scientists are coerced and incentivised through funding and research opportunities to adopt generally pro-governmental norms and approaches (Lee 1995). On the meso level, the researcher faces ever-growing barriers due to creeping problematic ethics procedures, poorly designed for such fieldwork and an increasingly formal set of ethics structures which encourages researchers to follow what they perceive to be the path of least resistance. And on the micro level, the researcher is unpracticed and untrained in a hostile security context, risking the welfare of themselves and a host of research subjects, gatekeepers and communities.

The impact of this has supported academic securitisation – the creation of a set of mechanisms which not only stifle primary research but acts to isolate and disable the researcher from drawing findings that are likely to challenge pre-existing assumptions about such groups. State structures are therefore able to mobilise a wide range of mechanisms to co-opt the researcher into supporting current articulations of power, which are bound together through a securitised palette of discourse.

Taking a critical reading, we can discern dominant actors (in this case, those with an interest in supporting the securitisation of political society) acting in ways that impact on academic culture (such as the ethics committee) and ultimately enforcing their interests on those in subordinate positions. The researcher themselves becomes complicit in this, taught to ignore the inequalities they are subject to and that they themselves exercise. This results in a *Pax Romana*, where the researcher is given the means to research through 'the active consent of the subordinate' (Steans and Tepe 2008: 140). The researcher becomes implicated in this process, to reproduce the fundamental structure of the system of dominant opposition.

The researcher is also co-opted by their place in class and status. The rise of the long 'War on Terror' has securitised civil society by opening up space for military and security discourses to combine with and reinforce concern about fragmented wage labour, immigration, education, and a number of other civil sites, to create an environment conducive to what Hallsworth and Lea call the 'securitisation of the life-world' (Lea and Hallsworth 2011). Elements of social life and civil liberties are traded for security, with citizens increasingly coming to accept the closing down and reconceptualisation of freedoms, such as pre-emptive arrests, or constraints of individuals suspected of 'connection' with terrorism. Upper classes and majority communities are least impacted, whilst the closing of civil liberties impacts most severely on minority groups – particularly Muslim communities, who already face severe restrictions on their ability to access education, employment, and to engage with the public arena and shape mainstream discourse (AI 2012). Whilst minority groups and those with limited means of accessing societal debate face forms of repression, the beneficiaries of this 'securitisation of the life world' can be broadly understood as the neoliberal and capitalist state (Lea and Hallsworth 2012). The researcher, largely embedded within generally more affluent, less working-class structures, and more likely to be from majority cultural backgrounds, is largely sheltered from the broader impacts of counterterrorism and more likely to reproduce it than find cause to systematically challenge it.

Whilst it is possible to establish a systemic form of complicity within academic research towards perpetuating securitisation processes, critical studies have, to date, only offered significantly limited means of emancipating the researcher from this environment. This has stifled attempts to break out from processes which prevent more primary research from taking root. The shortcomings of the critical turn are that, by apportioning too much blame on the bad practices of other researchers, it fails to set out a wider response to problematic power dynamics which keep the orthodox system dominant. What is needed is a more coherent and pragmatic response to the limiting of primary research in terrorism studies.

To break this cycle, a reconceptualisation of the risk of harm is proposed. Since much of the deficiencies in research stem from academia's complicity in securitised discourse, the transcending of such limitations is built here upon a discursive foundation. If we are to presuppose that 'language, entwined with power, frames and positions the response', it is important to act to reposition the discourse around which research occurs in an attempt to liberate the researcher, the field and its subject from its methodological malaise and its compromisingly close relationship with state security power.

EMANCIPATION

To challenge the barriers to research and the complicity of academia in securitisation mechanisms, the researcher must engage in challenge the current operations of social, economic and cultural hegemony within which it operates at the present time (Faubion 1994: 133). This can be attempted through exploring how we can adequately reposition "harm" and its role within such research.

At the micro level, a reorientation of harm is hampered by poor provision for training and support, with researchers having little protection from both the emotional stresses of research and little training for operating in hazardous environments. There exists a wealth of knowledge that is not being adequately utilised in academia, with skills being 'rarely shared and discussed' and practical findings which 'fail to be disseminated' (Lee 1995: 71). By creating greater opportunities for disseminating skillsets, as well as offering wider support networks for the researcher, scholars are better prepared and more likely to avoid difficulties in problematic regions. Initial guidance can come from the sharing of interdisciplinary methodologies, such as those used by contemporary anthropologists, archaeologists and geographers who often, in contrast to the orthodox terrorism scholar, 'carry out fieldwork in areas that may be quite remote' (Lee 1995: 11). Researchers in such fields have carried out far more difficult research and an interdisciplinary approach will encourage researchers to view their subjects not as something likely to cause them harm but as 'colleagues rather than subjects', as complex, 'humanised' actors. Researchers in such fields have experience of data collection in regions and communities that present a variety of relevant challenges, and such an interdisciplinary approach will encourage researchers in the study of 'terrorism' to view their subjects not as actors likely to cause them harm but as 'colleagues rather than subjects', as complex 'humanised' actors. This will support collaboration between fields, creating tangible benefits for researchers, and strengthening the tools at their disposal to conduct data collection in potentially challenging contexts (Barrett and Cason 1997: 123).

Further interdisciplinary approaches will support emancipation on the meso level. As Jones and Bhui declare, 'a new ethics of research into terrorism is needed', one which offers a more open approach amongst researchers and encourages greater flexibility of the ethics process towards the subject matter (Jones and Bhui 2009: 54). The supporting of new procedures which depart from strict adherence to the PPM model of biomedical sciences to ones which offer greater awareness of the ebb and flow of power within social science field research is critical. By reconceptualising 'harm' away from viewing the researcher solely as 'a potential threat to the participant of his research', academic ethics boards will be able to assess projects from a viewpoint whereby the power relationship between researcher and subject is understood as open to continual contestation and change (Sleat 2013: 16). The challenge of the PPM model will not force a lapse into the removal of sound ethics regulation, as Bauman suggests; rather, it offers the chance to diversify the nature of harm as more sensitive to the political scientist and challenge the current inherent structural disadvantage in managing power (Bauman 1993). There seems, at least anecdotally, a push for challenging the PPM forming amongst colleagues across Europe, who wish to emanate the more successful elements of Anglophone academic ethical processes whilst dispensing with those that stifle legitimate social science research in difficult areas.

On the macro level, social science needs to create a sustained challenge to current discourse. Through an active use of critical concepts, the researcher must join the critique of governmental and societal norms of 'terrorism' and security, working to expose power relations that sit behind their development. The researcher is thus encouraged to cultivate a necessary iconoclasticism to achieve this. Recast away from what Schmid and Jognman term a 'firefighter' of political violence, in favour of a 'student of combustion', academics can remove statist norms for more egalitarian approaches (Silke 2004: 58). Meanwhile, a society increasingly challenged on its securitisation will be more likely to re-cast the researcher beyond the binary malign/benign categorisations. We must work against a system that encourages the idea that 'an interest in terrorist material may be a marker for support and possible engagement in violent acts' and that researchers 'should be treated as suspects' (Jones and Bhui 2009). Rather, to chase away the chimera of terrorism, researchers could use their platforms critically and actively 'to engender crises of confidence in a society's ideological and institutional framework' (Sementelli and Abel 2000: 459). In this, we must be encouraged to blur the division between academic and activist, to tackle the imposing security structures we face.

In reorienting the discourse of harm which the researcher faces when conducting research, the social scientist can partly create an actor-based response to securitising power structures. First order critiques of practice and practitioners challenge the contemporary research field which perpetuates power imbalances by mapping the relief of constraints and coercion, planning the beginning of a voyage to firmer methodological ground.

LIMITATIONS

There are limitations in such critical approaches to terrorism research. Firstly, by relying on an emancipatory set of critical theories we run the risk of creating a 'confirmation bias' (Balzacq 2011). Such discursive emancipation, by developing 'the possibility of resistance and alternative worlds', tend to privilege speculation over empirical challenge (Grovogui and Leonard 2008: 170); by working to develop new processes free from current power paradigms, the researcher drifts into idealism and away from sincere rigour. In this case, such an approach becomes an exercise in post hoc storytelling that acts more as a methodological gloss than a solid theoretical foundation, the research 'never actually tests the theory, as researchers simply find what they're looking for' (Nyman 2013: 61). The approach simply swaps one hegemonic vision with a counter-hegemonic one, leaving academic enquiry, as Balzacq states, just as incomplete (Pasha 2008: 165).

The vision of the counter-hegemonic narrative can blind the researcher to the limitations of this approach; the 'rainbow of resistance' to power structures in themselves offer 'no real promise of transcendence and transformation' but rather a competing vision that can privilege the creation of new, repressive structures (Pasha 2008: 163). Critical scholars can miss the agency of other scholars whilst highlighting the many actors who benefit from counterterrorism, and there is limited appreciation that those who act to create a counter-narrative may be incentivised or seek aims that are less lofty than societal emancipation (Jackson, Smyth, and Gunning 2009: 44). As such, those who follow the critical approach of emancipation sometimes fail by their own standards in accepting that 'theory is always for someone and for some purpose' (Cox 1981: 128), ignoring the duality of both the 'potential and *limits* of resistance' to current power structures (Ayers 2008: 14).

Understanding the limits and diversity of state-centred power is a serious problem in critical terrorism approaches yet to be properly addressed. Whilst we should be aware of the huge scope of the power the state is co-opting and centralising under the auspices of counterterrorism, there will always exist limitations in the amount of power that can be accrued, just as there will be actors who are able to push back against the state from a lower position of privilege. Without accounting for activist response within securitisation theories, we risk creating a self-fulfilling process. Similar to al-'Azm's criticism of Said's *Orientalism* (al-'Azm 1980), we create a system in which the only means of breaking the processes of repression comes from the oppressor itself, and the agency for change is removed from the subaltern.[13]

Critical theory approaches have also been accused of relying too much on European experiences of political contestation (Jones 2008: 210). This is particularly problematic considering such emancipatory approaches are designed to lend 'a voice to the voiceless' (Toros and Gunning 2009: 105). Seeing, in this case, that the majority of actions by designated 'terrorist' groups are built around challenging the contemporary paradigm of the Western-centric post-Westphalian international and economic system, critical theory, with its reliance on Western political traditions, risks inadvertently sidelining alternative traditions and perpetuating hegemonic paradigms.

The overtly structuralist and rigid limitations of securitisation theories also risk simplifying authorities as operating in a monolithic manner or depriving activists of the means of changing or re-appropriating certain security practices. As such, critical theorists imperil the dialectic that takes place between paradigmatic actors. Hegemony, henceforth, becomes largely conceptualised as a 'one-direction power relationship... fashioned by the elite transnational class on its own terms and then forced or imposed on subaltern classes' (Germain and Kenny 1998: 17). These dominated groups are, in turn, given two options: either to resist assaults as best they can or capitulate in full and accept the status quo. Such an application of critical theory and the concept of hegemony misses the Gramscian act of contestation. By focusing solely on the power dynamics as a 'top down' phenomenon, what is missed is that, just as the structure bends the wills and actions of the individual, so 'structures are transformed by agency' (Gill 1993: 23).

CONCLUSION

Where does the researcher stand, in this process of contestation between state counterterrorism and critical studies? Are we beached upon the sands of this dialectic, destined to continue to engage as both accomplice and hostage of this securitisation 'terrorism studies', contrary to our best efforts? Whilst critical efforts at countering the inequalities of counterterrorism are floundering, we should remember that such theories are tricky in their application. One of the strengths of critical theories are their diverse methodological facets and this is, in some senses, also a weakness, risking them becoming diluted, inconsistent or methodologically unworkable (Germain and Kenny 1998: 8). Furthermore, by working with concepts such as hegemony and power outside of their originally conceived environments, we risk totalising them in instances that misunderstand the role of resistance (Germain and Kenny 1998: 18). Terms such as hegemony become 'reduced to a simple model of cultural control', ossifying power structures that are rather 'critically renewed, recreated and challenged, and in certain respects, modified' (Steans and Tepe 2008: 142). This runs counter to the aims of discursive analyses of historicising and contextualising paradigmatic norms.

Furthermore, utilising critical securitisation theory to understand such structural dynamics, in this context, reduces everything to a struggle over security, with the state-centric securitisation mechanisms cast as the key barriers to emancipation; desecuritisation, the enabler to achieving it. However, amongst key Copenhagen School scholars, securitisation sits within the context of 'no clear normative agenda'; Copenhagen scholars 'suggesting that desecuritisation is often preferable, never rules out securitisation as an option but rather suggests it is sometimes necessary' (Nyman 2013: 60). Critical terrorism scholars remove this potentially positive conceptualisation that security can have for change and, as such, limit the possibilities for researchers to use security or the state as a basis for positive change (Nyman 2013). For instance, whilst primary data offers a possibility to 'expose the gaps in understanding, and the cultural and political biases and misinterpretations in government, intelligence and media accounts' (Smyth 2009: 196), it fails to adequately account for the variation in standard and interpretation of primary research, ignoring the practical limitations that will continue to face the researcher in the field and the inability of them to escape the liberal-counterterror state.

All is not lost. The battle standard for challenging the role of security in academia has been raised by critical scholars and, whilst it seems that the message from the ivory towers of critical theories has not succeeded in their emancipatory aim, unable to dislodge the discursive sway of the long 'War on Terror', they have continued to nurture a critical flame which now sits quietly burning at the heart of much of contemporary mainstream research on 'terrorism'. Current critical and discursive theories offer only a limited framework to emancipate the researcher at present. Key shortcomings risk producing confirmation bias, problematic conceptualisations, dehistorical notions of power and limited means of matching theory with action in a workable practice. As such, the tackling of the problems of current critical approaches is vital and its development will be achieved through the drawing together of praxis and experiences from across spheres of knowledge and of new ethical practices that release the researcher from their current constraints, particularly around notions of 'harm'.

What this chapter does, therefore, is illuminate what is lacking. Critical terrorism studies are shown to be limited in their current guise, but they have driven the discussion in a new direction and a new generation of scholars will continue to challenge the securitised legacy of the long 'War on Terror' in new ways. Yet, what has been shown is that underneath the blank spaces and snarling metaphorical dragons on the map lies something far less intimidating than the uncompromising and colourful depictions of 'terrorism' and 'terrorists'. Critical terrorism approaches show there is more to be gained by filling in these spaces by venturing to engage with violent actors on a more human and genuinely interactive level, something which offers far more complex and interesting findings. Critical terrorism approaches are not enough in themselves to enable the researcher to achieve this, but they have changed the map for contemporary researchers and illuminated the routes that we now must traverse.

NOTES

1. 'The main argument of securitisation theory is that security is a (illocu-tionary) speech act, that by alone uttering "security" something is being done ... A securitising actor, by stating that a particular *referent object* is threatened in its existence, claims a right to extraordinary measures to ensure the reference object's survival. The issue is then moved out of the sphere of normal politics into the realm of emergency politics, where it can be dealt with swiftly and without the normal (democratic) rules and regu-lations of policymaking... [Thus] Security is understood to be a social and intersubjective constriction' (Floyd 2007: 329); The Copenhagen School refers to a small group of scholars formally based at the Copenhagen Peace Research Institute (COPRI) in Copenhagen, most notably Old Wæver and Barry Buzan, whilst the Welsh School is centred around a group of security studies scholars linked to the University of Aberystwyth.
2. 'When early cartographers mapped their universe they started with the settlements, connected these with travellers' routes and then, left with vast unknown spaces on their parchment, carefully quilled in the words, 'Here be dragons'. For these were the places where no-one ventured, or, if they did, never came back, or, if they returned, were never the same again ...' (Best 1988: 239).
3. 'Compromise is not what many terrorists usually have in mind except as part of a "salami" tactic to inch closer towards achieving all their professed goals. These "dangerous dreamers of the absolute" (as Karl Marx once called them) are often totalitarian in their mindset. Their ideology must therefore be targeted' (Schmid 2005: 229).
4. First developed in 1964, the Helsinki Declaration has – as of the time of writing – since been subject to six revisions: 1975, 1983, 1989, 1996, 2000 and 2008.
5. Where such sources are openly and externally available. Some universi-ties listed as Russell Group institutions have not been included here because they do not have a separate set of guidelines outside of those pro-duced by specific British research ethics institutions. For a list of Russell group institutions, see, www.russellgroup.ac.uk/our-universities/. The list of institutions from which ethics guidelines have been collected are as follows: Academy of Management; American Political Science Association; Association of Social Anthropologists; British Education

Research Association; the British Psychology Society; the Economic and Social Research Council; the British Sociological Association; Cambridge University; Durham University; King's College London; the London School of Economics; the Natural Environment Research Council; the Oral History Society; the Academy of Social Science' Oxford University; Queen's University Belfast; the RESPECT Project; the Social Research Association; University College London; the UK Research Integrity Office; the University of Birmingham; the University of Bristol; the University of Cardiff; the University of Exeter; the University of Liverpool; the University of Manchester; the University of Newcastle; the University of Nottingham; the University of Sheffield; the University of Southampton.

6. This did not include multiple instances of the same term within one sentence, paragraph or subsection.

7. The PPM model is so inadequately divorced from social sciences that some social science ethics processes still require academics to report on whether they will be using stem cells or organic material in their research.

8. '... prohibiting deception is akin to outlawing lying, something that at first blush might seem wonderful until it becomes apparent that lying and deceit lubricate daily life while serving large and small legitimate institutional purposes' (Haggerty 2004: 406).

9. 'Early 20th-century sociology was part of a larger muckraking movement to reveal and critique the abuse of workers, the exploitation of immigrants, inhumane housing conditions, outrageous exercises of criminal justice power, corrupt politician-business relations, and so on' (Katz 2013: 1137); 'REBS and IRBs require that the very people who abuse "vulnerable" populations consent to research that might reveal the abuse, such as the parents of runaway and intractable kids, police and judges who mistreat adults and juveniles, bathhouse managers who don't post HIV health warnings, hospital administrators with authority over staff who would report rule violations that injure patients, teachers who have sexual relations with students, employers who cheat their workers by not paying overtimes rates and by underfunding health plans, and ethics committee that may be shown to damage applicant's careers' (Katz 2013).

10. Irving Louis Horowitz here invokes Kai Erikson's famous statement in *Wayward Puritans (II)* when highlighting this process: 'Men who fear witches soon find themselves surrounded by them; men who become jealous of private property soon encounter thieves. And it is not always easy to know whether fear creates the deviance or deviance the fear, the affinity of the two has been a continuing course of wonder in human affairs' (Horowitz and Garn 1979: 1022).

11. 'Are researchers really expected to attempt to talk willing interviewees out

of speaking to them by presenting an exhaustive list of possible dangers of participation?' (Dolnik 2013b: 230-1)

12. One example in which a researcher has fallen foul of legal challenges is that of Bradley Garnett who conducted deep participation research during a PhD project with a group of urban explorers. Spending prolonged periods of time with this group on night-time excursions, Garnett also acted as the designated 'scribe for the tribe', detailing explorations and findings. Despite the research being approved by supervisors, a university ethics committee and successfully signing off his PhD after a defence with internal and external examiners, the British Transport Police took legal action against Garnett and a group of eight research participants. This centred around the collection of materials that were, according to the charge, 'illegally obtained information', and despite working through the doctoral process according to university regulations, the university refused to offer their support for him or the work. Even more concerningly, the British Transport Police seized his doctoral research findings, including personal text messages, quotes from his thesis, field notes, photographs, video footage and even chat logs from social media, all of which were connected 'off my person and from my house, which they raided while I was in custody after taking my door down with a battering ram' (Garnett 2014: 38).

13. 'If reciprocity between subject and object is impossible then, by the same token, the object cannot challenge the subject by developing alternative models ...' (Richardson 2000: 213).

BIBLIOGRAPHY

Amnesty International (AI) 'Choice and Prejudice: Discrimination against Muslims in Europe' (London: Amnesty International, 2012).

Aagaard-Hansen, Jens and Maria Veng Johansen, 'Research Ethics across Disciplines', *Anthropology Today*, 24 (2008).

al-'Azm, Sadik Jalal, 'Orientalism and orientalism in reverse', *libcom.org* (1980).

Ayers, Alison J., *Gramsci, Political Economy and International Relations Theory: Modern Princes and Naked Emperors* (New York: Routledge, 2008).

Balzacq, Thierry, *Securitisation Theory* (Abingdon: Routledge, 2011).

Barrett, Christopher B. and Jeffrey .W. Cason, *Overseas Research: A Practical Guide* (Baltimore and London: Johns Hopkins University Press, 1997).

Bauman, Zygmunt, *Postmodern Ethics* (Oxford: Blackwell, 1993).

BBC, 'Trojan Horse report finds "aggressive Islamist ethos" in schools', 18 July 2014.

Best, Simon, 'Here Be Dragons', *The Journal of the Polynesian Society*, 97 (1988).

Brachman, Jarret M., *Global Jihadism: Theory and Practice* (London: Routledge, 2009).

Bresler, Liora, 'Ethical Issues in Qualitative Research Methodology', *Bulletin of the Council for Research in Music Education* (1995).

Buzan, Barry, 'Will the "Global War on Terror" Be the New Cold War?', *International Affairs (Royal Institute of International Affairs 1944–)*, 82 (2006), pp. 1103–4.

Cox, Robert W., 'Social Forces, States and World Orders: Beyond International Relations Theory', *Millennium – Journal of International Studies*, 10 (1981), pp. 126–55.

Dodd, Vikram, 'Spying morally right, says thinktank', *The Guardian*, 16 October 2009.

Dodd, Vikram, 'List sent to terror chief aligns peaceful Muslim groups with terrorist ideology', *The Guardian*, 4 August 2010.

Dolnik, Adam, 'Conducting Field Research on Terrorism: A Brief Primer', *Perspectives on Terrorism*, 5 (2011).

Dolnik, Adam, 'The Need for Field Research', in *Conducting Terrorism Research*, Adam Dolnik (ed.) (London: Routledge, 2013a).

Dolnik, Adam, 'Up Close and Personal: Conducting Field Research on Terrorism in Conflict Zones', in *Conducting Terrorism Research*, Adam Dolnik (ed.) (London: Routledge, 2013b).

Enders, Walter and Todd Sandler, 'After 9/11: Is It All Different Now?', *The Journal of Conflict Resolution* 49 (2005), pp. 259–60.

Faubion, James D., *'Truth and Power': Power: Essential Works of Foucault 1954–1984* (London: Penguin Group, 1994).

Floyd, Rita, 'Towards a Consequentialist Evaluation of Security: Bringing Together the Copenhagen and the Welsh Schools of Security Studies', *Review of International Studies*, 33 (2007).

Gardner, Frank, 'MI5 chief Andrew Parker warns of Islamist threat to UK', BBC, 9 October 2013.

Garnett, Bradley, 'Access Denied', *Times Higher Education*, 2 (2014).

Germain, Randall D. and Michael Kenny, 'Engaging Gramsci: International Relations Theory and the New Gramscians', *Review of International Studies*, 24 (1998).

Gill, Stephen, 'Epistemology, Ontology and the "Italian School".' in *Gramsci, Historical Materialism and International Relations*, Stephen Gill (ed.) (Cambridge: Cambridge University Press, 1993).

Government, UK, 'Terrorism Act 2000', available at legislation.gov.uk (2000).

Grovogui, Siba N. and Lori Leonard, 'Uncivil Society: Interrogations at the Margins of Neo-Gramscian Theory', in *Gramsci, Political Economy and international Relations Theory: Modern Princes and Naked Emperors*, Alison J. Ayers (ed.) (New York: Palgrave Macmillan, 2008).

Grusin, Richard, *Premediation: Affect and Modality After 9/11* (London: Palgrave Macmillan, 2010).

Haggerty, Kevin D, 'Ethics Creep: Governing Social Science Research in the Name of Ethics', *Qualitative Sociology*, 27 (2004).

Halliday, Josh, 'Police warn sharing James Folley killing video is a crime', *The Guardian*, 20 August 2014.

Hennessy, Peter, *The New Protective State: Government, Intelligence and Terrorism* (London: Continuum, 2008).

Hoffman, Bruce, *Inside Terrorism* (London: Indigo, 1999).

Horowitz, Irving Louis and Stanley M. Garn, 'Social Science Research Ethics', *Science, New Series*, 206 (1979).

Howarth, David, and Yannis Stavrakakis, 'Chapter One: Introducing Discourse Theory and Political Analysis', in David Howarth, Yannis Stavrakakis and Aletta Norval (eds), *Discourse Theory and Political Analysis: Identities, Hegemonies and Social Change* (Manchester: Manchester University Press, 2000).

Ilardi, Gaetano Joe, 'Redefiniting the Issues: The Future of Terrorism Research and the Search for Empathy', in *Research on Terrorism: Trends, Achievements and Failures*, Andrew Silke (ed.) (London: Routledge, 2004).

Jackson, Richard, Lee Jarvis, Jeroen Gunning and Marie Breen Smyth, *Terrorism: A Critical Introduction* (London: Palgrave Macmillan, 2011).

Jackson, Richard, Marie Breen Smyth and Jeroen Gunning, *Critical Terrorism Studies: A New Research Agenda* (London: Routledge, 2009).

Jones, Branwen Gruffydd, '"Tell No Lies, Claim No Easy Victories": Possibilities and Contradictions of Emancipatory Strugging in the Current Neocolonial Condition', in *Gramsci, Political Economiy and International Relations Theory: Modern Princes and Naked Emperors*, Alison J. Ayers (ed.) (New York: Palgrave Macmillan, 2008).

Jones, Edgar and Kamaldeep Bhui, 'The New Ethics of Research into Terrorism', *British Medical Journal*, 338 (2009).

Juergensmeyer, Mark, *Terror in the Mind of God: The Global Rise of Religious Violence* (Berkeley: University of California Press, 2000).

Katz, Jack, 'Review of "The Seduction of Ethics: Transforming the Social Sciences", by Will van den Hoonaard', *Journal of Sociology*, 118 (2013).

Lea, J., and S. Hallsworth, 'Bringing the State Back in: Understanding Neoliberal Security', in *Criminalisation and Advanced Marginality: Critically exploring the work of Loïc Wacquan*, P. Squires and J. Lea (eds) (Bristol: University of Bristol, 2011).

Lee, Raymond M, *Dangerous Fieldwork* (Thousand Oaks: SAGE Publications, 1995).

McNeil-Willson, Richard, 'A Primer on the Impact of Islamic State on Counterterrorism Legislation', in *The Palgrave Handbook of Global*

Counterterrorism Policy, Scott N. Romaniuk, Francis Grice, Daniela Irrera and Stewart Webb (eds) (London: Palgrave Macmillan, 2017).

McNeil-Willson, Richard and Scott Romaniuk. due 2020. 'Counterterrorism has no Borders: Citizenship, Global Security Architectures and the Securitisation of Civil Society', in *The Palgrave Handbook of Civil Society and Security Policy*, Scott Romaniuk (ed.) (London: Palgrave Macmillan, due 2021).

Miller, David, and Rizwaan Sabir, 'Counter-terrorism as counterinsurgency in the UK "war on terror"', in *Counter-terrorism and State Political Violence*, Scott Poynting and David Whyte (eds) (London and New York: Routledge, 2012).

Munson, Ziad, 'Terrorism', *Contexts: All Politics is Social*, 7 (2008).

Nyman, Joanna, 'Securitisation Theory', in *Critical Approaches to Security: An Introduction to Theories and Methods*, Laura J. Shepherd (ed.) (London: Routledge, 2013).

Pasha, Mustapha Kamal, 'Return to the Source: Gramsci, Culture and International Relations', in *Gramsci, Political Economy and International Relations*, Alison J. Ayers (ed.) (New York: Palgrave Macmillan, 2008).

Ranstorp, Magnus, 'Mapping Terorrism Studies After 9/11: An academic field of old problems and new prospects', in *Critical Terrorism Studies*, Richard Jackson, Marie Breen Smyth and Jeroen Gunning (eds) (London: Routledge, 2009).

Reid, Edna, 'Evolution of a Body of Knowledge: An Analysis of Terrorism Research', *Informartion Processing and Management*, 33 (1997), pp. 91–106.

Richardson, Michael, 'Enough Said' in *Orientalism: A Reader*, Alexander Lyon Macfie (ed.) (Edinburgh: Edinburgh University Press, 2000).

Schmid, Alex P, 'Prevention of Terrorism: Towards a Multi-pronged Approach', in *Root Causes of Terrorism: Myths, Reality and Ways Forward*, Tore Bjørgo (ed.) (London: Routledge, 2005).

Schmid, Alex P. and A. Jongman, *Political Terrorism: A New Guide to Actors, Concepts, Databases, Theories and Literature* (Amsterdam: North Holland Publishing Company, 1988).

Schulze, Frederick, 'Breaking the Cycle: Empirical Research and Postgraduate Studies on Terrorism', in *Research on Terrorism: Trends, Achievements and Failures*, A. Silke (ed.) (London: Routledge, 2004).

Sementelli, Arthur and Charles F. Abel, 'Recasting Critical Theory: Veblen, Deconstruction and the Theory-Praxis Gap', *Administrative Theory and Praxis*, 22 (2000).

Silke, Andrew, 'The Devil You Know: Continuing problems with research on terrorism', in *Research on Terrorism: Trends, Achievements and Failures*, Andrew Silke (ed.) (London: Routledge, 2004).

Sleat, Matt, 'Generic Ethics Principles in Social Science Research', *Professional Briefings* (2013).

Smyth, Marie Breen, 'Subjectivities, "suspect communities", governments and the ethics of research on "terrorism"', in *Critical Terrorism Studies: A New Research Agenda*, Marie Breen Smyth and Jeroen Gunning Richard Jackson (ed.) (London: Routledge, 2009).

Steans, Jill and Daniela Tepe, 'Gender in the Theory and Practice of International Political Economy: The promise and limitations of neo-Gramscian approaches', in *Gramsci, Political Economy and Interantional Relations Theory: Modern Princes and Naked Emperors*, Alison J. Ayers (ed.) (New York: Palgrave Macmillan, 2008).

Taarnby, Michael, 'Professionalising high-risk research in academia', in *Conducting Terrorism Research*, Adam Dolnik (ed.) (Oxford: Routledge, 2013).

Toros, Harmonie and Jeroen Gunning, 'Exploring a Critical Theory Approach to Terrorism Studies', in *Critical Terrorism Studies: A New Research Agenda*, Richard Jackson, Marie Breen Smyth and Jeroen Gunning (eds) (London: Routledge, 2009).

Trent, Darrell M, 'The New Religion: Terrorism', *Human Rights*, 8 (1980).

Virgo, Graham, 'Possession of Articles', *The Cambridge Law Journal*, 67 (2008).

Vultee, Fred, 'Securitisation as a media frame: What happens when the media "speak security"', in *Securitisation: How Security Problems Emerge and Dissolve*, Thierry Balzacq (ed.) (Oxford: Routledge, 2008).

Wintour, Patrick, 'Blunkett Warns of Growing Danger', *The Guardian*, 13 March 2004, section Politics, Europe.

Wolfendale, Jessica, 'Terrorism, Security and the Threat of Counterterrorism', *Studies in Conflict Terrorism*, 30 (2007).

CHAPTER 7

Positionality and Access: Doing Surveys and Empirical Research in the Middle East

Bethany Shockley

This chapter demonstrates that collecting and analysing empirical data also involves careful attention to positionality and access. Its purpose is neither to defend quantification nor to instruct readers in a specific research methodology, but rather to discuss research challenges that are common to both qualitative and quantitative work. Researchers from differing methodological traditions often talk past each other, without understanding that shared difficulties may go by different names. For instance, survey researchers discuss *social desirability bias* and *interviewer effects*, which are related to what researchers from other traditions refer to as *positionality*. This chapter highlights obstacles that arise in the process of survey data collection and aims to explain key concepts in a way that aids understanding across research traditions. In so doing, the hope is to foster contemplation among those whose research trajectory leads them to empirical data collection in the Middle East and encourage them to produce quality research despite the obstacles.

The chapter begins by discussing common barriers faced by researchers seeking to access data in the Middle East, many of which are common to other parts of the developing world. Focusing on the growing field of survey research within the region, it identifies both challenges and opportunities for this type of research. The remainder of the chapter provides details regarding how issues of positionality shape each stage of the survey research process, including design, data collection, and analysis. It offers practical advice from both the broader literature on surveys in the MENA region and research experiences in the Arab Gulf region in particular.

ACCESSING DATA IN THE MIDDLE EAST

Researchers studying the Middle East, like those studying in other parts of the developing world, have legitimate cause to lament a lack of empirical data. This lack of data can stem from a number of circumstances beyond the researcher's control and inherent to doing research in authoritarian settings or those beset by political instability. Governments might not have the capacity, particularly in times of crisis, to collect and maintain information on income and expenditures, health and education quality, crime statistics, and other social outcomes. One can think of cases in the MENA region such as Yemen, Syria and Libya where reliable data on many basic social concepts simply may not exist. However, an equally frustrating situation for researchers results not from the lack of data per se, but from lack of access to existing data. Authoritarian and closed regimes are generally less transparent than their democratic counterparts, making it less likely that they will share the data they collect with academic researchers.

Rather than give up on testing a particularly theoretical relationship entirely, researchers may opt to analyse the data that do exist, even if the series is broken or values for some cases are *missing*, that is, inaccessible for whatever reason. This must be done with due regard for why the data are missing from the dataset. In many situations, the data that are missing may be systematically different from the data that researchers can observe and correlated with the outcome of interest. These data are referred to as *missing not at random* and under certain conditions can cause researchers to make incorrect inferences about the relationship between variables (Rubin 1976; Little 1988). Missing data problems and possible solutions vary with the nature of the study (Schafer and Graham 2002; Graham 2012).[1] More importantly, missing data constitute an important thought question for researchers. How do the data I collected (e.g. finance statistics, interviews, or test scores) differ from the data I was unable to access and therefore did not collect? Researchers may need to shift the focus or methodology of their study to avoid making incorrect inferences due to missing data.

Accessing survey data

Survey data are attractive to researchers struggling to access other forms of quantitative data not only because they potentially exist when other statistics are unavailable, but more importantly because they allow researchers to investigate theories of social behaviour not readily captured in other types of data. For instance, using public opinion data, researchers can study identity, perception, and attitude change processes rather than focusing exclusively on political or social outcomes. In addition, survey content can be controlled by the investigator and tailored to the research question. In the best case scenario, questionnaires are designed to include a rich and diverse set of covariates as well as multiple measures of concepts of interest. Since the content of the survey questionnaire can be controlled by the researcher, access to measures of all important theoretical constructs can be ensured in the research design process. Designing survey questionnaires is a complex process, however, and simply asking a question on a survey does not ensure that respondents will process the question and respond in ways that produce valid and reliable measures of the research concepts.

Accessing high-quality survey data

Prior to concerns about questionnaire design, researchers must consider the basic operations of the survey itself, including the sampling and fielding methods. How will survey respondents be selected? How will the survey be administered? Selecting a method that is well-suited to the aims of the research project is crucial to the overall quality of the data. Since surveys are highly scalable and can be useful for both smaller elite samples as well as larger samples of the mass public, some thought should be given to the *target population*. Once the relevant population is identified, the sampling method and fielding process should be discussed with the researcher's partner survey institute or company. A full overview of sampling methods is outside the scope of this chapter, which instead provides guidance for researchers desiring to access high-quality survey data in Middle East.

During the past decade, survey research has rapidly increased in popularity in the region, making survey data of varied quality more readily available. Researchers looking to partner with the survey firms in the region should consider the following issues. First, does the firm have access to necessary information and expertise to properly sample from the population? If the research goal is to make inferences about the population from the survey sample, some form of *probability sampling* is required, including simple or stratified *random sampling*. Probability samples are based on structured randomness that permits inferences because the probability of inclusion for each respondent is equal among respondents, at least in theory (Scheaffer et al. 2011). Thus, survey data from well-designed, population-based national probability samples often have strong *external validity*, allowing researchers to make statements about the population by asking only a couple of thousand respondents rather than the entire population.[2] However, survey firms in the Middle East often face difficulties in gaining access to the maps, census data, and human capacity necessary to produce nationally representative samples and thus high-quality data.

Secondly, does the survey firm follow best practices that are appropriate for the region with regard to contacting and interviewing respondents? For instance, when conducting face-to-face interviewers, it may be necessary to practice gender matching. Research from the Social and Economic Survey Research Institute (SESRI) at Qatar University has found that in Qatar, as in other parts of the Muslim world, it is not appropriate for a female respondent to be interviewed by a male interviewer without a male family member present in the room (Le et al. 2014). At the same time, the presence of any other person in the room may induce respondents to stick to socially acceptable responses. Although female interviewers can and sometimes do interview male respondents, if the survey contains sensitive questions pertaining to things such as health or sexual practices, it is desirable for the survey firm to implement gender-matching more strictly (Elamadi et al. 2010). Since deploying larger teams of mixed-gender interviewers is not cost effective, SESRI researchers developed a method that pre-specifies the gender of the respondent and deploys only same gender interviewers to that household (Le et al. 2014). Other aspects of interviewer effects will be discussed in the following section.

Finally, it is important to consider whether the survey firm is reasonably transparent about its practices and independent of government censorship. Informed researchers are encouraged to question survey research firms with regard to their sampling, interviewing, and field monitoring processes. Although all the details may not be available all of the time, particularly in closed-regime contexts, an unwillingness to be transparent calls for caution on the part of researchers. Many data collection entities in the region have to balance concerns about government monitoring and censorship with the agenda and needs of their clients and collaborators. Researchers should be aware of the position of the firm vis-à-vis the government and consider the trade-offs inherent in that position. For example, surveys conducted by government affiliates may reflect the interests of the regime, on the one hand, but also give researchers the needed clout to access vulnerable target populations on the other. It is therefore advisable to weigh the position of the firm alongside the access that it can provide to determine which firm can deliver the best quality data for a particular research project.

POSITIONALITY AND THE RESEARCH PROCESS: HOW IDENTITY SHAPES YOUR DATA

At the outset, it may appear that quantitative inquiry is less impacted by questions of positionality than research designs that rely on qualitative methods. This is, of course, an illusion. Quantitative researchers face challenges related to positionality that are equally daunting. This section discusses how identity shapes the survey research process before, during, and after data collection.

In each phase, researchers are challenged to consider who is involved in the research process and how their identities interact to produce the data that we observe and subsequently analyse. In Western contexts, social scientists are often able to utilise survey data collected by firms and institutions with long traditions of high standards for data collection. Often, the issues and potential problems discussed by this chapter have already been carefully studied and addressed by these entities, making it relatively innocuous to use such data without giving much thought to positionality. However, researchers seeking to use survey data from the Middle East rarely have this luxury, as survey research in the region is still developing.

Who writes the questions? Who will answer them?

Assuming that the researcher has selected a target population and survey firm, the subsequent stage of his or her research process involves drafting a questionnaire that will be administered by the firm during the data collection stage. The primary challenge of this stage is to create a questionnaire that is sensitive to the identities of the question writers and the respondents. Researchers often rely on phrasing and translations from previous surveys when attempting to measure concepts of interest. In some cases, international entities such as the World Health Organization (WHO) have validated scales in many languages, including Arabic, for a number of health-related constructs that researchers can leverage (WHO 2005). Researchers interested in political and social topics in the region may wish to review the Arab Barometer questionnaire for ideas on questionnaire design (Jamal et al. 2008). However, in order to measure many important concepts in the social sciences, researchers studying the Middle East usually need to adapt survey items written in a Western context to the local context, if not write questions from scratch.[3] In so doing, knowledge of both the international scholarly literature on the subject and local culture and practice are equally essential. Subsequent paragraphs discuss three common issues related to positionality and survey design and how researchers have applied various techniques to overcome their ill-effects in the case of Qatar.

One of the basic issues that researchers encounter in questionnaire design is that of establishing *conceptual equivalence* for cross-cultural measures (Hui and Triandis 1985; Okazaki and Sue 1995). Some concepts such as happiness or democracy are infamously difficult to quantify across contexts, but many researchers face challenges in effectively defining and measuring concepts that appear to be much simpler. Due to recent patterns of immigration and conflict in the region, national representative surveys inevitably involve respondents from different backgrounds and cultures, making it difficult to achieve conceptual equivalence. The author and her colleagues at the Social and Economic Survey Research Institute (SESRI) at Qatar University, recently sought clear answers to the question, 'Is this woman fat?' In order to study the acute impact of social media exposure on body image perceptions among young female Arabs in Qatar, the research team needed to identify images of models and celebrities that could be consistently considered thin, average, or heavy in terms of body weight. Knowing that local preferences traditionally favour a more curvaceous female body shape but that societal norms have shifted recently, the research team (a mix of Western and Arab residents of Qatar) decided not to entrust the classification of images solely to themselves. Instead, extensive *cognitive interviews* were conducted to determine how respondents from the target population classified images. Answers to the question 'Is this woman fat?' differed significantly between the research team and the respondents, illustrating the necessity of using tools such as cognitive interviews to determine concept equivalence. The study went on to find that, contrary to findings from Western populations, when Arab females are shown images of thin models they desire a fuller body shape for themselves (Khaled et al. 2017).

Researchers concerned with achieving conceptual equivalence also discuss the issue of *response scale heterogeneity*, sometimes referred to as *differential item functioning* (DIF) (Brady 1985; King et al. 2004). DIF occurs when respondents interpret questions and the concepts they measure in different ways based on their own culture and experiences. In addition to cognitive interviews, researchers can study and correct for DIF more directly using the *anchoring vignettes* approach (King and Wand 2007; Stegmueller 2011). Anchoring vignettes present hypothetical situations that concretely describe concepts of interest and ask respondents to rate both the hypothetical person and themselves on the same response scale. A study by Gengler and Mitchell (2016) implemented this approach among Qatari nationals. The survey included vignettes measuring economic well-being and political efficacy along with their demographic predictors. Findings revealed that individual-level variation in response thresholds can lead researchers to make dubious conclusions from more traditional self-assessment.

Secondly, in regions such as the Middle East where respondents are unfamiliar with surveys or are unaccustomed to giving opinions, it is natural for them to take the path of least resistance or to process the questions less carefully than they would under other circumstances (Stolte 1994; Krosnick, Narayan and Smith 1996). This *satisficing* behaviour can be evidenced in a number of ways, including respondents who say they do not have an opinion as well as through acquiescence, meaning that respondents disproportionately agree with the statement made by the interviewer because it is easy and they are unprepared to give a more calculated answer. Respondents who are willing to state that they do not have an opinion can be easily dropped from the dataset afterward, whereas acquiescence behaviour presents a greater challenge. How can researchers separate respondents who truly agree with a statement from those who are merely satisficing?

Questionnaires can anticipate satisficing behaviour in a number of ways, one of which is to vary the direction of statements on the survey so that respondents must disagree to convey the attitude of interest (Falthzik and Jolson 1974). Then, positive and negative statements measuring the same concept can be compared during analysis. For example, in a study of attitudes about women and society, some respondents agreed with two statements (one positive and one negative) that were logically inconsistent.[4] The research team leveraged the differences in responses to detect possible satisficing behaviour and take remedial measures such as excluding some respondents from analysis and selecting the negatively framed statement for use in econometric models. Other possible post-data collection solutions for satisficing include focusing analysis on only the highest category of agreement (that is 'strongly agree'), and conducting factor analysis (or other methods of latent trait extraction) to get beyond single question measures. However, the later solution is only available if the questionnaire design includes appropriate response scales and multiple measures of the same concept.

Elevated acquiescence in survey data may result from satisficing; however, it might also be the consequence of respondents selecting the most social desirable answer. *Social desirability bias* is particularly relevant in the Middle East and in other parts of the world where respondents want to avoid being rude or expressing disagreeable sentiments. Social desirability can be induced by the presence of interviewers and will be discussed in the next section on who collects the data. However, knowing that respondents are reluctant to reveal their true preferences with respect to certain topics can help researchers design questionnaires more effectively. In the author's experience, Islamic religiosity, gender attitudes, political views, and opinions about minority groups can all be shaped by social desirability bias. Researchers who study the Middle East are increasingly using indirect measures of these concepts, including *survey experiments*, to elicit more accurate opinions. Survey experiments involve the random assignment to treatment groups of some component of the survey process in order to estimate the effect of the treatment on an outcome of interest (Mutz 2011). Survey experiments include a wide range of techniques, including vignette and conjoint experiments, as well as randomisation of question ordering, response options and even interviewer characteristics.[5]

Religiosity is a very difficult concept to measure in the Arab Gulf. Self-reported measures of explicitly religious behaviours (for example, prayer or mosque attendance) as well as general questions about the importance of religion often fail to produce meaningful variation in this context. How can researchers know if this is because religiosity is genuinely high or because it is socially desirable to appear religious? One non-experimental solution used by researchers at SESRI involves using indirect measures of religiosity that avoid religious framing and sequences of questions about religion rather than asking about the impact of religion on some other social choice. For instance, useful proxy measures of religiosity have been obtained from batteries on diverse topics such as charitable giving and marriage choices (Shockley 2016). Respondents tend to discern the socially desirable response quickly, however, and indirect measures may not capture the entire story. In many cases, embedding an experiment into the questionnaire design is a more effective way to understand sensitive issues.

Sometimes researchers want to know about multiple issues that are potentially sensitive in isolation and certainly sensitive when combined, for instance, studying the impact of religiosity, gender, minority group identity, and other factors on voter preferences in authoritarian elections. Shockley and Gengler (2020) use a *conjoint experiment* to demonstrate, unsurprisingly, that answers to straightforward questions about the relative importance of each of these factors differ widely from those obtained in the experiment. When asked in straightforward manner, objective factors such as education and official qualifications were cited as the predominant reasons for favouring a political candidate. However, when respondents were given the opportunity to rate entire candidate profiles comprised of six pieces of randomised information, the group identity and religiosity of the candidate emerged as the unrivalled drivers of political choices. This finding calls into question the results of a number of social scientific surveys which paint an egalitarian and meritocratic picture of political proceedings in the Middle East that is largely the product of social desirability bias and unwarranted by political reality.

When crafting a questionnaire in the Middle East, many researchers worry not just about the quality of the answers they will get but also about whether or not they will face some form of opposition from the government or difficulties getting the necessary approvals to field the survey. While official connections are likely irreplaceable for alleviating such concerns, indirect methods of phrasing questions such as anchoring vignettes or conjoint experiments, can be useful in this regard. Since they ask respondents to evaluate hypothetical situations, they offer a more subtle approach to sensitive topics that is less likely to raise red flags with either respondents or the government. Finally, it is important to note that even carefully crafted questionnaires may produce unforeseen issues when they are implemented in the context of an actual interview, phone call, or web survey. Thus, a thorough pretesting of the questionnaire, if not a full pilot survey, should be built into the research plan as time and budget permit, in order to minimise the number of problems that arise during the data collection phase.

Who collects the data?

As previously alluded to, social desirability bias in survey data can result from the interaction of the identities of the interviewer (or survey enumerator) and the respondent. Just as researchers conducting ethnographic or linguistic studies must be conscious of the how their presence may alter the behaviour of those they are studying in order to avoid the *observer's paradox* (Labov 1981), survey research requires attention to *interviewer effects* (Weeks and Moore 1981; Davis and Silver 2003). Population-based public opinion surveys require fairly large teams of interviewers from various identity groups. As previously discussed, studies conducted by SESRI researchers have demonstrated the need for contextually sensitive survey practices with regard to the gender of the interviewer due to conservative social norms about gender mixing (Le et al. 2012).

Research from other parts of the Arab world has demonstrated that interviewer religiosity, as expressed through dress, also shapes survey participation and response. In a study conducted in Egypt, the religiosity of the interviewer's appearance, in particular the female interviewers' wearing of a headscarf, shaped answers to questions about religious practice (Blaydes and Gilluma 2013). Similarly, implied religiosity in interviewer dress affected responses to a broad range of questions in a Moroccan survey (Benstead 2014). In more conservative contexts, such as Qatar, all female interviewers use a headscarf when conducting interviews, however other relevant interviewer identity cleavages exist related to nationality. Using SESRI telephone survey infrastructure, Gengler, Le and Wittrock (2019) randomly assigned national interviewers to half to the respondents in the sample. Their study demonstrates that interviewer nationality, as measured by language dialect, impacted both completion rates and answers to some types of questions. In practice, social science researchers who employ a survey firm to conduct a substantive study are not generally interested in examining interviewer effects. However, all researchers should carefully consider the relevant 'who' questions with regard to interviewer characteristic and interviewing procedures and be aware of how interviewer identities may shape survey responses.

Who analyses and reports findings?

In the final phase of the research process, survey data are cleaned, analysed, and sometimes incorporated into larger cross-national datasets or multi-indicator indices. By using straightforward data analysis techniques, researchers can identify relationships in the data. Skeptical observers of the data analysis processes often assert that statistics can be manipulated at will by analysts. On the contrary, in the author's experience, issues of positionality in the region tend to push researchers toward *self-censorship* more than toward manipulation or falsification of results. Researchers in any context may choose not to report certain aspects of their findings that are potentially unflattering to powerful groups or actors who could react negatively. Working inside closed-regimes or in the context of political instability can heighten these concerns. Researchers citing or using secondary data, which they were not personally involved in collecting, including reports and publicly available documents, should bear in mind these tendencies. In addition, researchers involved in collecting their own survey data should be aware that local collaborators or institutions may be hesitant to publicly present or publish certain results. Researchers wishing to distribute controversial results are encouraged to submit them for publication in international journals, where they will likely go unnoticed by stakeholders.

As a final example of self-censorship, using data influenced by positionality can be problematic, even for large cross-national indices. For example, recent work by Shockley et al. (2018) demonstrates that survey respondents in authoritarian regimes exaggerate quality of governance scores. Due to their positions as economic and regime insiders, such respondents have incentives to paint a rosy picture of governance in authoritarian regimes. Consequently, global measures of governance, such as those produced by Transparency International, that rely heavily on executive opinion surveys are biased in consequence. The authors demonstrate the bias empirically by comparing executive opinion survey responses with corollary ratings of non-elites who are often outside the country. Researchers aiming to make cross-national comparisons about governance quality among democracies and their closed counterparts should think carefully about positionality when selecting aggregate indices to measure concepts of interest.

CONCLUSION: IMPROVING DATA QUALITY

As this chapter demonstrates, access and positionality are challenges faced by qualitative and quantitative researchers alike, though quantitative researchers know them by different names. In light of these pervasive issues, quantitative research in the Middle East may appear unduly daunting. However, the purpose of pointing out common challenges is to encourage high-quality research rather than to discourage the general undertaking thereof. In the process, researchers can glean practical guidance for working in the region.

As survey research in the Middle East grows in popularity, researchers have more firms and institutions with which to partner. This dynamic can create healthy competition and lower prices for survey clients, but it also widens the range of data quality. With different firms producing data of differing quality, it is necessary to distinguish between firms. Academics who aspire to high-quality data are advised to partner with firms that have access to the necessary information and expertise to conduct probability-based samples of the population in question. Researchers should actively question firms about interviewing and sampling procedures to determine if best practices are being followed.

Regardless of the firm or target population that is ultimately selected, positionality shapes the research process at every stage. As such, researchers are advised to employ a variety of techniques for measuring sensitive concepts, including survey experiments, vignettes and indirect questions, in order to mitigate social desirability bias. Where there are concerns about interviewer effects, interviewer characteristics, such as gender and race, can be controlled for in subsequent analysis. Finally, potentially sensitive results can be presented delicately to private audiences or reserved for publication in international journals so as to respect the security concerns of local collaborators and, in some cases, the respondents themselves. The Middle East remains an understudied region, with a long-standing dearth of data to lament. Fortunately, survey research has the potential to alter this status quo and enhance our understanding of these nuanced societies, provided that we continually strive to produce and use high-quality data.

NOTES

1. Interested readers are referred to Allison (2001) for an accessible guide to this issue.
2. A number of processes involved in random sampling, stratification, and post-survey weighting of data combine to make it likely that the data we observe in the sample are not systematically different from the data we did not observe. External validity refers to the extent to which the observed results can be generalised to other situations and people. For a discussion of how internal and external validity are impacted by sample selection in sociological data see Berk (1983).
3. Although not specifically targeted for Middle East researchers, Harkness et al. (2003) provides a solid introduction for readers wishing to know more about the issues surrounding comparative survey design.
4. The positively framed statement read, 'Men and women should share equal status in society' while the negatively framed statement read 'Leadership of the community should be only in the hands of men' (Shockley et al. 2020).
5. Druckman, Green, and Lupia (2011) offer a general treatment of experiments with applications to political science, while Mutz (2011) provides a very useful overview that focuses population-based survey experiments.

BIBLIOGRAPHY

Allison, P. D., *Missing Data: Sage University Papers Series on Quantitative Applications in the Social Sciences* (Thousand Oaks: SAGE Publications, 2001).

Benstead, L. J., 'Effects of interviewer-respondent gender interaction on attitudes toward women and politics: Findings from Morocco', *International Journal of Public Opinion Research*, 26(3) (2014), pp. 369–83.

Berk, R. A., 'An introduction to sample selection bias in sociological data', *American Sociological Review* (1) (1983), pp. 386–98.

Blaydes, L. and R. M. Gilluma, 'Religiosity-of-interviewer effects: Assessing the impact of veiled enumerators on survey response in Egypt', *Politics and Religion*, 6(3) (2013), pp. 459–82.

Brady, H. E., 'The perils of survey research: Inter-personally incomparable responses', *Political Methodology*, 11(1) (1985), pp. 269–91.

Christensen, L. B., B. Johnson and L. A. Turner, *Research Methods, Design, and Analysis* (Upper Saddle River, NJ: Pearson Higher Education, 2011).

Davis, D. W. and B. D. Silver, 'Stereotype threat and race of interviewer effects in a survey on political knowledge', *American Journal of Political Science* 47(1) (2003), pp. 33–45.

Druckman, J. N., D. P. Green, J. H. Kuklinski and A. Lupia (eds), *Cambridge Handbook of Experimental Political Science* (Cambridge, MA: Cambridge University Press, 2011).

Elamadi, D., H. Abdul Rahim, A. Diop, M. N. Khan, K. T. Le, E. Elawad and J. Wittrock, *First Annual Omnibus Survey: A Survey of Life in Qata* (Doha, Qatar: Qatar University, Social and Economic Survey Research Institute, 2010).

Falthzik, A. M. and M. A. Jolson, 'Statement Polarity in Attitude Studies', *Journal of Marketing Research*, 11(1) (1974), pp. 102–5.

Gengler, J. J., K. T. Le and J. Wittrock, 'Citizenship and Surveys: Group Conflict and Nationality-of-Interviewer Effects in Arab Public Opinion Data', *Political Behavior* (2019), pp. 1–23.

Gengler, J. and J. S. Mitchell, 'A hard test of individual heterogeneity in response scale usage: Evidence from Qatar', *International Journal of Public Opinion Research*, 10 (2016) edw025, http://doi.org/10.1093/ijpor/edw025.

Graham, J. W., 'Missing data theory', in *Missing Data* (New York: Springer, 2012) pp. 3–46.

Harkness, J. A., F. J. Van de Vijver and P. P. Mohler, *Cross-cultural Survey Methods*, vol. 325 (Hoboken: Wiley-Interscience, 2003).

Hui, C. H. and H. C. Triandis, 'Measurement in cross-cultural psychology: A review and comparison of strategies', *Journal of Cross-Cultural Psychology*, 16(2) (1985), pp. 131–52.

Jamal, A. A. and M. A. Tessler, 'Attitudes in the Arab world', *Journal of Democracy*, 19(1) (2008), pp. 97–110.

Khaled, S., B. Shockley, L. Kimmel, Y. Qutteina, K. T. Le (2017), 'The acute impact of exposure to images of models and celebrities on the desire for change in body size and body shape among young Arab women: a survey experiment', manuscript under review.

King, G., C. J. L. Murray, J. A. Salomon and A. Tandon, 'Enhancing the validity and cross-cultural comparability of measurement in survey research', *American Political Science Review*, 98 (2004), 191–207.

King, G. and J. Wand, 'Comparing incomparable survey responses: Evaluating and selecting anchoring vignettes', *Political Analysis*, 15(1) (2007), pp. 46–66.

Krosnick, J. A., S. Narayan and W. R. Smith, 'Satisficing in surveys: Initial evidence', *New Directions for Evaluation*, 70 (1996), pp. 29–44.

Labov, W., 'Field methods of the project on linguistic change and variation', in *Language in Use*, J. Baugh and J. Sherzer (eds) (Englewood Cliffs: Prentice Hall, 1981), pp. 28–53.

Le, K. T., J. M. Brick, A. Diop and D. Elamadi, 'Within-household sampling conditioning on household size', *International Journal of Public Opinion Research*, 25(1) (2012), pp. 108–18.

Le, K. T., A. Diop, J. Wittrock, D. Elamadi and E. Elawad, 'Gender pre-specified sampling for cost control', *International Journal for Public Opinion Research*, 26(4) (2014), pp. 441–52.

Little, R. J., 'A test of missing completely at random for multivariate data with missing values', *Journal of the American Statistical Association*, 83(404) (1988), pp. 1198–202.

Mutz, D. C., *Population-Based Survey Experiments* (Princeton: Princeton University Press, 2011).

Okazaki, S. and S. Sue, 'Methodological issues in assessment research with ethnic minorities', *Psychological Assessment*, 7(3) (1995), pp. 367–75.

Rubin, D. B., 'Inference and missing data', *Biometrika*, 63(3) (1976), pp. 581–92.

Schafer, J. L. and J. W. Graham, 'Missing data: our view of the state of the art,' *Psychological Methods*, 7(2) (2002), pp. 147–77.

Scheaffer, R. L., W. Mendenhall III, R. L. Ott and K. G. Gerow, *Elementary Survey Sampling: Seventh Edition* (Boston, MA: Cengage Learning, 2011).

Shockley, B., 'Women and political interest in Qatar: Moving ahead but not catching up', *Journal of Arabian Studies*, 6(1) (2016), pp. 53–73.

Shockley, Bethany, Noora Ahmed Lari, Engi Assaad Ahmed El-Maghraby, and Mohammad Hassan Al-Ansari, 'Social media usage and support for women in community leadership: Evidence from Qatar' in *Women's Studies International Forum*, vol. 81, p. 102374. Pergamon (2020).

Shockley B., M. Ewers, Y. Nardis and J. Gengler, 'Exaggerating good governance: Regime type and score inflation among executive survey informants', *Governance* (2018), ,00:1–22. http://doi.org/10.1111/gove.12330

Shockley, Bethany and Justin J. Gengler, 'Social Identity and Coethnic Voting in the Middle East: Experimental Evidence from Qatar' *Electoral Studies*, 67, p. 102213 (2020).

Stegmueller, D., 'Apples and oranges? The problem of equivalence in comparative research', *Political Analysis*, 19(4) (2011), pp. 471–87.

Stolte, J. F., 'The context of satisficing in vignette research', *The Journal of Social Psychology*, 134(6) (1994), pp. 727–33.

Weeks, M. F. and R. P. Moore, 'Ethnicity-of-interviewer effects on ethnic respondents', *Public Opinion Quarterly*, 45(2) (1981), pp. 245–9.

World Health Organization. 2005. Basic documents. http://apps.who.int/iris/handle/10665/43134

Conducting Ethnographic Research

Women, Conflict and the Everyday: Feminist Ethnographies in Palestine and Kurdistan

Sophie Richter-Devroe and Veronica Buffon

One of the core principles in feminist research is its aim to link research to emancipatory practices. Most feminist scholars today agree there is not one specific method that characterises feminist research. Rather, feminist research has defined itself largely through the challenges it launches against the epistemology of traditional science on various levels: methodologically, ethically as well as – importantly – politically. What unites feminist research across these varieties thus is its wish to affect and transform social and political realities. Feminist research should help to combat not only gendered discrimination, but all forms of oppression whether based on class, race, sexuality, ethnicity, or other factors. It should aim at transforming women's (and men's) lives and contribute towards achieving social justice. Feminist research thus is acutely aware of its political impact and, as such, demands a critical self-reflexive stance from the researcher at all stages of the research process.

In this chapter, we reflect on what feminist research practice means in the context of the Middle East and, more specifically, when conducting ethnographic work in politically-charged settings such as that of Palestine or Kurdistan. We rely on our long-term research experience in the Kurdish region of Turkey (Veronica Buffon) and Palestine (Sophie Richter-Devroe), and draw on the fieldwork we conducted there for our PhDs (Richter-Devroe 2010; Buffon 2017).[1]

During Veronica's multi-sited ethnography in the Kurdish region, she lived with her own family in the 'putative capital' of Northern Kurdistan, Diyarbakır, and in a nearby village where she was hosted by the family of a female 'traditional healer'. During the fieldwork, she engaged with various actors from the formal medical sector in the urban setting and also shared everyday activities with women in a small community in a village of Diyarbakır province. While Veronica conducted interviews that were more formal with men and women as professional figures in the health sectors, her engagement with ordinary women was informal and mainly took the form of participant observation, chats and conversations during rallies, protest or meetings in several healers' homes in different villages. Veronica built her strongest fieldwork relations with women through the participation in everyday activities and therapeutic practices in the village. The combination of different ethnographic tools contributed to revealing the ethnographic complexity of the inequality experienced by women in the health sector, by illustrating how formal and informal medical discourses and practices are intertwined and transformed.

Sophie's reflections in this chapter draw from her fieldwork in Palestine on the different forms of political activism that Palestinian women have engaged in since the 1993 Oslo Accords (see Richter-Devroe 2010, 2018). For this research, she spent about eleven months from 2007 to 2009 in the West Bank and East Jerusalem. She often stayed for prolonged periods with families in different towns and villages, conducting interviews, focus groups and participation observation in political events that focused on women's activism, peacebuilding or resistance. Approximately half of her interviews were with women (and a few male) activist or NGO leaders, many of whom had been engaged participants during the First Intifada. These interviews were more formal and structured, and offered important insights on how women's politics have changed over the last decades. The other half of the interviews she conducted with ordinary women (and some men) from different backgrounds in villages, towns, and refugee camps. Most of these informal interviews happened spontaneously, and they can be more accurately described as guided conversations. Staying in family homes, participating in women's everyday lives and sharing their daily work proved to be among the most fruitful occasions to gain insights into the practices and meanings of women's informal everyday survival, resistance, and coping strategies in Palestine.

Ethnographic fieldwork in Palestine and the Kurdish region thus for both of us entailed a variety of methods: more formal and structured interviews, informal conversations, focus groups as well as participant observation in different settings.

In this chapter, we critically reflect on our fieldwork experience, and engage with some of the core themes debated in feminist methodology and epistemology: the question of objectivity, self-reflexivity and positionality; the issue of representation and difference, as well as debates on politics, academia and activism.

REFLECTIONS FROM THE FIELD

In feminist methodology, a positivist claim to objective knowledge and truth is predominantly rejected. Rather, knowledge is understood to be partial

(Clifford 1986) and situated (Haraway 1988). Feminist researchers, in line with other constructivist and post-positivist scholarship in the social sciences and humanities, understand knowledge derived from interviews, informal conversations, focus groups, participant observation and other ethnographic methods to be constructed intersubjectively, power-laden and influenced by a multitude of issues. These issues include, for example, the location and timing of the interview, other people's presence, (the interviewee's perception of) the interviewer's identity (such as gender, age, socio-economic background, nationality, language skills, religious or political affiliation, etc.), and various other possible dynamics. A self-reflexive process in which the researcher thinks through her own positionality in the field, and influence on the data interpretation thus is core to feminist ethnography. Without denying the complexity, fluidity and contextuality of our identities in the field, we try to pinpoint below the most significant identity markers – whether ascribed or self-perceived – from which we approached our material, i.e. from which we understand, speak and represent.

Gender

Much has been written on the issue of whether and how gender affects the ethnographic encounter and, in particular, the interview situation.[2] Some contend that gender influences, firstly, the internal dynamics of an interview arguing that women respond differently to male interviewers (Williams and Heikes 1993); secondly, the methodology used during interviews assuming, for example, that women interviewers are more likely to lead non-hierarchical, open-ended, subjective and thus non-positivist interviews (Oakley 1981); and, finally, the quality of the interview data interpretation claiming that female scholars are more likely to accurately interpret women's words, since women use language differently from men (see Gilligan 1982).

Gender without doubt played a role in our field research. Nevertheless, we would not want to essentialise women's voices or nature. In line with other female scholars carrying out fieldwork in the Middle East, we found that as female researchers we could gain dual access to both men and women and thus 'actually enjoy[ed] *more* access than male researchers' (Schwedler 2006: 425; see also Abu-Lughod 1986/2000: 23). Many of our interviewees became friends, whom we met on a regular basis, who invited us for festivities, food or to stay overnight. It would have been more difficult, if not impossible, for a male researcher to establish such a close relationship with female research participants.

For example, Veronica stayed in a village in Diyarbakır province with the family of a female Sufi practitioner, who also acted as a healer. Sharing ordinary life and activities, Veronica created a strong relationship with the healer, the 'female patients', friends, and co-villagers. After a period of strong suspicion towards Veronica's presence in the village, her status as female researcher, wife and mother – at the time pregnant with her second child – helped in overcoming her research participants' initial mistrust. Veronica was accepted in the collective and convivial space of the healers' house, and invited to take part in the women-only *dhikr* several times. Such access to 'women's worlds' (Abu-Lughod 1993/2008) would have been impossible for a male researcher.

Just as Abu-Lughod noticed during her research with Bedouin women in Egypt, we also found that '[b]ecause relations in the women's world are more informal than in the men's, [we were] able to get beyond polite conversations more quickly' (Abu-Lughod 1986/2000: 16; see also Abu-Lughod 1985). For example, Sophie noticed during her fieldwork that the Palestinian women she spoke with were more likely to freely express their views on different forms of political activism in women-only groups rather than in mixed settings, especially their critical opinions on joint Palestinian–Israeli peace and dialogue projects. Contrary to Western stereotypical assumptions, which claim that female researchers face additional problems during their field studies in Arab countries, we thus found that we in fact enjoyed privileges.

To argue, however, that there is something specific about women's methodology or about ethnographies written by women 'in a woman's voice' ignores women's different standpoints, experiences and voices across cultures and other intersecting lines of division such as class, race, age, nationality, ethnicity, sexuality, etc. Such differences were, for example, apparent in the dialogue encounters that Sophie attended between Palestinian and Israeli women. While these encounters aimed to establish bridges across the national divide based on the participants' gender identity and their presumed feminine characteristics of 'care' and 'sisterhood', differences between the coloniser and the colonised could never be bracketed (see Richter-Devroe 2018).

An essentialist position that proclaims the singularity of 'a woman's view' – whether in methodology, political view or elsewhere – thus is untenable. Gender only constitutes one – and not necessarily the most significant – variable among many which influenced our fieldwork. There were other identity features (intersecting with gender), which gain importance in the Palestinian and Kurdish situation of heightened conflict and political polarisation.

East/West binaries

The dichotomous understanding of 'East' vs 'West' continues to be perceived as one of the main dividing lines distinguishing an 'insider' from an 'outsider' researcher. Those who attempt to study social, political, economic or cultural institutions and phenomena of the 'other', this narrative goes, will find it more difficult to make sense of what they see and hear during their fieldwork than so-called 'insiders' or native researchers.

Such culturalist arguments often falsely seek refuge and support from Edward Said's (1978) *Orientalism*. Said's critique of western Orientalist writers for (mis-)representing 'the East' has sometimes been misunderstood by culture-centric approaches as emphasising difference and dichotomies between 'East' and 'West'. In fact, however, Said argued that essentialising, constructing and knowing the other as different from the self has less to do with actual differences, but is a political act, a project of imperial domination aimed at establishing hierarchies and epistemic power over the (constructed) other. In line with several other postcolonial writers who criticised culture-centric approaches for reifying artificial dichotomies between 'us' and 'them' or 'East' and 'West' (Abu-Lughod 1989; Lazreg 1988; Hall 1996; Spivak 1988, Abu-Lughod 1993/2008), Said stressed that constructed binaries between self and other have their roots in real material and geopolitical differences between the North and South, East and West:

> If we no longer think of the relationship between cultures and their adherents as perfectly contiguous, totally synchronous, wholly correspondent, and if we think of cultures as permeable and, on the whole, defensive boundaries between polities, a more promising situation appears. Thus to see Others not as ontologically given but as *historically constituted* would be to erode the exclusivist biases we so often ascribe to cultures, our own not least. [emphasis added] (Said 1989: 225; see also Said 1993)

Paying attention to the impact that historical and political processes as well as current geopolitical constellations have on understandings of self and other thus unmasks cultural essentialism as a political project. Nevertheless culturalist arguments and dichotomous thinking which essentialise people and communities into 'East' and 'West' still hold sway in academic, popular and political discourses. In our conversations and interviews with Palestinian and Kurdish women such dichotomous interpretations and ideas of incompatibility were also sometimes voiced. Answers such as 'this is our culture, you know, it is difficult for you to understand' brought home to us the message that while essentialist binaries might have been deconstructed theoretically, this does not mean that they also have vanished from the popular, let alone political scene (see also Al-Ali 2000: 19–50; Hall 1996).

Yet, although our research participants sometimes initially packaged their understandings of 'East' and 'West' in terms of culture, they also stressed the historical and current political role of Europe and the US in perpetuating conflict, occupation and settler colonisation in Palestine and Kurdistan.

Constructions of 'East' vs 'West' have political roots and our research participants' occidentalist or self-orientalising answers should be seen as a reaction to geopolitical power constellations rather than reflecting cultural differences *per se*. Constructions of the other always are political projects, particularly in politically-heated and conflict-torn countries with a colonial history and present such as Palestine or Kurdistan. This becomes clear if one looks at the range of various 'others' that are constructed. Usually our research participants cast not only 'Westerners' as others, but also shored up their own identities against constructions of both internal political opponents. Often the divide between grassroots and elite was stressed, but more often the identified internal other was chosen along political lines.

Towards a historically-grounded feminist approach to self/other

It is impossible to identify and evaluate all variables that influenced our field research and our interpretations of the fieldwork material. The significance of each depends on the specific context of the encounter. While reflexive attention to difference and positioning is necessary to give an honest portrayal of the (inter-)subjective nature of data generation and analysis, we consider it similarly crucial not to reify difference by falling into the traps of individualistic-psychological or essentialist-culturalist approaches. Abu-Lughod has convincingly criticised the limited focus on (how to overcome) difference, as put forward particularly in reflexive ethnographic approaches of the 1980s (e.g. Clifford 1986):

> What worries ethnographers [in reflexive anthropology] now is not
> the history of the creation of the distinction between self and other,
> but how possibly to communicate across the divide, how to dialogue
> with the other. That there is an 'other', with the corollary that there is
> a self which is unproblematically distinct from it, is still assumed. To
> question that assumption would be to look at the relationship between
> anthropology, colonialism, and racism in the construction of the
> Western self. (Abu-Lughod 1993: 40)[3]

By prioritising the process to overcome difference, reflexive scholarship might in fact reify and essentialise difference, rather than tracing roots and processes through which difference comes about. Acknowledging that differences have roots in real material, political and historical processes, are largely constructed and not a natural stemming from 'culture,' helps to situate and contextualise people's actions and the meanings they attach to them. It helps to understand their practices as meaningful, and not something, that needs to be 'decoded' through false processes of trying to become an 'insider'.

It is at this point that feminist scholars, who have long debated and struggled with the difficulties of maintaining political force and unity while also acknowledging difference, can provide important insights to qualitative research. Rejecting essentialist universalist accounts on women's identity, intersectional feminist theory and praxis has stressed the need to acknowledge the differences that exist between women by class, race, sexuality, ethnicity, nationality and other intersecting variables (Mohanty 1984; Crenshaw 1991; Yuval-Davis 1999). Offering a corrective to both universalist 'global sisterhood' politics and particularist identity politics, this scholarship has also highlighted that women's identities, experiences, viewpoints and positionings are never stable, but are formed in interaction with and embedded in wider social and political structures (e.g. Haraway 1988; Harding 1991).

This fluidity also characterises a qualitative researcher's positioning in the field. As researchers, we were situated towards our research participants both as 'insider' and 'outsider' through various selves, some of which are more 'real', more perceived or more constructed than others. Among the many ascribed and self-perceived identities, we were relating to the people we interacted with as researchers, friends, women, as 'German' or 'Italian', as someone from the 'West', or as someone who supports the Palestinian or Kurdish liberation struggle. Rather than focusing on one of these – and particularly not the over-belaboured East/West divide – we thus prefer to follow Narayan's feminist deconstructive approach:

> Instead of the paradigm emphasizing a dichotomy between outsider/ insider or observer/observed, I propose that at this historical moment we might more profitably view each anthropologist in terms of shifting identifications amid a field of interpenetrating communities and power relations. The loci along which we are aligned or set apart from those whom we study are multiple and in flux. Factors such as education, gender, sexual orientation, class, race, or sheer durations of contacts may at different times outweigh the cultural identity we associate with insider or outsider status. (Narayan 1993: 671–2)

A feminist approach thus identifies aspects of the researcher's identity other than the East/West divide as crucial for the ethnographic encounter. During our encounters with interviewees, friends and research participants in Palestine and the Kurdish region the intersecting features discussed here of gender and geopolitical constellations (and derived constructions of East vs West) to various degrees defined our ethnographic encounters, our own as well as our interviewees' conceptualisations of self and other, and the intersubjective knowledge production in the field. Given the Palestinian and Kurdish historical and political context, the most important issue that defined not only our fieldwork, but also the process of textual production, however was our political positioning – a point discussed in more detail in the next section.

POWER, POLITICS AND REPRESENTATION

In the field we were regularly asked by our research participants about our political views on the Kurdish and Palestinian issue. Disclosing our critical viewpoints of Israeli policies in Occupied Palestine or Turkish policies in the Kurdish areas was unproblematic with most Palestinians and Kurds. Many of our interviewees drew up differentiations between 'good foreigners' (who are in solidarity with Palestinian and Kurdish resistance) and 'bad foreigners' (who support superficial peace and dialogue agendas). Our work, tracing different forms of Turkish and Israeli state violence, and Kurdish and Palestinian resistance to it, was associated with the former. In interviews with Palestinians and Kurds, disclosing our political positioning was thus often a necessary step towards establishing trust and a frank atmosphere.

These negotiations of political positioning were, however, more complex in interactions with Israeli and Turkish citizens, as well as with some Kurdish villagers who did not support the main Kurdish political party.

For example, Sophie's fieldwork involved regular participant observation in joint dialogue and peacebuilding projects between Israelis and Palestinians. In such joint Palestinian-Israeli meetings, particularly if without much critical political depth, Sophie sometimes refrained from revealing her views on Israeli politics or the fact that she resided in the West Bank. Israeli participants often interrogated her on why she had arrived together with the Palestinian participants, what her reasons for being in the meeting or in the West Bank were, if she had any institutional affiliations with Palestinian organisations, etc. She was often dragged into political discussions about current political events and Israeli policies, or asked to comment on particular incidents, or the nature of a particular joint Palestinian-Israeli project. In general, she tried to stay an observer during the joint meeting, but this was not always possible. Depending on her conversation partner, she sometimes had to shift between more neutrally and silently observing a specific research context, or more openly expressing her political views and commitment to ending Israeli settler colonisation in Palestine (Richter-Devroe 2018: 24–7).

Veronica, on the other hand, observed during her fieldwork that politics were more easily discussed with research participants in the urban setting rather than in villages. For example, in towns and cities, especially Diyarbakir, research participants would invite her for tea and talk about their or their family members' political history detailing stories of loss, violence and exclusion. Conducting fieldwork during the pre-election period in 2011, the political campaign was widely discussed and political divisions between supporters of BDP (*Barış ve Demokrasi Partisi; Partiya Aştî û Demokrasiyê*; Peace and Democracy Party) and of AKP (*Adalet ve Kalkınma Partisi*; Justice and Development Party) were visible in Diyarbakır also due to the strong presence of the pro-Kurdish party (BDP).

However, the political context had a different relevance in the village where Veronica was conducting part of her fieldwork. While in the city, the strong and visible presence of the state also materialised through the presence of policemen, armoured vehicles and helicopters (especially during the election time and public events such as international women's day, *Newroz* celebration, etc.), the state's presence was less evident in the village. In this latter setting, people from the village itself were involved in patrol activities. Under the command of the village leader, they were tasked with monitoring the incursion of PKK guerrillas. The constant presence (or phantom) of the police or military deeply shaped interactions with and among people. Veronica felt that villagers tended to be less open in discussing their political views. There was consequently also a much more pronounced mistrust towards a foreigner in the village. This obliged Veronica to negotiate her multiple and shifting positions, variously accentuating her support for the Kurdish party, her distance from the AKP party or a more neutral position in political discussion.

What these shifting positionings show is that our roles and identities as fieldworkers were never fixed. We were constantly 'shuttling between two or more worlds' (Visweswaran 1994: 119) and the different degrees to which we would reveal, feel ready to discuss and defend our political viewpoints reflected the uncertainties that fieldwork in this specific context of long-term military occupation entails. The ethnographic encounter thus is always intersubjective, fluid and power-laden.

Questions of power and political positioning exist not only during the ethnographic encounter, but remain equally crucial during the process of writing up. Representing the 'other' always entails a form of epistemic violence, particularly in the context of ongoing settler-colonial and oppressive practices in Palestine and Kurdistan. Some scholars (engaged in, for example, feminist participatory action research) therefore stress the need to bring to the fore as much as possible the voices and worldviews of the researched, advocating a strong cooperation between the researcher and researched. Our own data interpretation and analysis relied on such close cooperation and reciprocity with (particularly our key) research participants; it is not only *on*, but rather *with* and, as much as possible, also *for* Palestinian and Kurdish female activists that we aim to write. Yet, while we wanted to portray women's marginalised voices, we also remain wary not to naively 'romanticise' (Spivak 1988) them as necessarily or inherently emancipatory. Representing the marginalised, of course, is a politically important move, but it is not without pitfalls and problematics. The question of representation has been approached in academia both through *poetics* (i.e. experimentation with form and style) and *politics*.

The poetics of representation

Experimental reflexive anthropologists, in their criticism of the anthropologist-expert who, by writing about others, always engages in a process of subjugation through rhetorical means, have called for experimentation with representation through dialogical or polyvocal ethnography. Research participants should, in this view, 'begin to be considered as co-authors, and the ethnographer as scribe and archivist as well as interpreting observer' (Clifford 1986: 17). This co-production, according to Clifford, should not only be recognised and reflected upon by the researcher, but it should also determine the form of the text. Through a precise dialogical and polyphonic rendering of the interview situation, experimental anthropologists hoped to reduce the researcher's power over his/her subjects. Experimentations with texts, forms and styles strive to portray the ethnographic encounter more precisely, more 'realistically', and thus are an attempt to 'rescue representation'.

We have tried to include, as much as possible, the voices and narratives of our research participants in our writings, both through direct quotations from recorded interviews and paraphrasing of informal conversations (Richter-Devroe 2010, 2018; Buffon 2017). While always contextualising the interview/conversation material, we adopted only in a few instances dialogical or polyvocal forms of representation, which trace in much detail how a conversation evolved. Sophie included a transcription of a conversation between herself, a woman activist protesting against the construction of the Israeli Apartheid wall in her village, and a woman who accompanied Sophie during the interview in her PhD thesis (Richter-Devroe 2010: 28). The detailed textual representation of this specific interview passage provided an opportunity for Sophie to show how her own (perceived) positionality and identity in the field, as well as the specific power dynamics between all three people present, influenced the interview dynamics. As such, polyphonic, dialogical textual representations of fieldwork and interview material can help to illustrate how knowledge is generated intersubjectively during the ethnographic encounter.

Veronica's research on health revealed some of the difficulties that ethnographers might face in largely oral communities. For her, it proved difficult to describe, analyse and represent in written text the everyday conversation, information and tacit practices, which women would often simply dismiss as irrelevant. The women in the village mostly did not want to be recorded. For them recording was associated with the Turkish state's spying and policing techniques. Note-taking also was not always easy. Most of Veronica's research participants in the village were illiterate, and felt uncomfortable with her writing notes. They would thus ask her or their children to read aloud what she had written in her notebook, and explain. Transferring the everyday spoken word to written text, whether during fieldwork or in the process of writing up, thus poses a particular problem in largely oral communities for whom the written mode of knowledge production constitutes a somewhat foreign, but at the same time authoritative and potentially threatening element (see also Tedlock 1991).

Dialogical and polyphonic ethnography has been severely criticised for failing to solve the fundamental problem of power inherent in every act of representation: no matter which textual style the representation takes, power differences between researcher and researched always remain and the authoritative and final interpretive power still lies with the researcher. Abu-Lughod, for example, asserts that 'refiguring informants as consultants or "letting the other speak" in dialogic [...] or polyvocal texts – decolonisations on the level of the text – leaves intact the basic configurations of global power on which anthropology is based' (Abu-Lughod 1993/2008: 26; see also Abu-Lughod 1990: 11; Rabinow 1986).[4]

Geopolitical power configurations that structure and dominate the institution of research by mainly western-based scholars on mainly non-western 'subjects' are thus ignored and left intact. Said has identified reasons for the trend to focus on style and form rather than (geo)politics: '[T]here has been a considerable amount of borrowing [in anthropological writing] from adjacent domains, from literary theory, history and so on, in some measure because much of this has skirted over the political issues for understandable reasons, *poetics being a good deal easier to talk about than politics*' (Said 1989: 220–1 [emphasis added]).

By trying to solve the problem of power asymmetries between researcher and researched through textual experimentation – poetics – merely, experimental ethnography might not only fail to curb the risk of epistemic violence, but it might also risk adopting a depoliticised stance. This criticism should not be understood as an outright rejection of textual experimentation, but it highlights that an overemphasis on style and form might sidestep the most crucial issue: that representation is first and foremost a political issue.

The politics of representation

Traditional understandings of academic research expect the researcher to remain an apolitical, impartial outside observer. Impartiality, however, just as objectivity, is impossible in the field as well as when writing up. When Clifford asserted that '[e]thnographic truths are [...] inherently *partial* – committed and incomplete' (1986: 7, [emphasis in original]) he not only stressed the fact that knowledge production is subjective (and thus incomplete), but also that it is positioned (and thus committed). The researcher always is politically positioned towards his/her research subject and the context studied. Acknowledging that academic research necessarily *is* partial, however, does not provide answers to the fundamental question on whether it *should* be.

Scheper-Hughes (1995) in this regard, has argued that if anthropology is 'to be worth anything at all' in our times, it should be 'ethically grounded', 'morally engaged' and 'politically committed' (1995: 409). Research thus not only inevitably *is* partial and politically positioned but, according to Scheper-Hughes, also *should* be. In line with post-positivist feminist scholarship, Scheper-Hughes maintains that since scholarship never can be neutral and objective, researchers need to reveal and reflect on their own positionality, and work towards positive change in the research community. Such a position might be accused of bias, but for Scheper-Hughes, a 'militant anthropology' (1995), i.e. a committed scholarship that does not shy away from taking sides, is required, particularly in the contexts of political, social and economic injustice. Yet, those who provide reflexive accounts and think through the links between their scholarship and political positionings (see e.g. Swedenburg 1989) are regularly accused of bias and impartiality, and their scholarship is attacked and delegitimised as driven by political agendas and ideologies.[5]

We also faced such accusations of partiality during our respective fieldwork in Palestine and Kurdistan. Sophie recalls a discussion with an Israeli workshop instructor in a joint Palestinian–Israeli dialogue meeting, in which the instructor asked her to stay 'neutral' and refrain from expressing her judgements and views on the political situation. She was told that, as an 'outsider', she had no right to comment and that it would be more responsible for her to stay silent and not interfere. This exchange marked a crucial point in her fieldwork experience, and pushed her to reflect more critically on her own positionality as a so-called 'outsider', but also as regards her own commitment to and scholarship on Palestine, as well as the politics of research in Palestine more broadly (Richter-Devroe 2018: 20–7).

During her stay in the village, Veronica was regularly reminded by older men that 'we are not *Apoci*', that no one in the village was supporting Apo (Abdulla Ocalan). On one particular occasion, when the government (AKP) was providing free school bags and clothes, the men showed Veronica these gifts to demonstrate to her that the Turkish government took good care of the community, while the pro-Kurdish party was not providing any material help and support. As a witness to this generosity, Veronica should adopt a more critical and balanced view of the political situation, these men stressed, retell such stories once back in Europe, and refrain from participating in pro-Kurdish political activities in the city. In a similar way to Sophie's experience in Palestine, this incident highlighted to Veronica that research always is political, and what counts for some as 'impartial', carries a heavy and potentially biased political message for others.

Our experiences in the field thus made us reflect on the question of whether as researchers in politically-charged settings we should assume the role of 'neutral observer' or 'engaged witness'. Scheper-Hughes compares the role of the anthropologist to that of a witness:

> Observation, the anthropologist as 'fearless spectator', is a passive act which positions the anthropologist above and outside human events as a 'neutral' and 'objective' (i.e. uncommitted) seeing I/eye. Witnessing, the anthropologist as *companheira*, is in the active voice, and it positions the anthropologist inside human events as a responsive, reflexive, and morally committed being, one who will 'take sides' and make judgments. [emphasis in original] (Scheper-Hughes 1995: 419)

We support Scheper-Hughes call for a committed and reflexive positioning of the researcher as witness. In a strongly unjust context, such as that of Palestine or Kurdistan, saying nothing, not revealing one's anti-discrimination, anti-colonial and anti-occupation stance, and writing in an alleged 'impartial,' 'outsider's' voice, as the Israeli instructor demanded of Sophie or the Kurdish villagers of Veronica, would be a form of self-censorship and might even contribute to maintaining the status quo of injustice. Taking a stance against illegal and discriminatory Israeli and Turkish state policies thus, in fact, is not a pro-Palestinian or pro-Kurdish stance. It is a humanist position that responds to and aims to impact (geo-)political realities (see also Richter-Devroe 2019: 26–7).

TOWARDS A POLITICALLY-ENGAGED HUMANIST SCHOLARSHIP

Lila Abu-Lughod has called for a humanist scholarship noting that:

> ... the outsider self never simply stands outside; he or she always stands in a definite relations with the 'other' of the study, not just as Westerner or even halfie, but as Frenchman in Algeria during the war of independence, and American in Morocco during the 1967 Arab-Israeli war, or an Englishwoman in postcolonial India. What we call the outside, or even partial outside, is always a position *within* a larger political-historical complex. [emphasis in original] (Abu-Lughod 1993/2008: 40)

We do not consider ourselves as 'outsiders' to the Palestine question, or to the Kurdish issue in Turkey. Rather, we are politically and historically positioned towards this region and its people.

For Sophie, travelling to Palestine in the privileged positioning of a German passport holder, has highlighted the need to trace historical entanglements and act as 'witness' in Scheper-Hughes' sense to the injustices and violences of Israeli settler colonialism in Palestine. Veronica, as an Italian and UK-based researcher, also felt the need to act as 'witness' in Kurdistan.

Yet, at the same time, we were and are aware of the very different experience and safety that our status as foreigners, researchers and observers endowed us with in the field. This was also pointed out to us by Kurdish and Palestinian activists who stressed that we, unlike them, are not in danger of being arrested and that, in the worst case, we would simply be deported from the country. Their comments reminded us that it is important to recognise and pay attention to the very different ways of 'witnessing' that can be performed and enacted by (often privileged) researchers and their research participants.

Acting as witness, therefore, does not mean equating or overlapping our experience and subjectivity as ethnographers with that of our Palestinian and Kurdish research participants. When we apply the notion of 'witnessing' to our ethnographic work we remain wary not to establish an authority of the ethnographers-as-witness, but rather want to stress our commitment to the 'act of witnessing' in its specific genealogy. Veena Das argued that 'witnessing' takes the form of memories of violence, and goes beyond the simple remembering of traumatic past experiences. Multiple forms of violence and suffering, according to her, are experienced at both individual and collective level; they are embodied, and incorporated into the formation of the subject and the structure of the everyday (Das 2000). Our own experiences in and of the field, and our acts of witnessing thus remain crucially different to that of our research participants.

Yet, we believe that our fieldwork presence and, more importantly, our writing about what we witnessed can either work to sustain these injustices or work towards emancipatory social and political change. Particularly in strongly asymmetric contexts of conflict and colonisation, such as the Kurdish and Palestinian case, non-involvement, passive waiting and the refusal to take stands under the pretext of objectivity or cultural relativism can reinforce existing unequal power relations. Following an 'engaged, accountable positioning' (Haraway 1988: 590) by tracing and making visible our own entanglements in social, institutional and geopolitical relations of domination, we reject such a relativist stance, and instead propose a morally engaged and politically committed approach.

CONCLUSION

In this chapter we have reflected on our experience of doing fieldwork on and writing about Palestinian and Kurdish women's lives. Our discussion has drawn attention to two interrelated arguments: we argued, firstly, that it is crucial to avoid reifying dichotomies between self and other through psychologist or culturalist explanations. Instead, we stressed the need to recognise similarities and trace how historical and political structures shape(d) real material differences which in turn contribute to forging socially-constructed dichotomies between 'us' and 'them'. Secondly, we argued that research in highly asymmetric political 'conflicts' and contexts of occupation and colonisation cannot afford to fall into the traps of moral relativism and postmodern self-paralysis, but rather should be committed to some form of political positioning towards, moral engagement with, and positive transformation for the research community.

Such a historically grounded and politically positioned approach to the question of self and other offers ways to deconstruct culturally-essentialist binaries between researcher/researched, insider/outsider or indigenous/foreign. Following feminist scholar Nancy Fraser in her critique of narrow identity politics and her call for 'conceptualizing struggles for recognition so that they can be integrated with struggles for redistribution, rather than displacing and undermining them' (Fraser 2000: 109) we consider it important to acknowledge – but avoid reifying and essentialising – difference. (Perceived) cultural and identity differences, of course, do exist, and they do strongly influence what women (can) do and how they (and we) make sense and give meaning to their practices. But they are not natural or primordial. Culture is learned (Geertz 1973) and identity markers are products of processes of othering, often related to struggles for redistribution (Fraser, 2000)

We contend that once culturally-essentialist arguments are deconstructed, revealed as political projects and its historical and political roots and materialisations traced, forms of solidarity seem more possible. Rather than building on false assumptions of sameness between all women, feminist solidarity in and with Palestine and Kurdistan thus needs to look into history and politics in order to propose a joint political agenda of resisting injustice and colonisation (see also Richter-Devroe 2018: 27). Based on this joint political agenda a form of feminist solidarity and closeness might become possible. We have attempted to follow such a historically-grounded feminist politics, which recognises difference but strives for equality along humanist values, in our writings.

NOTES

1. Parts of this chapter draw on our PhD theses (Richter-Devroe 2010; Buffon 2017) and/or later reflections on the fieldwork material collected as part of the PhD research (Richter-Devroe 2018).
2. See Herod (1993) for a concise and clear overview of gender issues in interviewing and Ribbens and Edwards (1997); Maynard and Purvis (1994); Ramazanoglu (2002); Fonow and Cook (1991) for more detailed discussions on gender and qualitative research. See Visweswaran (1997) for a historical overview of feminist ethnography and Strathern (1987); Abu-Lughod (1990a) and Visweswaran (1988, 1994) for discussions of the possibilities, potentials and pitfalls of such a project.
3. See also Said (1989: 213–214) and Abu-Lughod (1986/2000: 17–19) for a similar account.
4. For insightful reflections on questions of power and responsibility in the context of research on Palestine, see Sukarieh and Tannock (2012).
5. See the debate between Ted Swedenburg (1989, 1992) and Moshe Shokeid (1992) in *Cultural Anthropology* which provides an insightful example of how a researcher's (Swedenburg's) reflexive account on his own positionality can be misconstrued and accused of bias and political ideology.

BIBLIOGRAPHY

Abu-Lughod, L., A Community of Secrets: The Separate World of Bedouin Women, *Signs*, 10 (4) (1985), pp. 637–57.

Abu-Lughod, L., *Veiled Sentiments: Honor and Poetry in a Bedouin Society*, Second Edition (Berkeley: University of California Press, 1986/2000).

Abu-Lughod, L., 'Zones of Theory in the Anthropology of the Arab World', *Annual Review of Anthropology*, 18 (1989), pp. 267–306.

Abu-Lughod, L., 'Can There Be A Feminist Ethnography?', *Women & Performance: A Journal of Feminist Theory*, 5(1) (1990), pp. 7–27.

Abu-Lughod, L., *Writing Women's Worlds: Bedouin Stories* (Berkeley: University of California Press, 1993/2008).

Al-Ali, N., *Gender, Secularism and the State in the Middle East: The Egyptian Women's Movement* (Cambridge: Cambridge University Press, 2000).

Buffon, V., *Kurdish Women and Traditional Healing in the Diyarbakır Province: Health, Medical Pluralism and Violence* (University of Exeter: PhD Thesis, 2017).

Clifford, J., 'Introduction: Partial Truth', in *Writing Culture: The Poetics and Politics of Ethnography*, J. Clifford and G. Marcus (ed.) (Berkeley: University of California Press, 1986), pp. 1–26.

Crenshaw, K., 'Mapping the Margins: Intersectionality, Identity Politics, and Violence against Women of Color', *Stanford Law Review*, no. 6 (1991), pp. 1241–99.

Das, V., 'The Act of Witnessing: Violence, Gender, and Subjectivity', in *Violence and Subjectivity*, V. Das, A. Kleinmnan et al. (Berkeley: University of California Press, 2000) pp. 205–25.

Fraser, N., 'Rethinking Recognition', *New Left Review*, 3 (2000), pp. 107–20.

Fonow, M. M. and J. A. Cook, *Beyond Methodology: Feminist Scholarship as Lived Research* (Bloomington, IN: Indiana University Press, 1991).

Geertz, C., *The Interpretation of Cultures* (New York: Basic Books, 1973).

Gilligan, C., *In a Different Voice: Psychological Theory and Women's Development* (Cambridge, MA: Harvard University Press, 1982).

Hall, S., 'When was the "Postcolonial"? Thinking at the Limit', in *The Postcolonial Question*, I. Chambers and L. Curti (eds) (London and New York: Routledge, 1996).

Haraway, D., 'Situated Knowledges: The Science Question in Feminism and the Privileged of Partial Perspective', *Feminist Studies*, 14 (3) (1988), pp. 575–99.

Harding, S., *Whose Science? Whose Knowledge? Thinking from Women's Lives* (Ithaca, NY: Cornell University Press, 1991).

Herod, A., 'Gender Issues in the Use of Interviewing as a Research Method', *The Professional Geographer*, 45 (3) (1993), pp. 305–17.

Lazreg, M., 'Feminism and Difference: The Perils of Writing as a Woman on Women in Algeria' *Feminist Studies*, vol. 14, no. 1 (1988).

Maynard, M. and J. Purvis, *Researching Women's Lives from a Feminist Perspective* (London: Taylor & Francis, 1994).

Mohanty, C. T., 'Under Western Eyes: Feminist Scholarship and Colonial Discourses', *Boundary 2*, 12: 3–13:1 (London: Taylor & Francis, 1984) pp. 333–58.

Narayan, K., 'How Native Is a "Native" Anthropologist?', *American Anthropologist*, 95(3) (1993), pp. 671–86.

Oakley, A., 'Interviewing Women: A Contradiction in Terms', in Doing Feminist Research, H. Roberts (ed.) (London: Routledge, 1981).

Rabinow, P., 'Representations Are Social Facts: Modernity and Post-Modernity in Anthropology', in *Writing Culture: The Poetics and Politics of Ethnography*, J. Clifford and G. Marcus. G. (eds) (Berkeley: University of California Press, 1986).

Ramazanoglu, C., *Feminist Methodology: Challenges and Choices* (London: SAGE Publications, 2002).

Ribbens, J. and R. Edwards, *Feminist Dilemmas in Qualitative Research: Public Knowledge and Private Lives* (London: SAGE Publications, 1997).

Richter-Devroe, S., *Gender and Conflict Transformation in Palestine: Between*

Local and International Agendas (University of Exeter: PhD Thesis, 2010).

Richter-Devroe, S., *Women's Political Activism in Palestine: Peacebuilding, Resistance and Survival* (Urbana: University of Illinois Press, 2018).

Said, E., *Orientalism* (New York: Random Books, 1978).

Said, E., 'Representing the Colonized: Anthropology's Interlocutors', *Critical Inquiry*, 15 (2) (1989), pp. 205–25.

Said, E., *Culture and Imperialism* (New York: Vintage Books, 1993).

Scheper-Hughes, N., 'The Primacy of the Ethical: Propositions for a Militant Anthropology', *Current Anthropology*, 36 (3) (1995), pp. 409–40.

Schwedler, J., 'The Third Gender: Western Female Researchers in the Middle East', *Political Science and Politics*, 39 (3) (2006), pp. 425–8.

Shokeid, M., 'Commitment and Contextual Study in Anthropology', *Cultural Anthropology*, 7 (1992), pp. 464–77.

Spivak, G., 'Can the Subaltern Speak?' in *Marxism and the Interpretation of Culture*, C. Nelson and L. Grossberg (eds) (Urbana: University of Illinois Press, 1988) pp. 271–313.

Strathern, M., 'An Awkward Relationship: The Case of Feminism and Anthropology', *Signs*, 12 (2) (1987), pp. 276–92.

Sukarieh, M. and S. Tannock, 'On the Problem of Over-researched Communities: The case of the Shatila refugee camp in Lebanon', *Sociology* vol. 47, no. 3 (2012).

Swedenburg, T., 'Occupational Hazards: Palestine Ethnography', *Cultural Anthropology*, 4, no.3 (1989), pp. 265–72.

Swedenburg, T., 'Occupational Hazards Revisited: Reply to Moshe Shokeid', *Cultural Anthropology*, 7, no. 4 (1992), pp. 478–95.

Tedlock, D., 'It's Not the Song, It's the Singing', in *Envelopes of Sound: The Art of Oral History*, R. Grele (ed.) (New York: Praeger, 1991).

Yuval-Davis, N., 'Ethnicity, Gender Relations and Multiculturalism' in Torres, R., L. Mirón, J. Inda (eds), *Race, Identity and Citizenship: A Reader* (Oxford: Blackwell Publishing, 1999).

Visweswaran, K., 'Defining Feminist Ethnography', *Inscriptions*, 3 (4) (1988), pp. 27–46.

Visweswaran, K., *Fictions of Feminist Ethnographies* (Minneapolis: University of Minnesota Press, 1994).

Visweswaran, K., 'Histories of Feminist Ethnography', *Annual Revue of Anthropololology*, 26 (1997), pp. 591–621.

Williams, C. and E. Heikes, 'The Importance of Researcher's Gender in the in-Depth Interview: Evidence from Two Case Studies of Male Nurses', *Gender and Society*, 7 (2) (1993), pp. 280–91.

CHAPTER 9

From the Ethical to the Practical: Cases of Working with Interpreters in Middle East Studies

Alex Mahoudeau and Yves Mirman

In an article critically reviewing his experience as a fixer and interpreter for Harvard researchers, Moe Ali Nayel describes a lack of empathy and several ethical issues which failed to be tackled by the team at the time (2013). Later, addressing researchers and journalists, he writes a fictional dialogue between refugees and their interpreter:

> Refugees: *'Are you enjoying filming our misery?'*
> Refugees: *'It's fine, you are like the others. You show up in the camp, film, leave, and we are still here.'*
> Interpreter: *'I used to reply: "but we want to tell the world about your story."*
> Interpreter: *'Always, with the same sarcasm, is the reply: "How much are you getting paid to tell the world our story?"'* (Nayel 2013)

This excerpt reveals the particular position of interpreters when conducting research in the Middle East, especially in situations where researchers aren't, as is ethnographic practice, embedded in the social groups they want to study for long periods of time: the interpreter is not merely a neutral and transparent agent, but becomes an actor of research, a way into the field and impactful participant to the activity of research. Stories like this – highlighting the different practical and ethical issues of working with interpreters – are plenty, and often shared between colleagues as jokes or anecdotes. Nevertheless, they present an opportunity to discuss the methodology of working with interpreters in social sciences.

Interpreters occasionally appear in research papers, theses and books, as 'research assistants', sometimes 'translators'. In the cases studied here, interpreters are also distinguished by their motivation for participating in the study; it is not always the promise of a payment. Despite this presence, the relationship with interpreters is, in anthropology, treated as a non-topic, given the requirement for researchers to master the local language: '[An] important aspect – so self-evident that it went without saying – was that anthropologists learn the language of the people they are studying. Of course, anthropologists never use interpreters' (Borchgrevink 2003). This doctrine started evolving with the reduction of the timescale available for the realisation of PhDs, and the centrality of learning the local language – in these cases, Arabic – while doing fieldwork. Similar to Borchgrevink, we started gathering data with the help of interpreters, while maintaining the conviction that this method was highly questionable. Indeed, it lacked the methodological discussion commonly held during informal and interstitial moments of exchange we had between ourselves, with colleagues, and with the interpreters.

This article explores the modalities of working with interpreters in contemporary qualitative fieldwork. We will build on several cases of investigations conducted in Lebanon and Jordan between 2012 and 2015, on local social movements in Palestinian refugee camps in Lebanon, on the cause of the missing people of the Lebanese Civil War and of the political detainees in Jordan, as well as on a review of the existing literature on the topic. As some researchers do on the topic (Temple and Young 2004), we need to specify that French is the native language of both authors, English the second language, and both speak and read MSA and speak Lebanese Arabic, without being fluent. We will first discuss the way in which the question of language can be approached from the perspective of a practical approach to methodology, before showing how, despite an epistemological rejection of the practice, the conditions of research have integrated interpreters into the practice of fieldwork. We will then discuss how the interpreter-researcher relationship can be thought of in terms of methods, given he has many opportunities to enter into fieldwork and managing time as a reflexive approach.

FACING EPISTEMOLOGICAL AND METHODOLOGICAL DILEMMAS

Bilingualism is a requirement for the comprehension of a studied group's culture in its entirety. Languages are not for ethnographers merely a way to access people, lead interviews, listen to conversations and objectify representations; they are the very objects of the study, ethnography consists partly of an emic-etic translation (Agar 2011). Specific anthropological controversies have led to methodological discussions and occasionally approached the topic. For example, when questioning Holmes' conclusions in his research on Samoa, Derek Freeman criticised the former's recourse to interpreters, as opposed to his own work conducted directly in the informants' native language (Freeman 1987).

In other disciplines practising ethnographic fieldwork, such a consideration has been maintained, often in a non-explicit manner. For instance, Stéphane Beaud and Florence Weber's guide to fieldwork investigation, one of the seminal references for French-speaking scholarship, presents a lack of mastering of the indigenous languages as a 'fault' in the field (Beaud and Weber 2010: 51). Similarly, Jean-Pierre Olivier De Sardan identifies linguistic incompetence as a particularly 'deplorable quirk' leading to over-interpretation (Olivier De Sardan 1995). Roger Keesing showed how the lack of ability to perceive the intuitions of the studied actors may lead a perfectly well-meaning researcher to over-interpretive extrapolations reifying common metaphors (Kessing 1985). As Bernard Lahire (Lahire 1996) insists, the role of the researcher is not simply to realise a bare translation of local meanings into the academic world. Following these authors one can associate interpretation in qualitative research to translation of meaning, hence the epistemological requirement, not only of bilingualism, but of a *practical bilingualism*, that is, of the ability to comprehend both the language and its use by the actors in order to interpret and avoid over-interpretation.

Mastering the language appeared, in our cases, as a tactical requirement to negotiating the researcher's presence, as much as the type of presentation of ourselves could open some doors and close some others. The case of the Palestinian refugee camps has been discussed extensively as an example of an over-studied field (Sukarieh and Tannock 2012), with the presence of researchers of various fields from Lebanese or foreign universities, NGOs and international organisations, journalists, activists, not to mention 'political tourists' (the expression used by several inhabitants of the Shatila refugee camp to describe mostly Europeans and Americans coming to 'see the camp'). This permanent presence of foreigners had a direct effect on the reaction the camps' inhabitants to Alex Mahoudeau (author) in their first meeting. Their representation of the researcher was moulded by many previous experiences, including in the question of the presence of interpreters, and can be perceived as an occasion of violent objectifications of the refugees from the research teams (Nayel 2013). The use of Arabic, to present yourself, share common courtesy, ask your own question and finally to avoid using 'gatekeepers', hence became a part of a strategy of integration we employed. On the contrary, Borchgrevink's approach describes a practical, relational approach of the competencies of the researcher in fieldwork.

Officially not speaking the language or being perceived as not speaking it well can similarly be an entrance to sensitive topics. Yves Mirman's (author) fieldwork on political detainees during 'hirak' contestations in Jordan in 2012 is a politically sensitive area of study. He was surprised at having gotten official access to State Security Court in Jordan, were some demonstrators were on trial. The political context, the people who gave him the access, and the fact that he was perceived as someone that does not speak fluent Arabic, could be clues to explain his access to a court heavily criticised by international human rights NGOs. Perceived as being less 'dangerous' than bilingual researchers – who are sometimes suspected of being spies, – he was able to observe different trials and emotions of lawyers and prisoners, as well as have face-to-face inter-actions with various actors of the tribunal. It is also an excuse to interrogate people on 'what's going on' and let them formulate in 'words' the meanings of what we observe but which it is not necessarily obvious to interpret, especially the complex juridical process. A native speaker, in a similar situation, would be unable to straightforwardly ask for explanations, their cultural competency often being assumed by informants. Being an outsider places one in a position where naiveté is forgivable, if not expected.

Despite bilingualism: the ethics of guilt, taboo and fieldwork mythologisation

> *'You do not speak Arabic well, hush! Do not said it in the research centre, this is evil!'*
> Informal conversation with a colleague.

In both the British and French cases, the question of interpreters appeared to be taboo in methodological discussion, reinforcing a feeling of incompetence in those relying on them. Relating to an interpreter was accepted as the least-worst solution, but the specifics of it were not discussed, such as the need to learn the local language or the presence of an additional 'fieldwork assistant'. Without questioning the grounding of the argument for bilingualism, a strong point remains the inclusion of interpreters to the investigation without chang-ing the context of enquiry. Practically, the methodological taboo surrounding the question of interpreters is balanced by conditions of realisation of research that compels it or strongly encourages it, while the 'fieldwork mystique' (Borchgrevink 2003), according to which any researcher should completely 'corner' their field, remains an essential element of research.

Languages are essential skills to acquire when pursuing a career in academia and speaking at least some Arabic is demanded for most positions in this field. With decreasing time allocated to PhD programmes, progressively restricted to three years both in France and the UK, the constraint of language learn-ing for non-natives gains in importance. While previous generations of PhD students could take the time to learn Arabic during their PhD, this has become less realistic. Derek Freeman was, after all, 'able directly to observe and then discuss with them in fine detail the realities of their behaviour' mainly because he was 'living in close association with members of Samoan polities for pro-longed periods'. But the capacity to practice sociological and anthropological fieldwork cannot be reduced to mere linguistic competences, even when accepting the necessity of bilingualism. *A contrario* a defeatist stance, admitting the impossibility of learning the local language without opening the methodological debate, seems to be merely a withdrawal of reflexion on positionality. Both approaches – 'fieldwork mystique' and defeatism – consist in idealising fieldwork and the 'good practices', either to sanctuarise it or to admit and apologise for a lower quality in its realisation. Instead, Jean Pierre Olivier De Sardan proposes an approach favouring a 'moral epistemology' which refutes both the idea of methodological 'tables of the law' and a lack of explicitation which can hide methodological laziness. For the author, the acknowledgement of potential biases and their discussion is indispensable:

> Fieldwork investigation has of course its biases (as do surveys). The 'field politics' are managed by navigating by sight among these biases. But one cannot escape them. The aims of the researcher are therefore much more modest. We have to minimise them, handle them, or control them. (Olivier De Sardan 2008: 91)

These previous remarks can appear as underlined by a certain feeling of guilt: if resorting to interpreters is epistemologically and institutionally contested, it still remains a non-negligible practice. If it remains a necessity to learn the local language on the field, the concrete conditions of realisation of a research could impose for at least a part of the period of data production to work with interpreters, instead of maintaining the taboo. The maxim of this 'ethic of guilt' is clearly that the debate does not lie between working or not with interpreters.

Gate-openers, privileged informants, and temporal resources: interpreters and the investigation process

Acknowledging the relative frequency of interpreters in social sciences (Temple and Young 2004) allows interrogating their place in investigation and its specific temporality. Entering the field with interpreters is a common practice that presents several advantages. They are a way to quickly acquire information on the limits of what can be safely said, and what is too sensitive, too personal, inappropriate to the context, or irrelevant. They provide a constant 'second chance' in interview by first checking the question, adapting the interview with the issue immediately, by hesitating to ask or demanding loudly to change it. As interpreters, they are considered an intermediate in a double way, for researchers and informants alike. For example, on the issue of the family of the missing in Lebanon during the Lebanese Civil War, a friend of Yves Mirman helped in translating an interview with an elderly mother of a missing person. After a long discussion, as a psychologist knowing how empathy is necessary in interviews, the interpreter advised him discretely to always accept the cookies made by this mother as a common appropriate cultural practice and change some overly-complex questions. The mother was aware of this discreet advice, playing with it during interview, becoming friendly with her. In the end, this face-to-face led the mother to provide more private details about the judicial process to the interpreter, as a more trusted person. This 'off the record' element, accessible thanks to the presence of this trustworthy outsider, was eventually kept out of the written research results, while still providing valuable knowledge on the more intimate aspects of the judicial process, left out by the translated parts of the interview.

A good adviser, the interpreter is also a 'local expert'. Their knowledge of several languages and cultures provides them with the status of 'cultural broker': they know the field, people, manners of speaking, ways to discuss, and so forth, especially valuable in the process of acquiring local categories. There are examples of access being denied because of the linguistic mistakes made by the researchers (Beaud and Weber 2010: 53); the use of interpreters can help to avoid this. Alex Mahoudeau's experience with the engagement of the interpreter has been a way to overcome this sort of mistake: after observing a demonstration organised by a group of local activists, he led a series of interviews with participants. One of the questions was: 'Explain to me why you went to this demonstration', that the interpreter translated in Arabic with the word '*muẓâharat*'. He was systematically corrected by the interviewees who rejected that word to prefer the word '*i'tiṣâm*', which translates to 'sit-in'. This 'misunderstanding' could have been badly taken by the interviewees, one of whom told him angrily: 'But you think it is politics everywhere', tension was quickly dispelled by the interpreter on the basis that the researcher knew the language poorly, and that he has translated it much too literally. This mistake proved eventually valuable, as it allowed clarifying the importance for this association to label its activities as social, non-conflictual, and mostly to distinguish their gathering from the ones – labelled as 'demonstrations' – organised for 'political' events, even though the event itself was contentious. The importance of this sort of practical knowledge also comes from integrating the interpreters when they are 'locals', into the very process of research: having had time to observe the research, the interpreter working with Alex Mahoudeau on these interviews had the time to develop a 'distant gaze' on a practice that he was a part of.

During the later phases of the investigation, partly at his request, integrating the interpreter into the interview process proved fruitful to the extent that his position as an observant, partly from the outside, had led him to develop critical personal perspectives on the routines of the organisation studied and its discourses. In these instances, the interpreter takes the role of a 'privileged informant', assuming the role of making 'confidences' to the researcher about oppositions or conflicts which are rarely displayed, and only hinted 'on stage'. Similarly for Yves Mirman, interviewing his friend and interpreter, questioning his sociological and moral positions in the studied field and their almost unavoidable evolutions during the investigations, was an occasion to put them into perspective with his interpretation and reactions during interviews.

Moreover, if we stop focusing exclusively on the understanding of the language, we discover how much 'un-explicit information' interviews provide. Emotions and feelings, unspoken reactions, disregards, refusals or reluctance of speaking, non-controlled reactions are often as important as common discussions mediated by reflection. After a number of interviews, hearing another time the official view that an interviewee wants to display in front of the recorder could be useful if completed by observation of non-spoken reactions (Beaud 1996). A similar method can be applied to emotions and feelings in collective action (Traïni 2010: 237).

Indeed, emotions vary from one culture to the other, but do not immediately and systematically relate to language. The presence of interpreters, as it mediates the comprehension of the content of the answers, provides additional time for observation of such emotions. In Jordan, Yves Mirman's interpreter and friend 'played' on that matter with the timing of the interview, practically giving ample opportunity to note observations. Between the questions, the time of the translation of the question, the answer, and the translation of the answer, it is a matter of managing time, noticing emotions and Arabic keywords, preparing next questions. Even if it does not provide the same type of fieldwork we need, the modalities of working with interpreters reveals an opportunity to mobilise other types of sources. It could be valuable especially when human and material sources become 'restricted', scattered or slightly audible, especially in 'difficult contexts', including the authoritarian one:

> Difficulty is a very subjective notion. It must be approached in a
> relational manner as well. (...) Thus, a research that requires knowing
> a foreign language can be considered as very difficult in that sense
> that it demands putting in place and in practice a series of linguistic
> adjustments, or relying on translation. (Boumaza and Campana 2007:
> 10)

In all cases, the interpreters are never only 'translators' (Temple and Young 2004) but have many valuable facets in the fieldwork.

QUESTIONING LIMITS: 'ENCLIQUAGE' AND THE POSITION OF INTERPRETERS

The means of accessing the field always influences the eventual gathering of data. The notion of 'encliquage' is particularly useful to describe the dilemmas of working with interpreters which, as 'privileged informants', are not simply an accompanier, but often a gate-opener, which will influence the researcher's anchoring into the field (Olivier De Sardan 2008: 94).

Because of the need to integrate other 'cliques' and 'triangulating' into one's field, working with different interpreters became essential. The interpreter, especially if playing the role of 'gatekeeper' at the same time, does not have access to the whole of the studied social world. In the case of an ethnographic field, marked by a certain density of inter-knowledge and interaction, being seen regularly in the course of interviews with a certain actor leads to the researcher being immediately associated with this interpreter, as a 'stigma' or at the contrary as a 'gate-openers'. Also, the variation of interpreters itself is for a part an answer to this situation, not only to avoid consensual 'stonewalling', but also to enlighten the relations between the various sub-groups of the studied field (Borchgrevink 2003). Mead explains that information coming from translators 'can only properly be controlled if the investigator has informants, and enough of them to check against each other' (Mead 1939), so to treat them with his or her own biases.

Second, it is possible that the researcher becomes oblivious to the power dynamics in his or her field. This leads to an attempt at describing their own field as an objective reality, without realising that this description itself contributes to the categorisation of the field. For instance, in Alex Mahoudeau's case, after several weeks of working with one specific organisation, one interpreter – a member of the organisation – suggested meeting with one of the Palestinian families from Syria living in the camp, in the context of a 'visit' he organised for several of the organisation's members. Several weeks later, the researcher received coincidentally and outside of his own study the request from two journalist friends to accompany them to the camp for an interview with a Palestinian family originating from Syria, which turned out to be the very same family. Interrogated by the researcher, a member of this family complained jokingly: 'Yes, they always bring me people to talk to me about my life and Syria. I don't even know why but that's what happens'. Because of the specific socio-economic condition and story of this family, the interpreter had clearly chosen them as an example of 'the reality of Palestinians originating from Syria in Lebanon'. On that account, working with interpreters invites raising particular attention to the question of the legitimacy of sources and their influence on the analysis. Benoît de l'Estoile invites, through a review of the relation between anthropology and the colonial policies in Africa, to question to what extent the 'true representations' carried by chosen, 'legitimate' actors on the field can be associated to an actor strategy consisting in obtaining confirmation of one's position by anthropology:

> Producing a certain model of the authentic African culture (or African cultures), the anthropologist endorses scientifically a certain way to truly be African, which leads to legitimising certain groups' claims and rejecting others. Anthropology can particularly, when it insists on tradition as a factor of social cohesion, appear as supporting the traditional authorities. (...) In fact, Sobhuza [a Swazi ruler particularly welcoming to anthropologists] expects from anthropology a legitimation of his power, especially when being challenged by some Swazi educated in missionary schools. (De l'Estoile 1997)

Gerald Berreman in his monograph, *Behind Many Masks*, offers a deepened reflexion on his fieldwork experience employing two interpreters. For him, the relationship of the interpreters to the field and the subjects of the study can be, in the last instance, the core element of the involvement of the researcher in his field. Each has his own relationship with people and their own role in society, and the opposition between what access to the field the author had with a high-caste Hindu interpreter and a Muslim interpreter varied, not only because of each interpreter's position, but also because of their own interests and perspectives on the field and the research (1962: 15).

In the end, different positions in the field present different types of translation. Therefore, rather than attempting to avoid this effect, it ought to be included as an element of the study itself. Translation is an interaction to be studied *per se*, as the position of the interpreter can lead him/her to 'jump the gap' and 'become' an actor again, for instance by reframing what the interviewee said. During Alex Mahoudeau's interviews, the interpreter regularly addressed term-suggestions to interviewees, who in parallel asked for confirmation to the interpreter on several occasions. Like any 'privileged informant', the interpreter therefore holds a specific place in the process of investigation, becoming a 'second degree' informant.

The difference remains between the researcher's presences in the field, mainly temporary, and that of the interpreter, generally deeply embedded in the field itself. Yves Mirman notices that involving his friend and interpreter into his fieldwork on the 'political detainees' in Jordan could be a risk for him. Even if the topics rely more on the judicial process and the juridical tools used by the lawyers, the fieldwork is still politically sensitive. He was potentially concerned by the process, getting in contact with interesting activists on national issues, learning practices of social sciences. However, the interpreter could be perceived as working with a 'foreign researcher' and was subject to possible stigmas that such position could lead to in the Jordanian political context. Trusting his knowledge of the 'sensitivity', in fieldwork where everybody suspects everybody, does not prevent us to be cautious and concerned.

The 'third man' in fieldwork always remains a subject of practical and ethical issue, including debates on collaborative work and the representation of 'others' in their own language (Temple and Young 2004).

SEEING A SCOPE OF POSSIBILITIES AND REFLEXIVITY

When working in 'distant' fields, our argument is that the changing conditions of realisation of the investigation incite to working closely with interpreters. For this reason, questions of translation cannot 'remain the domain of sociolinguistics or anthropology' (Temple and Young 2004). Indeed, all social sciences are concerned, both quantitative and qualitative. Therefore, we have attempted to address, rather than an anthropological debate on translation, a trans-disciplinary approach of the dilemmas of working with interpreters, based on qualitative studies. In no case should the acknowledgement of their presence on the field be reduced to an excuse for less reflexive research practices. We favour approaching this recourse in a 'guilty' way and avoiding the normalisation of what is, in any case, methodological makeshift. Despite the ease provided in terms of access to the field by the relationship with an interpreter, the very phenomenon of translation and the positionality of the interpreters incite to caution as well as critical and reflexive approaches.

Without offering given guidelines on how to manage relationships with interpreters, we have aimed at drawing attention to the pitfalls this practice can imply, which consists mostly in 'entangling' researchers in consensual, institutional, or partial perceptions of his or her field. On the contrary, we have insisted that considering interpreters as a 'third actor' of the investigation provides opportunities to include them in the critical production of data. Situating the place of the relation to interpreters in the 'times' of the investigation appears as a first element, as a mean to quickly access a field in which the local uses of a language is being learnt at the same time. Relating to interpreters in that sense is a way to quickly establish a 'layout' of the field, destined to be deepened with time. Second, including interpreters as members of the field and identifying relations of power, of inclusion and exclusion in the field, becomes central. The necessary entanglement implied by their position emerges, as the phenomenon of 'encliquage', as one of the elements of practicing research. Moreover, we insist on the inclusion of their interviews, common discussions and all our interactions into our studies, while questioning the writing of a common text together.

Berreman insists that '[in certain societies] the ethnographer is inevitably an outsider and never becomes otherwise. He is judged by those among whom he works on the basis of his own characteristics and those of his associates' (Berreman 1962: 21). Interpreters are objectively present in research, not merely as compensations for incompetence, but due to the structuration of a research industry. As such, their presence deserves to be considered as a question of methodology. We have discussed, in this brief overview, the possibilities of approaching their role and impact on research in a practical and ethical manner.

BIBLIOGRAPHY

Agar, Michael, 'Making sense of one other for another: Ethnography as translation', *Language & Communication*, vol. 31, 1 (2011), pp. 38–47.

Beaud, Stéphane and Florence Weber, *Guide de l'enquête de terrain* (Paris: La Découverte, 2010). Beaud, S., 'L'usage de l'entretien en sciences sociales: Plaidoyer pour l'«entretien ethnographique»', *Politix*, 9 (35): pp. 226–57 (1996).

Borchgrevink, Axel, 'Silencing language of anthropologists and interpreters', *Ethnography*, vol. 4, 1 (2003), pp. 95–121.

Boumaza, Magali and Aurélie Campana, 'Enquêter en milieu "difficile"', *Revue française de science politique*, 57, vol. 1 (2007), pp. 5–25.

Berreman, Gerald D., *Behind Many Masks* (Lexington: Society for Applied Anthropology, 1962).

De l'Estoile, Benoît, 'Au nom des 'vrais Africains', les élites scolarisées de l'Afrique coloniale face à l'anthropologie (1930–1950)', *Terrain*, 28 (1997), pp. 87–102.

Freeman, Derek, 'Comment on Holme's Quest for Real Samoa', *American Anthropologist*, 89, vol. 4 (1987), pp. 930–5.

Keesing, Roger M., 'Conventional metaphors and anthropological metaphysics: The problematic of cultural translation', *Journal of Anthropological Research*, vol. 41, 1 (1985), pp. 201–17.

Lahire, Bernard, 'Risking interpretation, Interpretative and overinterpretative relevance in social sciences', *Enquêtes*, 3, online (1996), available at http://enquete.revues.org/373 (last accessed 3 November 2017).

Mead, Margaret, 'Native language as fieldwork tools', *American Anthropologist*, vol. 41 (1939), 2, pp. 189–205.

Nayel, Moe Ali, 'Palestinian refugees are not at your service', *The Electronic Intifada*, online (2013), available at http://electronicintifada.net/content/palestinian-refugees-are-not-your-service/12464 http://electronicintifada.net/content/palestinian-refugees-are-not-your-service/12464http://

electronicintifada.net/content/palestinian-refugees-are-not-your-service/ 12464 (last accessed 3 November 2017).

Olivier de Sardan, Jean-Pierre, 'La politique du terrain', *Enquête*, 1, online (1995), available at http://enquete.revues.org/263 (last accessed 3 November 2017).

Olivier de Sardan, Jean-Pierre, 'La violence faite aux données', *Enquête*, 3, vol. 3, online (1996), available at http://enquete.revues.org/363 (last accessed 3 November 2017).

Olivier de Sardan, Jean-Pierre, *La rigueur du qualitatif, les contraintes empiriques de l'interprétation socio-anthropologique* (Louvain-La-Neuve: Academia-Bruylant, 2008).

Sukarieh, Mayssoun and Stuart Tannock, 'On the Problem of Over-researched Communities: The Case of the Shatila Palestinian Refugee Camp in Lebanon', *Sociology*, 47 (3) (2012): pp. 494–508.

Temple, Bogusia and Alys Young, 'Qualitative Research and Translation Dilemmas', *Qualitative Research*, vol. 4, 2 (2004), pp. 191–205.

Traïni, Christophe, 'From feelings to emotions (And back again) How does one become an animal rights activist?', *Revue française de science politique*, 2, vol. 60 (2010) (trans. by James Terry), pp. 335–58.

CHAPTER 10

Conducting Research in Arabic: Challenges and New Perspectives

Giorgia Ferrari

Conducting research in the language of the host community is of paramount importance to ensure a deep understanding of local realities and practices, and to gain access to published resources in their original language. In the case of researchers working with Arabic-speaking communities, this translates to mastering at least two different language varieties: the colloquial variety spoken by the members of the local community and the standardised variety used in formal contexts and in written and published resources. Although this binary distinction between language varieties is used commonly to represent the linguistic nature of Arabic, it provides a non-comprehensive description of the language that can be misleading for researchers and students approaching Arabic for the first time. This is because it portrays language varieties as a dichotomy solely based on linguistic functions (i.e. formal vs informal varieties) and it fails to provide insights into three aspects: the social values attributed to each variety; subjective choices that lead native speakers to switch between the two varieties; and the intrinsic heterogeneity that characterises both the colloquial and the standard varieties. In fact, both varieties are not fixed realities and there is a certain degree of mixing between their forms, vocabulary and phonology. In light of this, this chapter aims at enhancing a conceptual understanding among researchers working in the Arabic-speaking world of the linguistic and metalinguistic realities of its language varieties. It also aims to raise awareness of, and sensitivity to, their shared features instead of focusing solely on their differences. It is organised in three sections: the first part explores the historical development of Arabic language varieties and it defines their features; the second section tackles proficiency in Arabic as a foreign language; and finally, the third section introduces a learning approach that combines both varieties simultaneously.

While on the face of it this chapter looks as if it focuses on how to learn and teach Arabic, it is in essence referring to the employment of Arabic in the research of the region. The chapter examines the nature of the Arabic language and exposes the deficiencies in the way it is being taught in various educational contexts. Such a state of affairs make it difficult for researches to develop the linguistic competencies necessary to access their research subjects.

ARABIC LANGUAGE VARIETIES

In his seminal work *The Arabic Language and National Identity*, Suleiman states that, 'Arabic has many of the ingredients which make it eminently suitable to play the role of one of the primary markers of national identity in the modern period.' He describes Arabic as a symbol of collective identity, by virtue of its bond with religion and Islamic theology, as well as Arab nationalism (Suleiman 2003: 66–7). The kind of Arabic at issue here is an elevated form of Arabic, also labelled *al-'Arabiyya*, Classical Arabic, or *fuṣḥā* (Corriente 1976), and it is expressed through linguistic eloquence and sophisticated grammatical structure. It emerged in the sixth and seventh centuries CE and corresponds to the language of pre-Islamic poetry recited by nomadic tribes that lived in the Arabian Peninsula before, and in the early days of, the Islamic Revelation. Classical Arabic is also the language which is believed by Muslims to have transmitted the word of God in the Quran and it is therefore considered divine and sacred (Parkinson 1991: 38). It acted as the main vehicle for the dissemination of Islam as well as for intellectual and legal purposes during the expansion of the Islamic Empire, which started in the seventh century CE. The nomadic tribes that inhabited the Arabian Peninsula and who used Classical Arabic for their poetic composition, employed regional dialects as a means of daily communication. Although there is no overall agreement about the origin of the separation between the everyday spoken varieties and Classical Arabic, some evidence of different features between the two varieties was already evident between the pre-Islamic period and less than a century after its spread (Larcher 2001: 604–5). This implies that language variation is deeply and historically rooted in the nature of Arabic. The Islamic conquests entailed a linguistic contact with non-Arabic-speaking communities. A general fear that this contact could lead to the adulteration of Arabic, and therefore to the language of Islam, triggered a process of standardisation aimed at safeguarding Arabic's purity against the risk of being corrupted by foreign varieties (Eisele 2002: 7). The process of codification into fixed forms dates to as early as the eighth and ninth centuries (Van Mol 2003). It is within this process that the Bedouin began to be regarded by sedentary populations as the ideal type of Arab and their language as a focus for the preservation of the purity of the pre-Islamic period (Versteegh 2001: 37). This idealisation of the Bedouin was linked to a perception that linguistic purity was best attained by way of strict geographical restriction; accordingly, the more isolated and self-contained a tribe or social group was, the more likely it was to preserve its language unadulterated (Suleiman 2011: 203).

The process of standardisation of Classical Arabic served as a basis for the development of Standard Arabic, which has remained the modern iteration of Classical Arabic up to the present day. Standard Arabic shares most of its morphosyntactic rules with Classical Arabic and canonical Islamic literature, with only small simplifications that enhance its prestige as a model of eloquence and excellence (Mitchell 1986: 9). However, it tends to be more consistently different from Classical Arabic in style and lexicon (Ryding 2005: 9). This is because Standard Arabic is used in modern contexts such as news broadcasting, contemporary literature and academic writing, and therefore it needs expressions and terminology that did not exist in Classical Arabic. It is interesting to note that the distinction between Classical Arabic and Standard Arabic exists only in the analysis of Western research. Native Arab speakers conceive only one standard form, which is called *fuṣḥā* and represents the literary, eloquent and standard form as opposed to mere dialects (Bassiouney 2009: 27). The development of Standard Arabic allowed the codified language variety to continually evolve and remain in use as the standard form. It also enabled Standard Arabic's inheritance of the peculiar features of Classical Arabic, such as the symbolic embodiment of a mythical Arabness, its pan-Arab role and therefore its unifying role.

Despite the strong tendency towards the codification and dissemination of a unified and pan-Arab language, the linguistic situation within the Islamic Empire was extremely fragmented and vernacular forms continued to be used in everyday-life interactions and language performances. In this chapter, vernacular forms are included under the umbrella definition of Colloquial Arabic. There are several key linguistic differences between Standard Arabic and Colloquial Arabic. Firstly, they have different phonological systems; secondly their lexicon is divergent; and thirdly, Colloquial Arabic is characterised by a simplified morpho-syntax, particularly in the case-marking system which is preserved in Standard Arabic and absent in Colloquial Arabic (Holes 1995; Ibrahim 1986; Mansouri 2000). The linguistic trait that most distinguishes Colloquial Arabic and Standard Arabic is the medium of their performance: the former is written and the latter is spoken. This means that, although Standard Arabic has users with strong reading and listening comprehension and even occasional speaking and writing use, 'it is not a *spoken* language and therefore is nobody's native language' (Mitchell 1975: 70 [emphasis in the original]). This leads to a situation in which Standard Arabic synchronically has no native speakers, while Colloquial Arabic represents the actual native language and native speakers convey messages related to their personal or intimate spheres and opinions using Colloquial Arabic. Diachronically, in contrast, Arabic language speakers imbue the two varieties with a moral dimension, which elevates the status of Standard Arabic: Standard Arabic is perceived as preserving a pure state of the language whereas Colloquial Arabic is often seen a corruption of it (Grande 2012: 125). This highlights a dichotomy that affects modern Arabic-speaking communities, in which Standard Arabic represents the quintessence of Arabness although vernaculars are the authentic native languages. This being said, it is not uncommon to find Colloquial Arabic forms and colloquialisms inserted within Standard Arabic. According to Parkinson (1991: 38–9),

> Arabs, even highly educated ones, find it difficult and unnatural to use *fusha* spontaneously without referring to a prepared text which is then partially or entirely read. [Thus,] we can observe that the oral intervention of colloquial Arabic is becoming more and more frequent in these situations for purposes of better communication.

Moreover, and especially since the start of the Arab Spring, it has become more common to find Colloquial Arabic – instead of Standard Arabic as could be expected – employed on social media websites as a tool to express identity and belonging. This shows the existence of a division within the Arabic-speaking community as to how the role of language varieties is perceived, and what messages are conveyed by using one variety or the other.

At a first glance the Arabic linguistic reality might seem to be that of two markedly distinct varieties with specific and superimposed linguistic and moral dimensions that are shared by the entire Arabic-speech community. Instead, the Arabic-speech community shares the view that the two language varieties differ in the nature of their performance (Standard Arabic is written whereas Colloquial Arabic is spoken) and Classical/Standard Arabic play an irreplaceable role within Islam and as a pan-Arab nationalist symbol (Versteegh 2001); but the interpretation of roles, significance and use of the two varieties is more and more subjective to individuals, it is artificially constructed by each native speaker at their cognitive level and therefore lays in the native speakers' mind (Giolfo and Sinatora 2011: 115).

IS ARABIC A DIGLOSSIC LANGUAGE?

Arabic has been labelled a diglossic language since the late fifties, when Ferguson described the existence of two language varieties within the same linguistic situation as diglossia. He explained diglossia as a linguistic reality in which two distinct, codified and stable varieties of the same language 'exist side by side throughout the community, with each having a definite role to play' (Ferguson 1971/1959: 1). More specifically, the two varieties consist of a 'High' (hereafter H) or prestigious variety and a 'Low' (hereafter L) or inferior variety. Within a diglossic speech community speakers select the variety to be used in accordance with the distinct function it fulfils. Thereby, in one environment the high superimposed form is the only appropriate variety, whereas the ordinary form alone must be used in the other set of circumstances, with infrequent overlap. Ferguson does not distinguish between Classical Arabic and Standard Arabic in his representation of H. He identifies H as being related to the religious sphere as applies to Classical Arabic, but he also links it to situations where Standard Arabic is the usual means of communication, such as politics, news and modern literature. Ferguson claims (1971/1959: 6) that 'the importance of using the right variety in the right situation can hardly be overestimated' and he goes on to distinguish between the typical circumstances in which H or L are adopted. The former is appropriate for contexts such as sermons in church or mosques, political speeches, university lectures, news broadcasts, personal letters, newspaper editorials and poetry. It is also the variety used in formal schooling and higher education, as the language of instruction (Maamouri 1998: 31). In contrast, L is appropriate for conversations with family, friends and colleagues, radio soap operas and folk literature. Although it is generally agreed that diglossia can persist stably for centuries (Snow 2013: 65), it eventually vanishes due to social changes brought about by modernisation, with L replacing H in almost all domains (Hudson 2002). Ferguson lists the social developments that lead to the decline of diglossia, with L replacing H, as follows: firstly, the spread of literacy on a large scale; secondly, the rise of communication among distinct social and geographical segments of the community; and finally, a widespread desire for a national language that can serve as the symbol of independence and autonomy (1971/1959: 18–19). In the case of Arabic, it is unclear whether the social developments mentioned by Ferguson would lead to Colloquial Arabic replacing Standard Arabic or vice versa. This is because the Arabic literacy corpus is in Standard Arabic; Colloquial Arabic is predominant in the rise of communication among distinct social and geographical segment of the community would; and finally – as mentioned above – both Standard and Colloquial Arabic can serve as the symbol of identity. It is thus difficult to predict whether the spoken varieties of Arabic would take over, but it is likely that these will increasingly be adopted in formal and semi-formal domains and accepted over time (Belnap and Bishop 2003).

The claim that H and L reflect variation on the basis of occasions of use and are influenced by the linguistic environment, their addressee(s), the topic(s) and setting(s), does not consider social factors in determining language choice. While agreeing that external factors do determine language variation, this is also induced by subjective and individual elements and the role of individuals is fundamental in negotiating 'socially agreed patterns of language choice' (Bassiouney 2009: 12). Also, the theorisation of diglossic varieties that occur alongside each other and whose use is strictly determined by appropriateness of use, fails to see the two varieties as dynamic. Ferguson himself asserted that the reality of the Arabic language is more complex than the ideal description he depicted. An interesting example is provided by religious and political speeches: in some instances, when the speaker seeks to reach a greater audience or to be perceived as a member of the community (Holes 2004; Soliman 2008), the boundaries of the rigid dichotomy drawn by Ferguson are blurred, and these can be criss-crossed by speakers to convey specific messages. As far as literary production is concerned, nowadays it is not uncommon to come across literary texts that make partial use of Colloquial Arabic to convey messages related to everyday life or personal and intimate issues. Amer, Adaileh and Rakhieh (2011: 21) argue that the spread of literacy allowed speakers to employ a greater stylistic range when writing in Arabic, since many young Arabs see unmitigated SA as too formal for personal correspondence with peers. They prefer to use a variety of Arabic that is at least somewhat closer to Colloquial Arabic, if not primarily Colloquial Arabic. Diglossia could also be a consequence of 'an author's incomplete control of the prescribed variety' (Amer, Adaileh and Rakhieh 2011: 20) and this is because not all educated native speakers can produce grammatically correct Standard Arabic despite hearing and reading it every day, because they have little opportunity to practise it (Parkinson 1996: 92).

To summarise, although Ferguson is persuaded that speakers in a diglossic context have no freedom to choose which language variety to use, and that they passively abide by superimposed and socially determined boundaries (Amer, Adaileh and Rakhieh 2011: 20), the use of language varieties is in fact determined by speakers' subjective choices, sociolinguistic factors and their command of language varieties. This perspective sees Arabic as a unitary body, as one language that is part of one cultural system and that is conceptually divided into two complementary parts, Colloquial Arabic and Standard Arabic, and each one has both a linguistic and a metalinguistic nature as explained above. Individuals within the speech community have a peculiar linguistic behaviour that can vary from the behaviour of other individuals and it is forged by their cultural specificity (Giolfo and Sinatora 2011: 121).

THE NATURE OF AUTHENTICITY IN ARABIC

Albirini states (2016: 78) that language attitudes are key to understanding the prevailing assumptions about the language varieties used by speakers in a given linguistic community and he reports a positive change of native speakers' attitudes towards Colloquial Arabic. He also sheds light on increasingly favourable attitudes towards the mixing of Standard Arabic and Colloquial Arabic in social spheres that were traditionally assigned to Standard Arabic (2016: 118). His finding seems to reveal a possible change in the generalised attitudes of many educated Arabic speakers towards Colloquial Arabic that might no longer be seen as a challenger competing against Standard Arabic but, instead, as a complement to it. This could be because, nowadays, both varieties are needed to represent language unity and identity, which in turn might explain why diglossia is no longer viewed as a social problem by many educated Arabic speakers (Albirini 2016: 95). The switch between language varieties takes place when native speakers use both varieties simultaneously, or when they use vocabulary items that are formed by blending features of both language varieties. This affects the spoken sphere, and it also affects the written sphere, especially in vernacular writing on social media, due to their dynamic and communicative nature that brings them close to the oral sphere. It is important to note that the field of the sociolinguistics of spelling has pointed out that in vernacular writing, both the choice of a spelling variant that is supplied by the standard variety and the choice of a spelling that departs from an existing standard version in some way constitute a social action, i.e. they transport social meaning by either complying with or breaking existing norms (Hinrichs 2012: 326). Thus, it is important that researchers are aware of the features employed by native speakers in their written as well as oral production, as they carry deep social meaning. No less importance as their awareness of these features when they employ Arabic as a common tool in their research in whatever discipline and in whatever area of inquiry.

There exist different types of vocabulary items that result from a mixture of the two language varieties: neutral and mixed. The former refers to vocabulary in which the alternation between one lexical item in Colloquial Arabic and the other in Standard Arabic 'is only phonologocal' "(Bassiouney 2006: 30) and therefore it does not appear in the written word. This difference could be attributed to 'divergent vowel pattern' or 'realisation of consonants' (Bassiouney 2006: 33). For example the verb قال / qaːla/ (to say) can be realised phonologically as Standard Arabic by pronouncing it / qaːla/ as well as Colloquial Arabic by uttering it /ʔaːl/ or /gaːl/. The phonological variations at play here involve the pronunciation of the consonantق / q/ that is realised in Colloquial Arabic as a glottal stop /ʔ/, i.e. by hindering the airflow in the glottis (Watson 2002: 17), or as a voiced velar stop /g/, and the dropping of the last short vowel in the pronunciation of the verb. Neutral words also include words that appear to be Standard Arabic words because they may have some Standard Arabic features, but have no equivalent in Classical Arabic, and are therefore used in both codes. For example, this is the case of technical and academic vocabulary.

Mixed items instead merge features of the two varieties and Bassiouney (2006: 37) divides them into two forms:

> 1. Mixed forms that are mixed morpho-phonologically and lexically (within a word). [For example] the noun ʃeːʔ (thing). Lexically the noun is MSA, the ECA equivalent would be haːga. The glottal stop at the end also seems like an MSA phonological feature. However, the realisation of the vowel as eː rather than the MSA diphthong ay, is an ECA feature.
> 2. Mixed forms that are mixed by blending a bound morpheme from one code and a free morpheme from another. This category includes MSA verbs, for example, which are saliently MSA with MSA morpho-phonological features, but which have an ECA variable attached to them. The passive verb bi-tunaffadh (it is implemented) is a clear example.

Bassiouney gives us a significant insight into code mixing at the word level by exploring mixed and neutral items. This entails that authenticity in Arabic is a consistent blend of language varieties with different degrees of use depending on metalinguistic features as well as social variables. Metalinguistic features are subjective to native speakers. Among social variables we can identify the topic, the formality of the situation and the speakers' knowledge of Standard Arabic.

PROFICIENCY IN ARABIC

The linguistic reality of Arabic poses some challenges to researchers conducting research in Arabic-speaking countries and employing Arabic in their research. By considering Arabic as inherently structured around the abstract combination of two different linguistic poles, it appears clear that proficiency and fluency in Colloquial Arabic do not guarantee equivalent proficiency skills in Standard Arabic. Also, since switching and mixing between Arabic language varieties cannot be predicted, learners of Arabic as a foreign language need to be trained to recognise it, decode it and actively perform it. They also want to develop a deep understanding of its forms and facets in order to better grasp insights into how Arabic native speakers use the language in their everyday interactions. Thus, learning Arabic requires being exposed to both language variations, since this is real-life language use and it sets the basis upon which scholars and researchers make an informed decision as to which variety of Arabic to study in order to fulfil their academic purposes and similarly which Arabic to use in their research. If both varieties are needed to conduct specific research, and especially if the main objective is to use Arabic communicatively, then it is necessary to obtain proficiency in Arabic. This comprises focusing on both Standard Arabic and Colloquial Arabic, on switching between language varieties, and on metalinguistic features and social variables that trigger such switching. I will define communicative competence first, and I will subsequently outline the guidelines indicating Arabic proficiency from both the American Council on the Teaching of Foreign Languages (ACTFL) and the Common European Framework of Reference for Languages (CEFR).

Lightbown and Spada (2006: 196) define communicative competence as 'the ability to use language in a variety of settings, taking into account relationships between speakers and differences in situations.' Canale and Swain individuate four components of foreign language knowledge that are central to reaching communicative competence: linguistic or grammatical competence, which is knowledge of the target language's linguistic forms and structures; sociolinguistic competence, that is knowledge of language use in context; strategic competence, or knowledge of how to succeed in communicative situations and ability to compensate for limited language resources; and finally discourse competence, i.e. knowledge of how written and spoken languages are combined grammatically and meaningfully in different genres (1980: 28–9). They emphasise that learners should be provided with the information and experience needed in the communication process and that it is of essential importance to expose them to authentic communicative situations (Canale and Swain 1980: 28). They also state that the achievement of communicative competence in a foreign language involves all the components simultaneously without overemphasising one of them (Canale and Swain 1980: 27). The emphasis that Canale and Swain place on the importance of providing learners with sufficient sociolinguistic information and to expose them to authentic communicative situations implies that the development of communicative competence in Arabic is achieved through the development of linguistic, sociolinguistic and metalinguistic knowledge of language variation (i.e. the existence of different language varieties that are employed by native speakers through switching and mixing). Furthermore, the application of the features of communicative competence in Arabic entails that authentic spoken language must be part of discourse competence and authentic language, and therefore learners need to be exposed to it. In light of this, what is needed to achieve proficiency in Arabic is the ability to move and switch between language varieties, alongside the development of discrete linguistic abilities, in addition to the four language skills for complete communication, i.e. speaking, listening, reading and writing. As Ryding argues:

... the key to being a functional Arabic speaker is flexibility and interconnectedness: the ability to operate at all levels and, even more important, to be able to navigate between them as required by different social contexts. Those who learn Arabic as a foreign language, therefore, face a daunting challenge: competence in a full spectrum of language varieties. (2013: 4)

The guidelines from the ACTFL (2012) and the CEFR (2001) indicate language proficiency as the ability to efficiently communicate socio-linguistically in real-life circumstances. Most importantly, they emphasise the concept of different stages and competences within language proficiency, which is not 'an end result but a stage in a trajectory of development towards a specific outcome that more and more closely resembles the competence of an educated native speaker of a foreign language' (Ryding 2013: 6). The concept of stages allows for the differentiation between 'proficiency' and 'performance'. The former refers to the level of knowledge that the learner has of the target language. The latter reveals the communicative competence that the learner has at different stages of their learning process. The CEFR combines an approach to mastering a foreign language based on six different levels of proficiency, and it also focuses on using the language in authentic situations. This leads to the description of language use in authentic situations as provided by Younes (2015: 25): Standard Arabic used in reading and writing, whereas both Colloquial Arabic and Standard Arabic are used in listening and speaking. The difference in the latter group is that learners of Arabic at beginner levels need to master the skills of speaking and listening in Colloquial for use in ordinary conversation, whereas students at advanced levels need to be able to use Standard Arabic for delivering speeches or for formal interviews, and to adjust their Colloquial to produce a form that is suitable for semi-formal conversations.

As Giolfo and Salvaggio (2018: 6–7) contend, this

... implies that the language varieties used by language learners should be the ones to which native speakers would normally resort to in [real-life] situations. [...] When considering the six CEF levels, which include both 'ordinary conversations' and 'written and formal spoken purposes,' we should then be able to differentiate for each of the socio-communicative tasks the language variety normally associated with it in that particular context. [...] Basic levels mainly refer to daily situations in which learners have to cope with different basic tasks (fulfilment of needs of concrete types, introducing themselves, shopping, traveling, etc.). In Arabic these domains are not normally covered by SA but are instead predominantly associated with CA. However, more advanced levels involve, alongside more complex listening/speaking skills (which involve both CA and SA), the comprehension and production of increasingly challenging written texts. These despite being normally associated with SA can well consist of a mix of CA and SA or even CA only.

As previously explained, I consider proficiency not only as the ability to develop knowledge of language varieties in the language skills that distinguish their use, but also as the ability to move between language varieties. The switch between them is a response to different sociolinguistic requirements, as well as to express metalinguistic stances. Therefore, proficiency in Arabic comprises the ability to master two language varieties and the ability to perform switching and mixing between them.

LEARNING ARABIC AS A FOREIGN LANGUAGE

The field of learning Arabic as a foreign language is mainly characterised by teaching approaches that favour Standard Arabic over Colloquial Arabic and only rarely teach the latter. However, in order to achieve Arabic proficiency as it is outlined in the previous section, the study of both language varieties should take place. At present, there exist only a few approaches to Arabic teaching in which both Standard Arabic and Colloquial Arabic are included. I start by exploring the simultaneous method (Al-Batal 1992; Fakhri 1995; Al-Batal and Belnap 2006; Wahba 2006; Palmer 2007, 2008) and I subsequently proceed to outline integrated approaches (Younes 2009; Giolfo and Salvaggio 2018).

Within simultaneous approaches, Standard Arabic is taught concurrently with Colloquial Arabic and the two teaching tracks complement each other rather than compete (Ryding 2006: 17). There are specific reading and speaking goals for each track. According to this method, 'the Arabic classroom can and should be a place [where] multiple registers co-exist, as they do in real life' (Al-Batal and Belnap 2006: 397). Al-Batal argues (1992: 298) that the simultaneous approach seems to adequately deal with Arabic diglossia as it reflects in the classroom the linguistic situation that exists nowadays in the Arab-speaking world. This is achieved by introducing Standard Arabic as a written variety alongside one spoken dialect for communication. Three major shortcomings have been identified within the simultaneous approach. First, it 'does not account for variation in speaking brought about by situational, contextual, personal, and other factors' (Alosh 1997: 94). Second, speaking is restricted to Colloquial Arabic and reading and writing to Standard Arabic, thus creating an artificial dichotomy. Third, students run the risk of confusing the two varieties (Ellis 2001).

Integrated approaches differ to simultaneous approaches in that they start with one language variety and gradually integrate the other. There are two kinds of approaches: a Standard Arabic-based integrated approach that starts with Standard Arabic and gradually introduces Colloquial Arabic, and a Colloquial Arabic-based integrated approach that follows the opposite order. Ryding (2006: 16) calls the Standard Arabic-based integrated approach 'reverse privileging', as the vernacular language of the primary discourses of familiarity is postponed or minimalised, while the language of secondary and formal discourse is made central. She claims that it is discouraging and limiting for students to be denied early access to the vernacular skills with which they could informally interact with Arabic speakers. However, this approach is the most commonly used in Higher Education and dominates Arabic pedagogy (Eisele 2006: 218). Research conducted with students at the Universities of Exeter, Genoa and Milan, as well as personal research conducted in Jordan and Lebanon, showed that this teaching approach creates overwhelming duplication since learners study familiar and beginner-level vocabulary in the formal variety and they re-learn it again at a later stage. However, it gives learners a solid reference in Standard Arabic grammar, which can be used to develop knowledge in Colloquial Arabic grammar by contrast. The majority of students claimed they would have preferred a Colloquial Arabic-based integrated approach, but they also stated that when they were given support by the teacher in understanding how to link and connect the forms and vocabulary of the two varieties, they felt they could switch easily between them.

I am describing here the discussion of how best to learn and teach Arabic, but this not just about education. Such a process of learning is part of the development of a future researcher of the area, within area studies, who without proper knowledge of the language, in all its varieties, would not be able not maximise her abilities as a scholar in Middle Eastern Studies. Hence the following proposals of how to start learning Arabic are part of the tools kit for many researchers in the area of inquiry.

Younes (1990) and Giolfo and Salvaggio (2018) propose to start with Colloquial Arabic and integrate Standard Arabic. In these approaches, the emphasis is placed on familiar and informal vocabulary and contexts at the beginning of the programme, for which Colloquial Arabic is particularly appropriate. Reading and writing activities are also introduced at an early stage, and they are conducted in Standard Arabic through a clear separation of tasks performed in the two varieties. This separation becomes 'more fluid' as the level of proficiency of the learners increases (Giolfo and Salvaggio 2018: 7). As Younes (2009: 60) states, Standard Arabic:

> occupies an increasingly more [sic] prominent role in the curriculum with the move towards the less familiar, less concrete and more formal, but integration remains an important feature of the whole program.

An attempt is made to develop the four language skills simultaneously. Speaking activities are conducted in [Colloquial Arabic] throughout the course, while reading and writing are conducted in Fusha. One lesson typically involves work on more than one language skill, which results in a continuous and spontaneous movement from Fusha to [Colloquial Arabic] and vice versa as a function of the linguistic situation and the language material that are being replicated. Following common practice by native speakers, material presented in Fusha is discussed in [Colloquial Arabic], which contributes to the continuous movement between the two language varieties.

Data show that the opportunity to learn a variety of Arabic that can be used in daily conversations with native speakers greatly motivates students. By analysing phonology and grammar, Haddad (2006) concludes that cognitively it is preferable to learn a vernacular before Standard Arabic, but he argues that further research is needed in this area. 'Typically, two objections are raised against the integrated approach: the fear of confusing the learners, and the difficulty or cultural/political sensitivity of deciding which [Colloquial Arabic] should be introduced in the program to the exclusion of others' (Younes 2009: 63). According to Younes (2009: 63), confusion between Standard Arabic and Colloquial Arabic is minimised in the integrated programme because the two varieties are introduced in the classroom through language materials that keep their skills separate: Standard Arabic is presented through reading passages to be read and understood but not to be actively spoken, whereas Colloquial Arabic materials are introduced and regularly used as a foundation for speaking activities. The opportunity to develop the necessary skills to use in their proper contexts enables the students to develop a correct approach to the sociolinguistic realities of Arabic. Arabic learners who are going to conduct fieldwork research in Arabic would greatly benefit from features in their course as outlined by Ryding (2009: 50):

The challenges to our field lie in integrating authentic spoken discourse skills and strategies into traditional MSA curricula to the extent that they are necessary for communicative competence at any proficiency level. These challenges include the materials, sequencing, design, and teaching of primary discourse skills. [...] What our curricula need is restructured access to both the primary and secondary discourses of Arabic. The new architecture of Arabic as a foreign language –including curricular goals, sequencing, and text-type – needs to be constructed with full respect to issues of discourse type, interactive functional skills, the building of firm foundations, and expanded definitions of linguistic, cultural, and social norms and appropriateness. It includes written

Arabic as the cornerstone of literacy, and it includes spoken forms of
Arabic, both colloquial and educated, as cornerstones of spoken fluency.

Ryding (2009: 51) adds:

> This is not meant to imply that Arabic programmes should not
> teach individual dialects; but it does mean that, in the real world of
> Arabic usage, students need more than an acrolect [i.e. the H form]
> and a basilect [i.e. the L form]. They need to learn how to calibrate
> the formality of their speech, and how to distinguish and adjust to
> particular situations and regionalisms. [...] Learners need instruction,
> not just exposure. And part of that instruction incorporates the
> cultural and linguistic pragmatics of interactive discourse focusing on
> contextualized uses of language.

CONCLUSION

The field of teaching Arabic as a foreign language (TAFL) is mainly characterised by teaching methodologies that favour the teaching of Standard Arabic
and only rarely integrate it with the teaching of Colloquial Arabic. There are
two main reasons that have been brought forward in the literature for not incorporating Colloquial Arabic within Standard Arabic. First, Standard Arabic is
seen as a springboard for students to acquire any spoken dialect, and as a basis
of reference upon which to develop knowledge of Colloquial Arabic. Second,
Standard Arabic is claimed to be the variety used in formal and academic
contexts, and it is therefore considered appropriate to be taught to learners
of Arabic as a foreign language at higher-education level. This interpretation
of Arabic, mainly based on Ferguson's dichotomic distinction of H and L, is
not accurate and it does not reflect the reality of Arabic. Although Standard
and Colloquial Arabic have characteristic features that make them sociolin-
guistically more appropriate for certain situations rather than others, their use
is very often determined by a combination of social factors, pragmatics and
individual metalinguistic choices. This defines Arabic by being characterised
by language variation and heterogeneity rather than by two distinct varieties
and it means that it is very rare to find situations in which a pure variety, be it
either Standard Arabic or Colloquial Arabic, is used. For this reason, learners
of Arabic as a foreign language need to study both language varieties and they
also need to be exposed to the switching between Arabic language varieties and
learn how to decipher its use.

BIBLIOGRAPHY

ACTFL, ACTFL proficiency guidelines (2012), available at http://www. actfl.org/sites/default/files/pdfs/ACTFLProficiencyGuidelines2012_FINAL.pdf (last accessed 15 June 2019).

al-Batal, M., Diglossia Proficiency: The Need for an Alternative Approach to teaching', in A. Rouchdy (ed.), *The Arabic Language in America* (Detroit: Wayne State University Press, 1992).

al-Batal, M. and R. Belnap, 'The Teaching and learning of Arabic in the United States: Realities, Needs, and Future Directions' in *Handbook for Arabic Language Teaching Professionals in the 21st Century*, K. Wahba, Z. A. Taha and L. England (ed.) (Mahwah: Lawrence Erlbaum Associates, 2006).

Albirini, A., *Modern Arabic Sociolinguistics* (Oxford: Routledge, 2016).

Alosh, M., *Learner, Text, and Context in Foreign Language Acquisition*, (Columbus: Ohio State University National Foreign Language Resource Center, 1997).

Amer, F. H., B. A. Adaileh and B. A. Rakhieh, 'Arabic Diglossia: A Phonological Study', *Argumentum*, 7 (2011), pp. 19–36.

Bassiouney, R., *Functions of Code Switching in Egypt: Evidence from Monologues* (Leiden: Brill, 2006).

Bassiouney, R., *Arabic Sociolinguistics* (Edinburgh: Edinburgh University Press, 2009).

Belnap, R. K. and B. Bishop, 'Arabic Personal Correspondence: a Window on Change in Progress?', *International Journal of the Sociology of Language*, 163 (2003), pp. 9–25.

Canale, M. and M. Swain, 'Theoretical Bases of Communicative Approaches to Second Language Teaching and Testing', *Applied Linguistics*, 1 (1980), pp. 1–47.

Council of Europe (CEFR), *Common European Framework of Reference for Languages: Learning, Teaching, Assessment* (Cambridge: Press Syndicate of the University of Cambridge, 2001).

Corriente, F., *From Old Arabic to Classical Arabic Through the Pre-Islamic Koine: Some Notes on the Native Grammarians' Sources, Attitudes and Goals* (Manchester: Manchester University Press, 1976).

Eisele, J. C., 'Approaching Diglossia: Authorities, Values and Representations', in *Language Contact and Language Conflict in Arabic*, A. Rouchdy (ed) (London: Curzon, 2002), pp. 3–23.

Eisele, J. C., 'Developing Frames of Reference for Assessment and Curricular Design in a Diglossic L2: From Skills to Tasks (and Back Again)', in *Handbook for Arabic Language Teaching Professionals in the 21st Century*, K. Wahba, Z. A. Taha and L. England (ed.) (Mahwah: Lawrence Erlbaum Associates, 2006).

Ellis, R., 'Introduction: Investigating Form-Focused Instruction', *A Journal of Research in Language Studies*, 51 (2001), pp. 1–46.

Fakhri, A., 'Arabic as a Foreign Language: Bringing Diglossia into the Classroom', in *The Foreign Language Classroom: Bridging Theory and Practice*, M. A. M. Haggstrom, Leslie Zarker, J. A. Wieczorek (ed.) (New York: Garland, 1995).

Ferguson, C., 'Diglossia', *Word*, 15 (1959), pp. 325–40.

Ferguson, C., Language Structure and Language Use: Essays by Charles Ferguson (Stanford: Stanford University Press, 1971).

Grande, F., 'Arabic Language Teaching and Valorization of Roots: the Italian Experience', in *Mother Tongue and Intercultural Valorization: Europe and its Migrant Youth* (Milan: Franco Angeli, 2012), pp. 123–47.

Giolfo, M. and F. Sinatora, 'Rethinking Arabic Diglossia. Language Representations and Ideological Intents', in *Multilingualism. Language, Power and Knowledge*, P. Valore (ed.) (Pisa: Edistudio, 2011).

Giolfo, M. and F. Salvaggio, *Mastering Arabic Variation. A Common European Framework of Reference integrated model* (Rome: Aracne Editrice, 2018).

Haddad, Y. A., 'Dialect and standard in second language phonology: The case of Arabic', *SKY Journal of Linguistics* 19 (2006), pp. 147–71.

Hinrichs, L., 'How to spell the vernacular: a multivariate study of Jamaican e-mails and blogs', in *Orthography as Social Action: Scripts, Spelling, Identity and Power*, A. Jaffe, J. Androutsopoulos, M. Sebba (eds) (Berlin/Boston: Mouton de Gruyter, 2012), pp. 325–58.

Holes, C., 'Community, Dialect and Urbanisation in the Arabic-Speaking Middle East', *Bulletin of the School of Oriental and African Studies*, 58 (2) (1995), pp. 270–87.

Holes, C., *Modern Arabic: Structures, Functions, and Varieties* (Washington, DC: Georgetown University Press, 2004).

Hudson, A., 'Outline of a Theory of Diglossia', *International Journey of the Sociology of Language*, 157 (2002), pp. 1–48.

Ibrahim, M. H., 'Standard and Prestige Language: A Problem in Arabic Sociolinguistics', *Anthropological Linguistics*, 28 (1986), pp. 115–26.

Larcher, P., 'Moyen arabe et arabe moyen. Linguistique arabe: sociolinguistique et histoire de la langue', *Arabica*, 48 (4) (2001), pp. 578–609.

Lightbown, P. M. and N. Spada, *How Languages are Learned* (Oxford: Oxford University Press, 2006).

Maamouri, M., Language Education and Human Development: Arabic Diglossia and its Impact on the Quality of Education in the Arab Region. Discussion Paper prepared for The World Bank Mediterranean Development Forum, Marrakesh (Philadelphia: University of Philadelphia Literacy Institute, 1998).

Mansouri, F., *Grammatical Markedness and Information Processing in the Acquisition of Arabic [as] a Second Language* (Munich: Lincom Europa, 2000).

Mitchell, T., 'Some Preliminary Observations on the Arabic Koine', *Bulletin of the British Society for Middle Eastern Studies*, 2 (2) (1975), pp. 70–86.

Mitchell, T., 'What is Educated Spoken Arabic?' *International Journal of the Sociology of Language*, 61 (1986), pp. 7–32

Palmer, J., 'Arabic Diglossia: Teaching Only the Standard Variety Is a Disservice to Students', *Arizona Working Papers in SLA & Teaching*, 14 (2007), pp. 111–22.

Palmer, J., 'Arabic Diglossia: Student Perceptions of Spoken Arabic After Living in the Arabic-Speaking World', *Arizona Working Papers in SLA & Teaching*, 15 (2008), pp. 81–95.

Parkinson, D., 'Searching for Modem Fusha: Real-Life Formal Arabic', *Al-'Arabiyya*, 24 (1991), pp. 31–64.

Parkinson, D. B., 'Variability in Standard Arabic Grammar Skills', in *Understanding in Arabic Essays in Contemporary Arabic Linguistics in honor of El-Said Badawi*, A. Elgibali (ed.) (Cairo: American University in Cairo Press, 1996), pp. 91–101.

Ryding, K. C., *A Reference Grammar of Modern Standard Arabic* (Cambridge: Cambridge University Press, 2005).

Ryding, K. C., 'Teaching Arabic in the United States', in *Handbook for Arabic Language Teaching Professionals in the 21st Century*, K. Wahba, Z. A. Taha and L. England (ed.) (Mahwah: Lawrence Erlbaum Associates, 2006).

Ryding, K. C., 'Educated spoken Arabic: a flexible spoken standard', *NECTFL review* 64: Spring/Summer (2009), pp. 49–52.

Ryding, K. C., *Teaching and Learning Arabic as a Foreign Language: A Guide For Teachers* (Washington, DC: Georgetown University Press, 2013).

Snow, D., 'Revisiting Ferguson's Defining Cases of Diglossia', *Journal of Multilingual and Multicultural Development*, 34 (2013), pp. 61–76.

Soliman, A., *The Changing Role of Arabic in Religious Discourse: A Sociolinguistic Study of Egyptian Arabic* (Unpublished Doctoral Dissertation) (College Park: University of Maryland, 2008).

Suleiman, Y., *The Arabic Language and National Identity: A Study in Ideology* (Edinburgh: Edinburgh University Press, 2003).

Suleiman, Y., *Arabic, Self and Identity: A Study in Conflict and Displacement* (New York: Oxford University Press, 2011).

Van Mol, M., *Variation in Modern Standard Arabic in Radio News Broadcasts: A Synchronic Descriptive Investigation Into the Use of Complementary Particles* (Leuven: Peeters Publishers, 2003).

Versteegh, K., *The Arabic Language* (Edinburgh: Edinburgh University Press, 2011).

Wahba, K., 'Arabic Language Use and the Educated Language User', in *Volume 36 of Handbooks of Linguistics and Communication Science*, W. Kassem, Z. A. Taha and L. England (eds) (Mahwah: Lawrence Erlbaum Associates, 2006).

Watson, J. C. E., *The Phonology and Morphology of Arabic* (Oxford: Oxford University Press, 2002).

Younes, M., 'An Integrated Approach to Teaching Arabic as a Foreign Language', *Al-'Arabiyya*, 23 (1990), pp. 105–22.

Younes, M., 'The Case for Integration in the Arabic-as-a Foreign-Language Classroom. Educated spoken Arabic: a flexible spoken standard', *NECTFL review* 64: Spring/Summer (2009), pp. 59–67.

Younes, M., *The Integrated Approach to Arabic Instruction* (Abingdon: Routledge, 2015)

Research through Text, Symbols and Technology

CHAPTER 11

Problems of Method: Applying 'Western Literary Theory' to Arabic Texts

Hannah Scott Deuchar

The title assigned to this chapter, 'Applying "Western Literary Theory" to Arabic Texts,' appears to propose a single method for the study of Arabic literature, one predicated on the stability of, and hierarchical relationship between, three categories: 'Arabic texts,' 'literary theory,' and 'the West.' In fact, of course, the slightest literary-historical investigation reveals the contingency and ambiguity of all three, while their relations to one another in the field of literary studies are by no means so simple as the title suggests. As such this chapter will rather treat 'Applying Western Literary Theory to Arabic Texts' as a basic methodological problem, tracking its appearance in recent discussions of critical methods in Arabic literary studies, and discussing some of the alternatives – of which there are of course many – proposed for it. A single case study provides the entry point into these larger debates: the scholarship on, and the literary work of, the nineteenth-century Levantine author Aḥmad Fāris al-Shidyāq (1805–87). Although Al-Shidyāq was for much of the twentieth century a somewhat neglected figure, recent decades have seen a resurgence of interest in the author, a major figure of the period from roughly 1850–1920 known in Arabic as the Nahḍa, or 'renaissance.'[1] Al-Shidyāq's own irreverent approach to questions of literary form, language and tradition stands as a reminder that the starting point for the study of Arabic literary texts must surely be the questioning of such categories as 'literature' and 'theory,' particularly in the light of the ways in which these categories have been shaped by modern histories of colonialism and domination.

Al-Shidyāq was celebrated in his time as a journalist, grammarian and literary scholar.[2] As well as editing a major early Arabic journal, Al-Jawā'ib, and publishing a travelogue (Kashf al-mukhabba' 'an funūn ūrūbā, 1881) and treatises on grammar and Arabic language, in 1855 he produced a four-volume fictional work, al-Sāq 'alā al-sāq fī-mā huwa al-fāriyāq (Leg over Leg; Concerning the

Nature of the Fāriyāq). The text is highly digressive and linguistically playful, mixing literary forms from lengthy lists of obscenities, to scholarly discussions of grammar, to classical odes; it is broadly structured around the life and travels of the eponymous Al-Fāriyāq, whose name collapses that of the author, Fāris al-Shidyāq. The difficulty not only of reading but of classifying this text within narratives of modern Arabic literature contributed to its relative marginality, but since the 1990s attempts have been made once more to find a way to respond to the challenges of *al-Sāq*, largely by scholars well-versed in what this chapter's title calls 'Western literary theory'.

The text itself is highly and often comically self-reflexive. Four chapters, for instance, are written in the major classical Arabic narrative form of the *maqāma*, in rhymed prose;[3] but they are also framed by ironical passages on the difficulty and absurdity of rhymed prose as a style (Al-Shidyāq 1855/ 2014, vol. 1: 49). Elsewhere, the author's own translations of Chateaubriand and Lamartine's Orientalist writings are mobilised in a discussion of Arabic and 'Frankish' literary style, concluding with a description of a donkey written in each (Al-Shidyāq 1855/ 2014, vol. 1: 119). In text that travels France and its just-established colonies, the political stakes of these absurdist translation games are clear. As such, that critics' recent attempts to reassert the text's importance have consistently entailed assigning it a single, recognisable, prestigious, 'modern' genre – most often a novel, even the title of 'first Arabic novel' (e.g. Ashour 2013),[4] or an autobiography – is surprising. Even in the case of a text designed to obfuscate categorisation, the impulse to render *adab* legible, and in Anglo-European terms, apparently remains difficult to resist.[5]

Despite, or perhaps because of, the relative idiosyncrasy of his writings, scholarly work on Al-Shidyāq and especially on *Al-Sāq* has crystallised central methodological issues in the field of Arabic literary studies, particularly as pertains to the vexed question of 'theory'. Recent scholars' inclination towards reflexive philological work, alongside Al-Shidyāq's own early games with notions such as 'textual authority' and 'language', provokes the suggestion that any viable critical methodology for Arabic literary studies must restructure the relationship, and indeed the distinction, between 'theory' and 'text': remembering, firstly, that 'theory' is (only) text; and secondly, allowing the 'Arabic text' to 'theorise' too.

WHAT IS ARABIC LITERATURE?

The first question for the student of Arabic literary studies is, rather obviously, 'What is meant by Arabic Literature?' This question is not an easy one: the caution inherent in this chapter's title, which refers to '*literary* theory' but then, non-committally, to Arabic *texts* (not 'literature') indicates the parameters of the problem. As recent scholarship on 'world literature' has emphasised, the dominance of an Anglo-European understanding of 'literature,' comprising a series of sanctioned forms, such as the novel or the poem, cannot be naturalised: the creation of 'world literary space,' and the decision about what is or is not considered 'literature' within it, is embroiled in the long history of colonial activity, culminating with the rise of the nation-state and the global expansion of capitalism (Damrosch 2003) (Casanova 2007) (Tageldin 2012) (Apter 2013) (Allan 2016). Throughout the twentieth century, as Comparative Literature and literary studies were institutionalised, 'other' literary histories, including the history of Arabic literary production and culture, have been rewritten according to teleological and Eurocentric accounts of, for instance, the inevitable rise of the realist novel, the author as social critic, and so forth (Tageldin 2012) (Allan 2016).

Scholars such as Michael Allan and Shaden Tageldin have recently noted that although the Arabic concept '*adab*' is today translated as 'literature', it has for centuries encompassed a constellation of meanings bearing little or no relation to the English word in its current definition (Allan 2016: 5–6) (Tageldin 2012: 233–5). The term '*adab*' is associated historically with something like 'culture', in the sense of training, etiquette, good breeding, and even morality. In Arabic dictionaries from the thirteenth to the nineteenth centuries, entries for *adab* include the verb *a-da-ba*, whose primary significance was the act of inviting someone to a repast or banquet, but which also signifies the disciplining of the mind, acquisition of manners, and so on (Ibn Manḍḥūr 1290: 43) (al-Bustānī 1867–70: 5). Here, the noun is associated with such qualities as grace and charm (*ḍharf*) and good or moral behaviour (*ḥasan al-tanāwul*) honour or generosity and civility: it is specified indeed that ' *'ilm al-adab 'ilm al-arabiyya'* – 'the science/knowledge of *adab* is the science/knowledge of the Arabic language.' It is also noted that the textual corpus produced by an *adīb*, a literate (mostly) man further possessing the requisite qualities of good breeding, etiquette, etc., was also known as *adab*. This corpus encompassed poetry and a range of prose genres, from narrative episodes to histories and scientific work; a complex written style replete with punning and wordplay was valued by many, though debates over literary style were themselves a significant part of *adab*.

The term's meaning, at least as recorded in the dictionaries, thus arguably produced an explicit and circular relationship between the *habitus* and the text of the *adīb*: adab is the quality of good breeding and morality; the textual record of this quality's production; and the means of producing it. Well into the nineteenth century, therefore, the concept of *adab*, particularly in terms of the particular symbiotic relationship it articulated between 'text' and 'man,' exceeded both the form (fictional, narrative, often novelistic prose) or social function (representation and critique of 'society', itself a new term) with which the English category 'literature' would become associated in this period (see e.g. Williams 1988: 185–6).

Unfortunately, this important distinction between *adab* and 'literature' was for much of the twentieth century seemingly lost. This loss had a significant effect on the study and historiography of *adab*, especially that *adab* now referred to as modern Arabic literature. In the modern period, as noted already, the relationship between Western and Middle Eastern literatures played out against a colonial history of the dominance and even erasure of one 'literary' world by another. The standard translation, employed above, of the term 'Nahḍa' as 'renaissance' itself indicates the ways in which narratives of Arabic literary and cultural change in the long nineteenth century have been inflected by European periodisation and aesthetic norms. The changes undergone by Arabic literary language and form in this period have historically been attributed to Arab intellectuals' translation and 'imitation' of European fictional norms, along with an expanding press and rising literacy (Allen 1988; Hafez 2001). Such narratives conform to what Kamran Rastegar terms the 'novelist-nationalist' paradigm, which presumes a teleological process of Europe-oriented 'development' culminating in the ideal political form of the nation state, and ideal cultural form of the national novel; all other literary production is assessed for its success or failure in contributing to this 'development' (Rastegar 2007: 4).

Past approaches to Aḥmad Fāris al-Shidyāq have exemplified this tendency. For decades his linguistically complex, genre-bending writing posed a challenge to smooth narratives of nineteenth-century Arabic literary 'progress' towards Western generic norms, and as such his texts were frequently sidelined, or, most often dismissed as idiosyncratic, as late as 2001.[6] However, the first chapter of *Lan Tatakallama Lughatī* (*Thou Shalt Not Speak My Language*) (2002) by Abdelfattah Kilito, a searing discussion of Arabic literature, translation and bilingualism, is a wry anecdote illustrating the seeming impossibility of rendering classical Arabic forms legible to Western audiences, and the distortions that are inevitably wrought on them to do so (Kilito 2002: 10–12). The book plays with the modest proposal of, simply, refusing to translate, but Kilito reads Al-Shidyāq as an author who foresaw his own erasure in a new age of Western cultural and military dominance. Through readings of *al-Sāq ʿalā al-sāq fī-mā huwa al-fāriyāq* and other writings, including Al-Shidyāq's panegyric poem to Queen Victoria, Kilito presents the author as brilliant but bitter, his shifting between genres and forms an attempt to announce his place in a newly unstable literary (and worldly) geography (Kilito 2002: 80–99). Since then, many others have returned to Al-Shidyāq, according him a central place in critiques and reassessments of the Arabic Nahḍa and its historiography. In particular, they too have returned to *al-Sāq*, whose eclectic combination of both classical Arabic and contemporaneous European literary forms had proved off-putting for so long.

RECOURSE TO THEORY

That it is to '(Western) literary theory' that the most recent studies of *adab* and particularly of al-Shidyāq have turned in order to *remedy* this situation might seem paradoxical. A problem of past scholarship has apparently been scholars' apparent inability to approach Arabic texts *without* recourse to 'Western theory': that is, to approach the Arabic text without recourse to a host of dominant notions regarding what constitutes literature, and how to read it. Theory can and has been defined in many ways, but the layman's definition offered by the *Oxford English Dictionary* (OED) dictates 'an explanation of a phenomenon arrived at through examination and contemplation of the relevant facts; a statement of one or more laws or principles which are generally held as describing an essential property of something.'(*Oxford English Dictionary* 2000). If, then, theory is to be understood as 'laws' constructed from the examination of 'relevant facts,' the problem historically has been that while the 'facts' considered 'relevant' to dominant notions of literature are the literary histories of select Anglo-European nations, particularly Britain and France, the 'laws' extrapolated from them have come to be treated as universal.[7]

However, 'literary theory' is of course more commonly accorded a different meaning, one which gestures towards its potential as, precisely, a tool for the disruption or critique of categories and paradigms presumed universal. The OED defines 'literary theory' as follows: 'An approach to the study of literature, the arts, and culture that incorporates concepts from disciplines such as philosophy, psychoanalysis, and the social sciences; *esp.* such an approach intended to challenge or provide an alternative to critical methods and interpretations that are established, traditional, and seen as arising from particular metaphysical or ideological assumptions' (*Oxford English Dictionary* 2000). Terry Eagleton, reflecting on the institutionalisation of 'theory' since the publication of his seminal *Literary Theory* in 1983, further critiques the academy's 'marketplace' tendency to present theory as a kind of discipline, rather than a critique of disciplinarity itself: 'Theory at its best poses questions to these other pursuits ...literary theory is a kind of meta-discourse. Rather than figuring as one way of speaking about literature among others, it adopts a critical stance to other forms of critical analysis' (Eagleton 2008: viii). Much of what is considered literary theory, he points out, did not even originate in the study of literature, but in philosophy, psychoanalysis, sociology, etc.: its impulse may be utopian or liberatory (Eagleton 2008: ix). Literary theory, for Eagleton, connects scholars from the Russian Formalists through post-structuralism and psychoanalysis; it concerns itself not with 'what texts mean', but with the nature of meaning itself. It should be noted that the works Eagleton himself canonises as 'theory' were produced entirely in the Western academy, i.e. in Western Europe and America.[8]

'(Western) Literary theory', in Eagleton's reading, should thus not only permit but be predicated upon the interrogation of the very categories and assumptions that produced it. In this reading, the importance of literary theory to the scholarly reassessment of Arabic literary texts, histories and canons over the past decade becomes clear. It was, for instance, by extending modes of philology and close reading advocated by Edward Said in his readings of Erich Auerbach (Said 1984) that more recent scholars such Shaden Tageldin (2012) and Jeffrey Sacks (2015) launched their exploration of Arabic categories like *adab* – a step without which any study of 'Arabic literature' is decidedly limited. Engagement with other kinds of literary theory, from the sociological work of Bourdieu to post-structuralism and post-colonialism,[9] has produced exciting new readings of the work of al-Shidyāq; however, it has also revealed new problems. Scholarship from the past decade by Kamran Rastegar (2007), Tarek el-Ariss (2013), Jeffrey Sacks (2015) and Nadia Bou Ali (2017), indicates that too often, recourse to literary theory has helped to release scholars from Anglo-European literary paradigms only to replace the latter with its own models.

An important contribution of most of these scholars has, however, been a commitment to self-reflexivity on the part of the critic. In the light of structuralism's killing of the author (e.g. Barthes 1967) and post-structuralism's invocation of the endless disruption and deferral of meaning in language (e.g. Derrida 1968), it is difficult for the literary scholar to claim authority for their own reading of a text; more difficult still, in the light of postcolonial theorists' assertion of the colonial dynamics at work in the humanities as a discipline (e.g. Spivak 1983), to justify a reading informed solely by the theoretical giants of the Western academy. For instance, Kamran Rastegar's *Literary Modernity Between the Middle East and Europe* (2007) makes sustained use of Bourdieu's notions of value and the field to argue against the notion of European 'influence' on Arabic texts, identifying instead a form of 'transactional intertextuality' in Arabic, Persian and French travel writing, including *al-Sāq* (Rastegar 2007: 5–7). However, Rastegar is careful to acknowledge the historical and geographical contingency of Bourdieu's own paradigms, rooted as they are in the study of bourgeois French society (Rastegar 2007: 32).

Tarek el-Ariss appears to go further: *Trials of Arab Modernity* (2013) addresses selected Arabic texts, including several by al-Shidyāq, through the notion of 'affect', invoked via Massumi as an intense, non-conscious experience that is itself resistant to critique. El-Ariss argues that evocations of illness and physical disgust in Al-Shidyāq's travel writings perform the simultaneous incorporation and rejection of European 'civilisation' and 'modernity' that exemplified Nahḍa attitudes (El-Ariss 2013: 54). Using Natalie Melas's work on Spivak's comparative 'ethic of reading', el-Ariss further advocates a mode of close reading in which critic and text are suspended in 'a dynamic back and forth with … no guarantees or certainties' (El-Ariss 2013: 15). This notion of comparison is also explored by Jeffrey Sacks, who proposes in *Iterations of Loss* (2015) a philology that operates as 'a critique of the domesticating force of legibility,' capable of 'discombobulating' linguistic categories (Sacks 2015: 19). Sacks sets out from Derrida's assertion of loss as an essential dimension of language (Sacks 2015: 11) to read Arabic literary texts as records of the timeless material and epistemological violence of colonialism, especially colonial language reform. Sacks promises readings concerned not with 'bringing literary works to the light of clarification' but remaining in what Apter termed the 'aporia of comparison' (Sacks 2015: 19).

The invocation of comparability seems designed to impose a measure of equality between the Arabic literary text, the critical study, and the theoretical texts engaged by the critic. If this equality were maintained and explored, it might certainly go some way towards undoing the power inequities that have structured the study of Arabic literature – even producing a space in which, perhaps, to rethink the very notion and function of 'theory' and 'literature'. However, equality proves quite difficult to maintain. Rastegar's acknowledgement of Bourdieu's potential incompatibility with the literary worlds of nineteenth-century Arab and Persian is, for instance, just an acknowledgement: the book produces subtle and thoughtful readings of the connections between three literary traditions, but it does so by importing Bourdieu's schema fairly exactly (e.g. Rastegar 2007: 32). Differently, and more recently, Nadia Bou Ali's essay on al-Shidyāq and Buṭrus al-Bustānī makes a point of translating *adab* as 'culture' rather than 'literature' (Bou Ali 2017: 47). Yet it becomes clear that this translation, which is never examined or justified in detail, serves an end other than fidelity to the Arabic concept. It permits Bou Ali to describe the Nahḍa as overwhelmingly concerned with interrogating 'culture' – and, further, through semantic resemblance to fit it into an existing Marxist narrative about the 'retreat of politics' in 'culturalism' (Bou Ali 2017: 48). Aspects of this reading incidentally contradict other recent studies, including the chapter preceding hers in the same volume.[10]

El-Ariss too makes a point of mobilising Arabic, rather than English, concepts as the starting point for his study: *kashf*, which he translates as 'revealing' and later 'unveiling'; *ta'riya*, 'stripping'; *ḥadātha*, 'modernity', and so on (El-Ariss 2013: 18). The term '*kashf*' is taken from the title of al-Shidyāq's non-fictional travelogue, and El-Ariss uses its translation as 'unveiling' to bring in, via Deleuze and Kafka, interesting observations about the body and language in al-Shidyāq's text (El-Ariss 2013: 76); but the translation is not the standard or only one, and indeed could be seen as a translation choice indebted more to the European theoretical interventions than the historic usage of the term. Further, and although El-Ariss performs some philological work with the Arabic term (El-Ariss 2013: 78), the way in which '*ḥadātha*' is used for the most part reveals it as translated *back* from the major critical-theoretical frameworks of (European) 'modernity'. El-Ariss acknowledges that these frameworks guide his own work (El-Ariss 2013: 20), and so in addition to the fact that in al-Shidyāq's period, *ḥadātha* does not in fact appear to have been used to mean anything like 'modernity',[11] this perhaps renders the El-Ariss's insistence that the study is driven by Arabic concepts slightly – by no means entirely – disingenuous. El-Ariss's mobilisation of 'affect', while it permits him to attend to the as-yet neglected aspects of the bodily and physical in Al-Shidyāq's writings, also leads him to dismiss 'representation' as a worthy object of critical study (El-Ariss 2013: 14). *Al-Sāq*, and other nineteenth-century texts, produced as they were during a period when notions of literary language and form were suddenly in flux, are much concerned with the concept and critique of verbal 'representation', which has a different status and history within *adab*: the dismissal is perhaps hasty.

Consistently acknowledging, as he does, the implication of his own work in colonial legacy of the professional academy (Sacks 2015: 23), Jeffrey Sacks is faithful to his stated intention not to allow his own critical voice to overpower the Arabic texts; his focus is, after all, the enduring 'indeterminacy of language' (Sacks 2015: 85).[12] The critical philology he advocates and puts into practice, for instance, is drawn from Said's critiques of Orientalist philology, but also from violent loss of *adab* as a 'language event' (Sacks 2015: 78). Al-Shidyāq, moreover, is treated seriously here as a philologist and even a theorist of language; sometimes, perhaps, a little seriously, as the mischief and irony at work in, for instance, al-Shidyāq's claim to understand words by sound and not meaning – a claim that both mocks and cites *adab*'s history of wordplay – is in Sacks's earnest Derridean reading (Sacks 2015: 97).

Sacks, too, has a tendency to treat Derrida alone as the authority on language, the truth of whose pronouncements on, for instance, iterability and loss are expanded but also proven by the writings of al-Shidyāq and Darwish (Sacks 2015: 24). For the most part, this does not distort: al-Shidyāq's self-reflexive texts are responsive to Derridean readings. Indeed, concerned as they are with genre and gender, power and play, deferral and refusal of meaning, his writings often seem to have anticipated the theoretical concerns of the late twentieth and twenty-first century. Quite apart from the question of how far individual scholars allow their theoretical readings to overpower the Arabic text, this casts a new light on al-Shidyāq's recent return to prominence. If al-Shidyāq is redeemed because his work happens to dovetail with the concerns of recent critical theory, has the paradigm according to which Arabic texts are validated or discarded according to their relevance to Anglo-European models really been escaped?

A MATTER OF APPLICATION

Of course, contemporary critical theory is frequently produced by scholars working on and in non-Euro-American contexts, including some of the scholars read here; the bugbear of 'Western theory' is becoming a little outdated. Even so, the question is, perhaps, useful to keep in mind – especially given that the analysis above seems to suggest that it is not so much 'literary theory', Western or otherwise, in itself that is potentially problematic for Arabic texts, but the ways in which Arabic literary texts are permitted to relate to 'theoretical' ones. The problem, in other words, is one of application. I will end therefore by examining the notion of 'applying' theory, returning to al-Shidyāq's *al-Sāq ʿalā al-sāq fī-mā huwa al-fāriyāq* to ask how scholars and students might better apply ourselves to the work of reading and writing about Arabic texts.

As noted above, recent scholars of Al-Shidyāq have invoked a notion of 'comparability' to denote the ways in which their readings situate Arabic texts alongside other literary or theoretical texts. These scholars thus avoid the (rather outdated) notion of 'applying' theory; but in a sense, they are quite true to the verb's etymology. The verb 'to apply' came to Middle English via Old French from the Latin *'plicare'*, meaning 'to fold', which combined with the prefix *'ad'*, 'to', produces *'applicare'*, 'to fold or fasten to'. 'Fold' implies a single fabric, made to incline in upon itself; 'fasten' implies the addition of a second body, linked to the first. In the space between 'fold' and 'fasten to' there is surely something to be learned about the delicate job of reading 'literature' and 'theory' together: connecting the latter to the former without obscuring it; conceiving both, in fact, as part of the same textual material. 'Folding' further carries the possibility its opposite, 'unfolding'. Theory should not (only) be brought to the literary text, but permitted to unfold from within it.

Al-Sāq ʿalā al-sāq, after all, itself performs and examines the practice of extracting meaning from a text, and the notion of meaning itself – an interrogation Eagleton, for one, considers definitive of 'literary theory'. To take a single and obvious example, the lengthy poem which opens *al-Sāq's* first volume offers strict instructions to the reader regarding the ways in which they are to interpret the text: they must read closely if they are to reach its 'hidden' meanings, and are under no circumstances to skip any lines (Al-Shidyāq 1855/2014: 17–19). The next chapters launch a laughing challenge to that exhortation by digressing from their narrative to record lists several pages long of, among other things, words for female genitalia (Al-Shidyāq 1855/ 2014: 41), and synonym-lists of the same kind, often rhyming and alliterative, will irrigate the text throughout (e.g. Al-Shidyāq 1855/2014: 65, 91, 229, 257).

If the reader concludes that they are, in fact, released from the obligation to the read the lists, they are forced to confront their own relation to the text, admitting defeat before it, and to the author, whose authority they have refused. If they attempt in spite of the challenge to do as they were first told, reading each word of the list, they are forced into a new relation to language: to read for meaning becomes impossible because of the endless proliferation of meanings, performed *ad absurdum* on the page. And *ad absurdum* is important, because language is always, here, conceived also as a form of play; no more so, of course, than in the genitalia-list, where the undoing of meaning is compounded by obscenity. That *al-Sāq*'s very first list should use linguistic excess to relate linguistic play to sexual play, and linguistic to sexual difference, is significant for a text heralded by some as an early feminist work.

If this sounds Derridean, perhaps it is – but it is also more, and other. Derrida worked in postcolonial France from the legacy of Saussure and Benveniste, Sartre and Heidegger; Al-Shidyāq, writing in the early decades of European colonisation of the Middle East and North Africa, had entirely different interlocutors, and he wrote from the tradition not of *philosophie* but of *adab*. His intertexts include Rabelais and Sterne, but also a range of Arab grammarians, and *udabā'* from al-Hamadhānī to Al-Shirbīnī; his contemporaries included lexicographers and linguists such as Buṭrus al-Bustānī, Rifeā 'a al-Ṭahṭāwī, Naṣīf al-Yāzijī and, in a later generation, Jurji Zaydan. Al-Shidyāq's dialogue with these and other writers, and his place in a tradition of *adab* that did not distinguish between or even name 'literature' and 'theory', animate and inform his experiments, leading him in directions different to those of the later theorists to whom he bears a resemblance.[13] Timothy Mitchell (1989), Shaden Tageldin (2011), and Jeffrey Sacks (2015) have, as noted, begun to address and to learn from the large body of linguistic and literary theory, beyond Al-Shidyāq, produced in Arabic in the nineteenth century alone; Lara Harb (2013) and, more recently, Matthew Keegan (2017) are undertaking similar work in the field of classical Arabic literature. Much, however, remains to be done.

CONCLUSION

Using recent scholarship on Aḥmad Fāris al-Shidyāq as a focal point for addressing larger debates about critical methodology in the field of Arabic literature, this chapter has analysed scholarly debates in the light of al-Shidyāq's own work in an attempt to highlight some of the persistent problems within the field, and to indicate possible directions for the future. Historically, a consistent problem has been the tendency to constitute Arabic literature as an object according to Anglo-European understandings of literature and literary history, ignoring the different aesthetic sensibilities, modes of production, and philosophies of language that animated *adab*. Somewhat paradoxically, it is in the aftermath of 'literary theory', concerned as it is with critiquing the production of meaning, that more recent scholars have acknowledged and tried to address this problem. Returning in different ways to the notion of *adab*, these scholars have sought new methods of reading and writing Arabic literary texts that avoid inserting these texts into pre-ordained models or paradigms, but allow them to 'speak', as it were, for themselves, and for their own content or form to direct the critical reading.

These attempts, this chapter suggests, have not always been entirely successful, but they indicate an important shift. A will to resist the privileging of 'theory' over Arabic 'literature', and a willingness to reconsider the relationship between them, will be an important part of future critical methodologies. More important, however, will be the acknowledgement that significant theories of literature and language are produced in, as well as proven by, Arabic literary texts – sometimes through styles and forms quite alien to contemporary notions of how 'theory' is articulated. The work of acknowledging, examining, and finding new ways to read these texts is the major unfinished task of Arabic literary studies.

NOTES

1. The Nahḍa was a period of significant cultural and political change in the Middle East; its precise dates, like much else about the period including its problematic, if convenient, translation as 'renaissance', remain up for debate.

2. He is for instance given a significant place in the section on the Nahḍa in Jurji Zaydan's canonical 1903 collection of the biographies of modern luminaries, *Tarājim Mashāhīr al-Sharq* (*Famous Men of the East*) (Zaydan, 1970).

3. The episodic *maqāma* form emerged in the twelfth century. Further reading: (Kilito, 2001) or (Hämeen-Antilla, 2002).

4. Radwa Ashour's *Al-Hadātha al-Mumkina* (2013) critiques the Nahḍa as a total epistemic break, making her celebration of al-Shidyaq as a novelist still more surprising.

5. As will be discussed in the following section, there are exceptions: Sheehi refuses to assign a genre, noting that 'categorization of *al-Saq*'s genre is

antithetical to its very composition' (Sheehi 2004: 123); El-Ariss (2013) and Sacks (2015) concur.

6. See reference to Sabry Hafez above. In Arabic, however, one finds Fawwaz Traboulsi and Aziz al-Azmeh's important monograph on Al-Shidyāq (1995), which affirmed him as a major literary and political figure not in spite but because of his linguistic and generic experimentation.

7. On this process, see scholarship mentioned above by Apter (2013), Allan (2016) etc. on the institutionalisation of world and comparative literature.

8. Eagleton has a notable disdain for the theoretical school known as postcolonial studies, some of which was produced outside the Western academy; he considers it largely derivative of earlier theory (Eagleton 2002).

9. Whether postcolonial thought ought to be considered part of Western theory is a topic discussed elsewhere by Gayatri Spivak (1983), but its existence as a body of work certainly complicates easy references to 'Western theory'. Some of the scholars of Arabic literature discussed here have been considered part of the post-colonial movement, but their work arguably exceeds the traditional concerns of post-colonial theorists.

10. Bou Ali works from Andrew Sartori's work on Bengal (Bou Ali 2017: 50), not mentioning the possibility that her work on Greater Syria might require adaptation of Sartori's insights. In the chapter preceding hers, Hussein Omar makes convincing arguments against the application of South Asian paradigms to the Naḥḍa (Omar 2017).

11. Baudelaire is not credited with coining the term in French until the late nineteenth century; at one point el-Ariss compares al-Shidyāq to Baudelaire p. 73, coming uneasily close to asserting al-Shidyāq's 'modernity' by his resemblance to the French poet.

12. Perhaps performatively, Sacks' writing is so wary of passing judgement as to be often rather difficult to follow.

13. His extraordinary mobilisation of obscenity to approach the relation between sexual and linguistic difference is especially worthy of lengthier consideration.

BIBLIOGRAPHY

Al-Bagdadi, N., *Print, Script and the Limits of Free-thinking in Arabic Lettres of the 19th Century: The case of al-Shidyaq*, *Al-Abhath* (2000), pp. 99–122.

Al-Bustani, B., *Kitab Muhit al-Muhit, ay, Qamus Mutawwal li-lughat al-Arabiyah* (Beirut: Bayrut, 1867–70).

Ali, N. B., 'Corrupting Politics', in *Islam After Liberalism* (London: Hurst, 2017), pp. 47–64.

Allan, M., *In the Shadow of World Literature: Sites of Reading in Colonial Egypt* (Princeton: Princeton University Press, 2016).

Allen, R., *The Arabic Literary Heritage: The Development of its Genres and Criticism* (Cambridge: Cambridge University Press, 1988).

Al-Shidyaq, A. F., *Al-Saq 'ala al-Saq fi ma huwa al-Fariyaq Vol I–IV* (New York: New York University Press / Library of Arabic Literature, 2014/ 1855).

Apter, E., *Against World Literature: On the Politics of Untranslatability* (London: Verso, 2013).

Ashour, R., *Al-Hadatha al-Mumkina: Al-Shidyaq wa-l-Saq 'ala al-Saq, al-Riwaya al-Ula fi al-Adab al-Arabi al-Hadith* (Cairo: Dar al-Shorouk, 2013).

Barthes, R., *The Death of the Author*, volumes 5–6 (Aspen: University Press of Colorado, 1967)

Bou Ali, N., 'Corrupting Politics: the Arab *Nahda* and Liberalism Revisited', in *Islam After Liberalism*, D. Faisal Z. Kazmi (eds.) (London: Hurst, 2017).

Casanova, P., *The World Republic of Letters* (Cambridge, MA: Harvard University Press, 2007).

Damrosch, D., *What is World Literature?* (Princeton: Princeton University Press, 2003).

Derrida, J., *Marges de la Philosophie* (Paris: Les Editions de Munuit, 1972/ 1968).

Eagleton, T., *Literary Theory: An Introduction 3rd (Third) Edition* (Duluth: University of Minnesota Press, 2008).

El-Ariss, T., *Trials of Arab Modernity: Literary Affects and the New Political* (New York: Fordham University Press, 2013).

Hämeen-Antilla, J., *Maqama: A History of a Genre* (Weisbaden: Harrassowitz Verlag, 2002).

Hafez, S., *The Genesis of Arabic Narrative Discourse: A Study in the Sociology of Modern Arabic Literature* (London: Saqi Books, 2001)

Harb, L., *Poetic Marvels: Wonder and Aesthetic Experience in Medieval Arabic Literary Theory* (New York University: PhD Thesis, 2013).

Ibn Mandhur, M., *Lisān al-'Arab* (Beirut: Dār Ṣādir, 1968).

Keegan, M., *Commentarial Acts and Hermeneutical Dramas: The Ethics of Reading in al-Hariri's 'Maqamat'* (New York University: PhD Thesis, 2017).

Kilito, A., *Lan Tatakallama Lughati* (Beirut: Dar al-Tali'ah lil-Tiba'ah wa-al-Nashr, 2002).

Mitchell T., *Colonising Egypt* (Cambridge: Cambridge University Press, 1989).

Omar, H., 'Arabic Thought in the Liberal Cage', in *Islam after Liberalism*, Z. K. Faisal Devji (ed.) (London: Hurst, 2017), pp. 17–46.

Oxford English Dictionary (Oxford: Oxford University Press, 2000).

Rastegar, K., *Literary Modernity between the Middle East and Europe – Textual Transactions in Nineteenth-century Arabic, English and Persian Literatures*

(Oxford: Routledge, 2007).

Sacks, J., *Iterations of Loss: Mutilation and Aesthetic Form, Al-Shidyaq to Darwish* (New York: Fordham University Press, 2015).

Said, E., *The World, the Text, and the Critic* (Cambridge, MA: Harvard University Press, 1984).

Spivak, G., 'Can the Subaltern Speak?', in *Marxism and the Interpretation of Culture* (Chicago: Board of Trustees of the University of Illinois, 1983), pp. 271–315.

Tageldin, S., *Disarming Words: Empire and the Seductions of Translation in Egypt* (Berkeley and Los Angeles: University of California Press, 2011).

Tageldin, S., 'Proxidistant Reading: Toward a critical pedagogy of the nahdah in U.S. comparative literary studies', *Journal of Arabic Literature* (2012), pp. 227–68.

Traboulsi, F and Aziz al-Azmeh, *Ahmad Faris al-Shidyaq* (London: Riad El-Rayyes, 1995).

Williams, R., *Keywords* (Second Edition) (London: Fontana Press, 1988).

Zaydan, J., *Tarajim Mashahir al-Sharq fi al-qarn al-tāsi' 'ashar* (Beirut: Dar Maktabat al-Hayah, 1970).

CHAPTER 12

YouTube and Ethnography in the Middle East: Creative Access in Difficult Places

Kenny Schmitt

YouTube became a useful resource in my ethnographic work by frustration and chance. I was exploring the impact of Israel's occupation on Muslim religious practices in Jerusalem, and was having difficulty accessing al-Aqsa Mosque, the sacred centre of Islam in the city. As a non-Muslim, Israel only permitted me to enter during tourist visiting hours, and those hours never coincided with Muslim prayer times. Then one afternoon in February 2014 while I was interviewing a Muslim leader, I began venting my frustration – How can I do this research if it's impossible to observe something as simple and vital as prayer at al-Aqsa Mosque? Appreciating my frustration and sensing the importance of my research, he asked me his own question: Do you receive al-Aqsa's weekly email?' No, I answered. I had never heard of such a thing. He then offered to add me to the listserv and told me to expect an email soon. A few days later that email came, and it had links to twenty-some YouTube videos from the previous week's religious activities at the mosque. There were videos of small-group teachings, calls to prayer, Quranic recitations, lectures, and the Friday *khutba* (the weekly sermon). All the videos in the email had been posted on one YouTube channel. And that channel had over 2,500 videos (al-Aqsa 2015).[1] I instantly had a glut of relevant material rich for observation. But how did the material relate to the ethnographic methods I had used in the research thus far?

YouTube was founded in 2005 and has since gathered over 1-billion users. Approximately 300 hours of video are uploaded every minute (YouTube 2015). The social media platform (and others like it) has become so influential that *Time Magazine* named 'You' person of the year in 2016 (Grossman). And 'You' referred to the millions of people across the globe uploading videos. The cover design was a computer with a mock-up version of YouTube on the screen. The website has changed the way people relate socially and globally.

Some have begun calling YouTube 'the archive of now' (Little 2015). And unquestioningly, this archive has opened new and expansive horizons for ethnographic research. But 'the archive of now' has also forced ethnographers – like me – to consider a host of new methodological questions. In this chapter, I address one: What sort of opportunities and benefits, complications and limits may ethnographers encounter by including YouTube videos in their methodological toolkit when they conduct research in conflict zones? I argue first that since people's social interactions today are both online and offline that ethnographers have little choice but to include both. Assimilating these interactions into a single ethnographic frame strengthens the reliability of research findings. In Middle Eastern conflict zones specifically, researchers also gain access to otherwise restricted locations and circumvent personal risk. The videos reconfigure temporal and spatial limits, allowing researchers access to past events and to be virtually present in multiple sites simultaneously. But, ultimately, ethnographers are limited by what video-posters choose to show them. Including the videos challenges ethnographers to rethink the influence of their identity on data collection; what constitutes participation, and what it means to use the method ethically. I conclude the chapter by discussing one unexpected benefit and a lesson learned the hard way by including the videos. As my discovery of al-Aqsa Mosque's YouTube videos changed the course of my ethnographic research in Jerusalem, I intend these insights to benefit students and scholars conducting ethnographic research in contexts where various forms of conflict create different ethnographic opportunities and challenges.

LOCATING YOUTUBE IN AN ETHNOGRAPHIC CONTEXT

In 1993, the anthropologist Debra Spitulnik observed that despite the vast proliferation of mass-media, anthropologists had neglected their study, leaving the resource for other academic disciplines. She argued that anthropologists should incorporate these resources into their methodological frame since they impacted 'the *total social fact* of modern life' (293). Interestingly, in 1993, Spitulnik was discussing television, radio, recorded music, and print material – not the internet. Despite her summons, ethnographers continued to rely on traditional methods of participant observation and ethnographic interviews. With time, however, some anthropologists began exploring mass media resources from ethnographic perspectives (Ginsburg, Abu-Lughod et al. 2002). But when it came to the internet specifically, their primary concern was with the online world as a social domain itself (Horst and Miller 2012; Miller and Slater 2001; Wilson and Peterson 2002). They drew few analytical links between people's online and offline behaviours. The focus was on the textual material people created online, analysing chatroom logs, discussion groups, and emails (Campbell 2006; Soukup 2000). But as the possibilities for online interactions evolved, developed and diversified; ethnographers began discussing these new forms of interaction as well. They studied textual material, alongside images and videos and other platforms for communication (Pauwels 2005; Pink 2004). Thus, social media sites such as Facebook, Twitter and YouTube were brought into the methodological frame.

In recent years, a small (but growing) group of ethnographers have argued that effective ethnography today must not limit itself to studying either online or offline social interactions. Effective ethnography, they claim, must take a blended approach (Coleman 2010; Hallett and Barber 2013; Hine 2015). Angela Garcia, the boldest of the group, has asserted, '*virtually all* ethnographies of contemporary society should include technologically mediated communication, behavior, or artifacts' (2009: 57). Her logic is clear and compelling: when research subjects actively engage with web-based materials – their production and consumption – the material cannot be ignored. Ethnographers can no longer create artificial dividing lines between people's online and offline lives with an 'either-or' approach. Social and cultural realities today include both, and ethnographic methods should reflect that.

The new social and cultural reality has challenged ethnographers to think critically about their methods (Boellstorff, Nardi, et al. 2012; Garcia, Standlee, et al. 2009: 73–5; Hine 2005). On a fundamental level, they have concluded that traditional research methods such as participant observation and ethnographic interviews must not be abandoned, but augmented. The underlying logic is that putting online and offline data in conversation allows ethnographers to validate their insights through triangulation. According to Norman Denzin, triangulation is the 'combination of methodologies in the study of the same phenomenon' (Denzin 1978: 297). Assimilating people's online and offline interactions into a single ethnographic project strengthens the reliability of research findings.

Ethnographers of the Middle East have been leaders in the analytical project of understanding the relationship between people's online and offline social interactions. One key figure has been Lila Abu-Lughod. In her 1997 article, 'The Interpretation of Culture(s) after Television', she argued 'that we are only beginning to find the right point of entry for the ethnographic work... that it would take to draw out the significance of television's existence as a ubiquitous presence in the lives and imaginaries of people in the contemporary world'. Television had come to the Western Desert Bedouins of Egypt, she observed, and it had transformed their culture. She, thus, set a precedent for ethnographers to analyse and understand how technology and media were transforming Middle Eastern people's lives. And as technology evolved and developed, so have the ethnographic methods. Other ethnographers of the Middle East have shown a keen interest in the dynamics between mass media and religion (Abu-Lughod 2006; Bunt 2000; Eickelman and Anderson 2003; Hirschkind 2006; Kong 2001). Charles Hirschkind, in particular, has examined the devotional discourse and ethical formation happening on discussion threads of *khutbas* posted on YouTube (2012). In recent years, ethnographers have paid attention to the major regional transformations and their links to people's Social Media use. The Arab Spring, for example, a social movement calling for liberation and regime change, was facilitated by people's virtual connections online (Eltantawy and Wiest 2011; Howard, Duffy et al. 2011). The Islamic State, also known as ISIS and *da'ish*, has made the internet and social media sites its principle means of recruitment and propaganda for its global terrorist agenda (Nissen 2014). But aside from the clear links between online activity and social movements in the region, ethnographers of the Middle East have had two additional reasons to include YouTube videos into their methodological frame – access restrictions and personal risks.

ACCESSING RESTRICTED LOCATIONS AND CIRCUMVENTING PERSONAL RISKS

Since the Middle East is marked by political upheaval, researchers assume certain risks. The mere act of going to the region means being exposed to personal hazards. Scholars have discussed these risks at length (Nordstrom and Robben 1995; Swedenburg 1989), but when YouTube videos are brought into the methodological frame, two particular risks are reconfigured – access limits and threats to personal safety. These two reconfigurations played out dramatically in my ethnographic work in Jerusalem.

As I explained at the article's outset, my access to Al-Aqsa Mosque in Jerusalem was severely limited. Since 1967, when Israel began its occupation of East Jerusalem, Israeli Border Police have controlled entry and exit to the compound. They decide who enters and when – this includes Muslims and non-Muslims, tourists and researchers. As a result, even if Muslim officials employed by the Islamic *waqf* (endowment) gave me permission, I still had to obtain approval from Israeli authorities. Over a five-year period, I was only able to negotiate both sides of the approval once. And even then, I passed through Israeli security and was accompanied by a *Waqf* employee; two facts that made my visit hardly worth labelling ethnographic. My visits were otherwise limited to tourist visiting hours. But even when I entered as a tourist, I had to be cautious not to visit too often because I did not want to alert Israeli authorities to my presence. I had no desire to get trapped in lengthy interrogations with security officials, demanding I divulge sensitive information about my research participants or explain the details of my project. My interviewees could easily be harmed, and I could quickly be deported. And these limits only concern access to the site.

Once I was on the compound, I had to navigate a different set of challenges. First, I was confined to the visiting hours, as I mentioned, which meant that I was never present during Muslim prayer times. The schedules never overlap. Second, while camera-carrying tourists were more-or-less benign, some had caused problems previously, forcing Muslim authorities to restrict visitors to the open-air surface of the compound (Hasson 2015). As a result, I could not enter the physical structures on the site – the Qibli Mosque, the Dome of the Rock, the Islamic Museum, and so forth – the very places where Muslims perform their religious rituals. Finally, my visits always coincided with the visits of Israeli settlers. And since some of them desire to destroy the Mosque and rebuild the new Jewish Temple, their presence made a tense, occasionally dangerous situation. Muslims felt threatened (Inbari 2007; Schmitt 2017). Thus, whenever I was on the compound at the same time as Israeli settlers, there was a tenuous dynamic. Sometimes the tension was palpable. Skirmishes could breakout on a moment's notice, putting me in physical danger.

The access limits and threats to personal safety I encountered at al-Aqsa Mosque illustrate why I was thrilled to learn of al-Aqsa Mosque's YouTube channel. The videos allowed me to side-step these challenges. I had access to events that were otherwise off limits, and I didn't have to assume as much personal risk. While the argument could be made that these particular dynamics were unique to Jerusalem; they are broadly transferable to other field-sites in the Middle East. Whether someone is researching Moroccan Berbers, Turkish state officials, Iranian street protests, or anything in between; researchers must navigate the difficulties of gaining access to restricted places and side-step threats to their safety. YouTube videos give ethnographers more access and allow them to avoid a few risks.

RETHINKING TIME AND SPACE

Beyond gaining access to al-Aqsa Mosque and averting personal risk, YouTube videos reconfigured the way I related to time and space. I was in Jerusalem throughout the Summer Gaza war of 2014, and my apartment was 3 kilometres from Muhammad Abu Khdeir's abduction site. He was a fifteen-year-old youth from East Jerusalem immolated and murdered by three Israelis (Carlstrom 2014; Ihmoud 2015). This event sparked a particularly intense period of the war, and Israeli forces blocked off access to my neighbourhood. Massive protests broke-out close to home, lasting for what seemed to be weeks. Initially, I tried to observe the action personally; but after a few close encounters, I decided to remain within the confines of my house. From the relative safety of my apartment, I did two things: I called Palestinian friends and watched YouTube videos of what was happening in the streets. Jerusalemites were posting material constantly. And as I watched the videos, I began to notice that they were changing the way I related to events temporally and spatially.

YouTube videos are primarily a source of visual and aural material. They can include images, videos, and sounds. Since they can be uploaded by anyone with access to a camera and the internet, their content and scope vary immensely. And ethnographers who observe YouTube videos are – by default – observing images and sounds that have already happened. They are watching the past.[2] This causes a significant shift in the temporality of ethnographic observation. With traditional ethnographic methods, researchers are limited to the present. They can only observe the events for which they are physically present. This also implies that without being in the right place at the right time, ethnographers miss events. But with YouTube videos, ethnographers have easy access to the past. They can observe events that were uploaded ten minutes before or ten years ago. The dynamic is particularly useful viewing events ethnographers have missed and for seeing them at their own convenience. Several benefits emerge from this.

YouTube videos change the ethnographic act of note-taking entirely. Ethnographers are no longer faced with the dilemma of taking out their distracting notebooks and recording devices. And as is well known, these tools influence the dynamic of ethnographic interactions (Emerson, Fretz et al. 1995). The distraction is eliminated watching the videos. Ethnographers can take as many or as few notes as they desire with no inconvenience to research subjects in the slightest. What is more, they can pause, rewind and replay the videos without disruption to the person or people being observed. And unlike the ever-fading memories of researchers (even with all their notes), videos do not fade or distort with time. They preserve cultural artefacts in a medium that can be revisited whenever. During the Summer Gaza war, I regularly found myself viewing events from previous days since I often learned of events after they happened. I also jotted notes with no concern of distraction.

From the spatial perspective, researchers using YouTube videos participate in events virtually where they were absent physically. This dynamic became particularly important for my research during the war. Since the conflict overlapped with Ramadan and my research was concerned with religious practices, I was particularly interested in this time period. The most sacred night of the month is the Night of Power (*Laylat al-Qadir*). In Jerusalem, the night is typically filled with religious rituals, a sense of celebration and anticipation. It is a night to encounter the divine. Approximately 400,000 Muslims spend the night in al-Aqsa Mosque in any given year (Ma'an 2013; Reuters 2012). But the Night of Power was anything but typical in 2014. The

Israeli Defence Force (IDF) deployed an additional 4,000 soldiers in the city. No West Bank Muslims were permitted to enter the city (an accommodation Israel typically makes during Ramadan in spite of its normal movement restrictions).[3] At al-Aqsa Mosque, only Muslims above fifty years of age were allowed to enter (Nasson 2014). Palestinians were incensed. A massive protest was staged toward the Qalandia Checkpoint. Thousands trampled the barriers at al-Aqsa's gates. Some youths set fire to the Israeli police station abutting the sacred mosque. Israel used crowd dispersal methods to extinguish the confrontations. That night, only 14,000 Muslims entered al-Aqsa Mosque, a mere fraction of a typical year. These circumstances (aside from making a very tense evening) presented an excellent opportunity for me to collect data. I spent the evening breaking fast (*iftar*) with Palestinian friends and then watched dozens of YouTube videos in the following days. I saw countless protest videos at Qalandia. I watched people pray alongside one another at al-Aqsa's gates. I even saw a grainy video of the confrontations between Israeli soldiers and Palestinian youths at the Israeli police station abutting al-Aqsa Mosque. I saturated myself in events throughout the city. What I realised afterwards is that YouTube had allowed me to be present in multiple locations simultaneously and throughout the night. Ethnographic time and space were wholly redefined. The relevance of this dynamics should be obvious to ethnographers. Having the typical temporal and spatial limits widened to include easy access to the past and having the ability to be virtually present in multiple locations simultaneously is a substantial benefit to almost any research context.

The benefits of temporal and spatial reconfigurations aside, working with YouTube videos does have limits. Researchers can only observe what the camera operator and video uploader allow them to see. If the camera is not recording or the video is deemed unworthy of posting – for whatever reason – researchers simply never see the events. Ethnographers only view the material video-posters deem relevant. This is ethnographically limiting. Additionally, without direct contact between uploader and researcher, ethnographers are left with many unanswered – and ethnographically relevant – questions: Why did the videographer choose to record what they did? Was this video edited? If so, why? Was the motive stylistic (wanting to highlight a specific moment), logistic (not wanting to waste time uploading a long video), or political (wanting to capture a seditious or inflammatory act). Researchers are in the dark about these questions. There are clear limitations. Ethnographers can, however, gain valuable insights from other available information. They can easily find other videos the author has posted. They can track view-counts to gauge the popularity of various videos. They can track whether or not the videos were linked to other social media sites, and those sites may include other additional commentary or discussion. Ethnographers can also gain a rough sense of how much time and effort someone put into their videos by considering their production quality; they can gain a sense of how invested the person is in the medium of communication and so forth. Each information source provides relevant data that benefits ethnographers and their research. Thus, while the method is limited, in that ethnographers can only view events through the narrow frame of a camera lens, the medium does present particular data-collection opportunities, ones that reconfigure time and space.

RESEARCHER IDENTITY, ETHICS AND PARTICIPATION

Ethnographers are well-aware of the implications of their identity on the data collection process (Holstein and Gubrium 2003; Mann and Stewart 2000). But with YouTube videos, their identity has little – if any – bearing on the videos people post. Rarely would someone consider that his or her video might be observed by an ethnographer. This is a clear advantage. My experience in East Jerusalem illustrates the point. With traditional ethnographic methods, I spent hours engaged with the community explaining who I was, where I was from, and why I was asking questions. On one hand, addressing these questions was a normal part of ethnographic fieldwork, providing opportunities for me to gain access and trust. But on the other, when interlocutors found out that I was American or that I was not Muslim, they often altered the course of our conversation. Some wanted to know what I thought of American foreign policy, democracy, human rights and so forth. Others thought it was presumptuous of me to think I – as a non-Muslim – could understand Muslim religious practices. By incorporating YouTube videos, I was able to expose myself to people, their views, and circumstances without the distracting influence of my presence. The videos allowed me to transcend the influence of my personal identity.[4]

This line of reasoning, however, leads to a fundamental question about ethnographic methods – does watching a video constitute participation? Can someone be a 'participant observer' when they are only virtually present? I argue, yes, but with a qualification: only if the researcher uses the data as a supplement to traditional ethnographic methods. On a broad scale, ethnographers working in various online environments have addressed this dynamic (Mann and Stewart 2003). When ethnographers observe passively, remaining completely anonymous, their data-collection process has been labelled 'lurking'. And, unsurprisingly, researchers have different perspectives on this method's advisability and ethics (Garcia, Standlee et al. 2009: 58–9). They do agree, however, that the technique is best used as a way to gather information about the behavioural norms of their research subjects before engaging actively. Researchers learn how to act appropriately before making their presence known (Kozinets 1998; Shoham 2004). I regularly experienced this benefit in my research. I acquainted myself with organisations, activities and individuals before I engaged personally. I entered many situations with a clear sense of who I might encounter and what those people might be doing before I went. This helped me know how to act and what to say. The technique improved my times of participant observation. Beyond this, the tactic also enhanced my ethnographic interviews. I recall, for example, interviewing a leader from al-Aqsa Mosque. The week before we met, I watched several of his teachings on YouTube. Then when I asked him specific follow-up questions about the material, he was surprised and honoured that I had been so closely engaged with him.

Another tactic I used to engage with the videos actively was to seek out the people who posted them. I asked why they made the videos, what else had been happening, and what they thought of those experiences. One time, for example, a friend showed me all the videos he posted from the Night of Power 2014. His comments were a rich source of ethnographic data, and I gained a more nuanced sense of how he understood the experience. Watching YouTube videos became a form of participate observation because they facilitated more effective direct interactions. And as a post-script to this point, the researcher's identity begins to influence data production at point of contact, whether online or in person (See Garcia, Standlee et al. 2009: 70–2). This must be taken into account.

Whether ethnographers actively engage or not, they must think critically about the broader social and political dynamics that shape the videos people post. Video-posters are typically concerned with who may watch the video in a general sense – who is 'out there' on the internet. They want to communicate something. And a helpful way for ethnographers to understand this communication is identity-performance on the internet (Campbell 2006; Shoham 2004). Considering what sort of goal or persona (individually and collectively) people are trying to create by posting videos is a fundamental ethnographic task. And in the Middle East, the task is particularly important since YouTube videos often have political import. In Jerusalem, for example, Palestinians were routinely aware that the Israeli government was regularly observing the material they posted. They knew that others had been arrested and jailed for posts Israel deemed inappropriate. I often heard stories such as the one where a Palestinian youth was sentenced to eight months in jail for social media 'incitement' (Ma'an 2015). I also learned that not only did surveillance influence people's behaviours, but people's perception of possible surveillance did, too. Shireen, for example, a conservative Muslim from Jerusalem, put a piece of paper over her smartphone camera out of fear that the Israeli government was violating her privacy by recording her every move – even her daily prayers.[5] For some people, threats of arrest, jail-time, and surveillance were major deterrents to being active on social media; for others, the threats incentivised them because they thought their messages expressed legitimate critique that needed an avenue of expression. Since people's perception of who's 'out there' on the internet influences the material they post, ethnographers must understand the broader political and social dynamics that inform who they perceive to be out there.

Finally, including YouTube videos raises an important ethical question: what should ethnographers make of informed consent?[6] Standard ethical practice is for research subjects to know they are participating in a study, and they should agree to be included. But since YouTube videos are available for public viewing, the dynamic of consent is changed. Ethnographers can assume that video-posters have given their consent by posting their material in the public domain. This gives researchers some latitude. But as a general rule of thumb, researchers should anonymise their participants' names in any published materials, even if the people's real names are publicly accessible through the videos. One final note, some studies have shown that ethnographers can put their research subjective at risk by revealing their identity online (Garcia, Standlee et al. 2009: 59). Ethnographers should always take stock of the ethical implications of their methods, even when watching YouTube videos.

AN UNEXPECTED BENEFIT AND PRACTICAL TIPS FROM EXPERIENCE

After I decided to include YouTube videos in my ethnography, I discovered one unexpected and practical benefit. The videos were an exceptional resource for language learning. While reviewing videos, I paused, rewound, and re-listened to segments countless times. The process strengthened my Arabic skills exponentially. The videos also added value to my lessons with language tutors. Whenever I encountered difficult vocabulary or idiomatic expressions, I asked my tutors to explain. Tutors gave me an understanding of the subtleties of their language; nuance that was not readily apparent to me as a non-native speaker. As a result, Palestinians on many occasions during participant observation and ethnographic interviews told me that because of my language skills I was one of them – a Palestinian. The skill added to my ability to gain trust and access. I attribute much of that trust and access to the valuable resource YouTube videos become for my language development.

I did encounter one complication that caused great frustration. When I began writing up the ethnography, I had trouble re-accessing some videos. Most were easy to access since I kept good records of titles, authors, dates and permalinks. The problem arose, however, when I encountered inactive links. Authors had taken down their videos, or YouTube had censored them. On multiple occasions, for example, I came across a message from YouTube saying,

'This video has been removed for violating YouTube's Terms of Service'.[7] It had not occurred to me while I was in the field that YouTube would remove the content for being too provocative, violent, or inciting. Looking back, that should have been obvious. I lost much valuable ethnographic material this way. Fortunately, since I had used some videos for language learning and had needed to access them without an internet connection, I downloaded many to my hard-drive. Those videos remained useful even when their permalink had been disconnected. For ethnographers working on the Middle East in conflict zones where censorship is a real possibility, this practical tip can save much headache and frustration – when you find a relevant YouTube video, download it immediately. It may be gone quickly.

Throughout the writing process, I wrestled with how to best assimilate the video material into the written ethnography. I could not merely include a permalink, expecting people to interrupt their reading to watch the videos. To solve the problem, I chose to do two things: First, I wrote a 'thick description' of the video's content (Geertz 1973), including transcriptions of what was said in the video. And second, I took a screen-shot of the video at a compelling or relevant frame and included the shot as a picture in my text. I always made sure the screen-shot included the navigation buttons and time-tracker YouTube places at the bottom of the screen. This allowed me to quickly communicate to readers that the image they were viewing was, indeed, a video snap-shot.

As I mentioned at the chapter's outset, YouTube may best be understood as the 'archive of now'. And that archive has changed the way everyone, everywhere in the world relates. Ethnographers of the Middle East would be wise to consider this transformation and include analysis of YouTube videos into their methodological frame. It will benefit them in myriad ways. The data has been stored and made available – ethnographers need only engage.

NOTES

1. The original YouTube channel has been taken down. For an equivalent resource, see al-Aqsa, khutab wa duruws al-masjid (2017), 'Khutab Wa Duruws Al-Masjid Al-Aqsa', *YouTube*, <http://www.youtube.com/channel/UCqZSTOX5S638tX_zLk2lIkQ/videos> (last accessed 30 January 2018).
2. Technically, some YouTube content can now be watched in the present since the website has allowed users to create live-feeds.
3. Since the early 1990s, Israel has made movement restrictions a ubiquitous part of the Palestinian experience. For details, see Dolphin, Ray, and Graham Usher (2006), *The West Bank Wall: Unmaking Palestine*, Ann Arbor, MI: Pluto Press, 43.

4. As a qualification, I am speaking very narrowly of data-collection. An ethnographer's perception and analysis of the data is a different issue. Researcher identity influences the way data is understood and interpreted regardless of the data source. For studies evaluating the influence of researcher identity on the knowledge construction process, see Abu-Lughod, Lila (1989), 'Zones of Theory in the Anthropology of the Arab World', *Annual Review of Anthropology*, 18: 267–306; Said, Edward W. (1989), 'Representing the Colonized: Anthropology's Interlocutors', *Critical Inquiry*, 15:2, 205–25; Spivak, Gayatri Chakravorty (1988), 'Can the Subaltern Speak?", in Cary Nelson and Lawrence Grossberg (ed.), *Marxism and the Interpretation of Culture*, Basingstoke: Macmillan Education.

5. Shireen is a pseudonym. Personal interview, Ras al-Amud, Jerusalem, June 2014.

6. For three helpful resources, see Johns, Mark D. and Shing-Ling Sarina Chen, Jon G. Hall (2003), *Online Social Research: Methods, Issues, and Ethics*, New York: Peter Lang International Academic Publishers; Buchanan, Elizabeth A. (2003), *Virtual Research Ethics: Issues and Controversies*, Hershey, PA: Information Science Publishing; Mann, Chris, and Fiona Stewart (2000), *Internet Communication and Qualitative Research: A Handbook for Researching Online*, London: SAGE Publications.

7. See, for example Arafat, Yasser (2012), 'Abu 'Umar Yasser Arafat (Wa Hum Fi Ribat Ila Youm Al-Deen)', *YouTube*, <http://www.youtube.com/watch?v=YoJTaxDJECs> (last accessed 3 June 2014).

BIBLIOGRAPHY

Abu-Lughod, Lila, 'The Interpretation of Culture(S) after Television', *Representations* (1997), 59: pp. 109–34.

Abu-Lughod, Lila, *Local Contexts of Islamism in Popular Media* (Leiden: Amsterdam University Press, 2006).

Abu-Lughod, Lila, *Veiled Sentiments: Honor and Poetry in a Bedouin Society* (Oakland: University of California Press, 2000).

Abu-Lughod, Lila, 'Zones of Theory in the Anthropology of the Arab World', *Annual Review of Anthropology*, 18 (1989), pp. 267–306.

al-Aqsa, al-Msjed, 'Al-Quds: Al-Msjed Al-Aqsa', YouTube (2015), available at http://www.youtube.com/user/almsjd (last accessed 30 January 2018).

al-Aqsa, khutab wa duruws al-masjid, 'Khutab Wa Duruws Al-Masjid Al-Aqsa', YouTube (2017), available at http://www.youtube.com/channel/UCqZSTOX5S638tX_zLk2lIkQ/videos (last accessed 30 January 2018).

Arafat, Yasser, 'Abu 'Umar Yasser Arafat (Wa Hum Fi Ribat Ila Youm

Al-Deen)', YouTube (2012), available at http://www.youtube.com/watch?v=YoJTaxDJECs (last accessed 3 June 2014).

Boellstorff, Tom, Bonnie Nardi, Celia Pearce, T. L. Taylor and George E. Marcus, *Ethnography and Virtual Worlds: A Handbook of Method* (Princeton: Princeton University Press, 2012).

Buchanan, Elizabeth A., *Virtual Research Ethics: Issues and Controversies* (Hershey: Information Science Publishing, 2003).

Bunt, Gary, *Virtually Islamic: Computer-Mediated Communication and Cyber Islamic Environments* (Cardiff: University of Wales Press, 2000).

Campbell, Alex, 'The Search for Authenticity: An Exploration of an Online Skinhead Newsgroup', *New Media & Society*, 8: 2 (2006), pp. 269–94.

Carlstrom, Gregg, 'East Jerusalem Clashes Follow Teen's Murder', *Al-Jazeera English*, 3 July 2014, available at http://www.aljazeera.com/news/middleeast/2014/07/palestinian-youth-body-found-amid-tension-2014727956766566.html (last accessed 30 January 2018).

Coleman, E. Gabriella, 'Ethnographic Approaches to Digital Media', *Annual Review of Anthropology*, 39: 1 (2010), pp. 487–505.

Denzin, Norman K., *The Research Act: A Theoretical Introduction to Sociological Methods* (New York: McGraw-Hill, 1978)

Dolphin, Ray, and Graham Usher, *The West Bank Wall: Unmaking Palestine* (Ann Arbor: Pluto Press, 2006).

Eickelman, Dale F. and Jon W. Anderson, *New Media in the Muslim World: The Emerging Public Sphere* (Second Edition) (Bloomington: Indiana University Press, 2003).

Eltantawy, Nahed and Julie B. Wiest, 'Social Media in the Egpytian Revolution: Reconsidering Resource Mobilization Theory', *International Journal of Communications*, 5 (2011), pp. 1207–24.

Emerson, Robert M., Rachel I. Fretz and Linda L. Shaw, *Writing Ethnographic Fieldnotes* (Chicago: University of Chicago Press, 1995).

Garcia, Angela Cora, Alecea I. Standlee, Jennifer Bechkoff and Yan Cui, 'Ethnographic Approaches to the Internet and Computer-Mediated Communication', *Journal of Contemporary Ethnography*, 38 (2009): pp. 52–84.

Geertz, Clifford, *The Interpretation of Cultures* (New York: Basic Books, 1973).

Ginsburg, Faye D., Lila Abu-Lughod and Brian Larkin, *Media Worlds: Anthropology on New Terrain* (Berkeley: University of California Press, 2002).

Grossman, Lev, 'You – Yes, You – Are Time's Person of the Year', *Time*, 25 December 2016.

Hallett, Ronald E. and Kristin Barber, 'Ethnographic Research in a Cyber Era', *Journal of Contemporary Ethnography*, 43: 3 (2013), pp. 306–30.

Hasson, Nir, 'Report: Israel, Jordan in Talks to Readmit Non-Muslim Visitors to Temple Mount Sites', *Haaretz*, 30 June 2015, available at http://www.haaretz.com/news/diplomacy-defense/.premium-1.663644 (last accessed 30 January 2018).

Hine, Christine, *Ethnography of the Internet: Embedded, Embodied and Everyday* (New York: Bloomsbury Academic, 2015).

Hine, Christine, *Virtual Methods: Issues in Social Research on the Internet* (London: Bloomsbury Academic, 2005).

Hirschkind, Charles, *The Ethical Soundscape: Cassette Sermons and Islamic Counterpublics* (New York: Columbia University Press, 2006).

Hirschkind, Charles, 'Experiments in Devotion Online: The Youtube Khutba', *International Journal of Middle East Studies*, 44: 1 (2012), pp. 5–21.

Holstein, James and Jaber F. Gubrium, *Inside Interviewing: New Lenses, New Concerns* (London: SAGE Publications, 2003).

Horst, Heather A. and Daniel Miller, *Digital Anthropology* (London: Bloomsbury Academic, 2012).

Howard, Philip N., Aideen Duffy, Deen Freelon, Muzammil Hussain, Will Mari and Marwa Mazaid, 'Opening Closed Regimes: What Was the Role of Social Media During the Arab Spring?', *Project on Information Technology & Political Isla*m (PITPI) (Seattle, 2011).

Ihmoud, Sarah, 'Mohammed Abu-Khdeir and the Politics of Racial Terror in Occupied Jerusalem', *Borderlands*, 14: 1 (2015), pp. 1–28.

Inbari, Motti, 'Religious Zionism and the Temple Mount Dilemma – Key Trends', *Israel Studies*, 12: 2 (2007), pp. 29–47.

Johns, Mark D., Shing-Ling Sarina Chen and Jon G. Hall, *Online Social Research: Methods, Issues, and Ethics* (New York: Peter Lang, 2003).

Kong, Lily, 'Mapping 'New' Geographies of Religion: Politics and Poetics in Modernity', *Progress in Human Geography*, 25: 2 (2001), pp. 211–33.

Kozinets, Robert V., 'On Netnography: Initial Reflections on Consumer Research Investigations of Cyberculture', *Advances in Consumer Research*, 25 (1998), pp. 366–71.

Little, Mark, 'YouTube at 10: The Archive of Now', *Algazeera English*, 23 April 2015, available at http://www.aljazeera.com/indepth/opinion/2015/04/youtube-10-archive-150423104559567.html (last accessed 30 January 2018).

Ma'an, News Agency, 'Palestinian Sentenced to 8 Months Prison over Facebook Posts', *Ma'an*, 19 May 2015, available at http://www.maannews.com/Content.aspx?id=765515 (last accessed 30 January 2018).

Ma'an, News Agency, 'Thousands Head to Al-Aqsa Mosque for Ramadan Prayers', *Ma'an*, 19 July 2013, available at http://www.maannews.com/Content.aspx?id=615182 (last accessed 30 January 2018).

Mann, Chris and Fiona Stewart, *Internet Communication and Qualitative*

Research: A Handbook for Researching Online (London: SAGE Publications, 2000).

Mann, Chris and Fiona Stewart, 'Internet Interviewing', in *Handbook of Interview Research: Context and Method*, James Holstein and Jaber F. Gubrium (ed.) (London: SAGE Publications, 2003).

Miller, Daniel and Don Slater, *The Internet: An Ethnographic Approach* (London: Bloomsbury Academic, 2001).

Nasson, Nir, 'Two Palestinians Killed in W. Bank Clashes with Israeli Security Forces', *Haaretz*, 24 July 2014, available at http://www.haaretz.com/news/diplomacy-defense/1.607157 (last accessed 30 January 2018).

Nissen, Thomas Klkjer, 'Terror.Com – IS's Social Media Warfare in Syria and Iraq', *Military Studies Magazine: Contemporary Conflicts*, 2: 2 (2014), pp. 1–8.

Nordstrom, Carolyn and Antonius C. G. M. Robben, *Fieldwork under Fire: Contemporary Studies of Violence and Survival* (Berkeley: University of California Press, 1995.

Pauwels, Luc, 'Websites as Visual and Multimodal Cultural Expressions: Opportunities and Issues of Online Hybrid Media Research', *Media, Culture & Society*, 27: 4 (2005), pp. 604–13.

Pink, Sarah, 'Making Links: On Situating a New Web Site', *Cambridge Journal of Education*, 34: 2 (2004), pp. 211–22.

Reuters, 'Palestinians Flock to Jerusalem as Restrictions Eased for Ramadan', *Haaretz*, 16 August 2012, available at http://www.haaretz.com/news/israel/palestinians-flock-to-jerusalem-as-restrictions-eased-for-ramadan-1.458519 (last accessed 30 January 2018).

Said, Edward W., 'Representing the Colonized: Anthropology's Interlocutors', *Critical Inquiry*, 15: 2 (1989), pp. 205–25.

Schmitt, Kenny, 'Ribat in Palestine: The Growth of a Religious Discourse Alongside Politicized Religious Practice', *Jerusalem Quarterly*, 72 (2017), pp. 26–36.

Shoham, Aviv, 'Flow Experiences and Image Making: An Online Chat-Room Ethnography', *Psychology and Marketing*, 21: 10 (2004), pp. 855–82.

Soukup, Charles, 'Building a Theory of Multi-Media CMC: An Analysis, Critique and Integration of Computer-Mediated Communication Theory and Research', *New Media & Society*, 2: 4 (2000), pp. 407–25.

Spitulnik, Debra, 'Anthropology and Mass Media', *Annual Review of Anthropology*, 22 (1993), pp. 293–315

Spivak, Gayatri Chakravorty, 'Can the Subaltern Speak?', in *Marxism and the Interpretation of Culture*, Cary Nelson and Lawrence Grossberg (ed.) (Basingstoke: Macmillan Education, 1988).

Swedenburg, Ted, 'Occupational Hazards: Palestine Ethnography', *Cultural Anthropology*, 4: 3 (1989), pp. 265–72.

Wilson, Samuel M. and Leighton C. Peterson, 'The Anthropology of Online Communities', *Annual Review of Anthropology*, 31: 1 (2002), pp. 449–67.

YouTube, 'YouTube for Press', YouTube (2017), available at https://www.youtube.com/yt/press/statistics.html (last accessed 30 January 2018)

CHAPTER 13

Reading the Signs:
Towards a Semiotic Approach
in Islamic Studies

Pierre Hecker

The purpose of this chapter is to reflect upon how to make use of semiotics in Islamic studies. The author holds the opinion that the semiotic toolkit as laid out as follows allows us to analyse representations of Islam in a wide array of fields, whether it be fashion, music, politics or religious practices in everyday life.

The methodological lens we wear not only determines the way we look at 'things' but also what questions we ask and what answers we generate. In this sense, semiotics directs our focus to the study of signs and the meanings that are being attached to them. The way we read and decode the various signs that are the subject of our research is a matter of conventions and positionality. Signs never speak for themselves. They only assume meaning when situated in a particular context and interpreted from a clearly defined perspective. If the context (and/or the perspective) of interpretation changes, the meaning of the sign may change as well. Consequently, we also must be aware that our own position within the field might have an effect on our academic analysis. Semiotics provides a methodological framework that helps us reflect upon questions of positionality and contextualisation and, furthermore, avoid a purely descriptive research approach. The particular focus on Barthean semiotics as outlined below furthermore places emphasis on questions of ideology and power, which is an aspect still often neglected in Islamic studies.

This chapter begins with an introduction to key concepts of semiotics, including Ferdinand de Saussure's dyadic model of the sign as well as Roland Barthes' idea of modern-day myths. With the help of three case studies – namely a video clip by French band Zebda, a discussion on conventions and arbitrariness as related to the Koran, and, on a related note, a visual analysis of Islamic fashion photographs – it then demonstrates the potentials of using Saussurean and Barthean semiotics in Islamic studies. Not only can Islamic fashion and popular music videos be conceptualised and analysed as a system of signs, but also the holy scriptures of Islam, notably the Koran and the Prophet's Sunnah.

SEMIOTICS FOR BEGINNERS

Semiotics is commonly referred to as the study of signs. A *sign*, in a semiotic sense, can be basically anything provided that it stands for something else or, more precisely, as long as 'someone interprets it as "signifying" something else' (Chandler 2007: 13). Consequently, signs manifest as words, images, sounds, colours, flavours, odours, gestures, facial expressions, objects and eventually any 'thing' that can be perceived through our sensory organs and interpreted in accordance with particular codes (that is, sets of conventions) that we have previously been socialised with. Through signs, human beings make sense of the world around them and, from this perspective, they can be considered vehicles of human communication. Indeed, without signs, communication cannot take place, and all communicative acts are anchored in particular systems of signs. Language is the most important of these systems, but it is still only one among many that shape our everyday lives; non-verbal signs also form systems and are thus often similarly referred to as 'languages' (Hall 1997: 18–19). Fashion, for instance, is one of those sign systems that constitute modern societies; others include music, religion, theatre, television, and film. The conventions according to which these sign systems 'operate' need not be learned and acquired through processes of socialisation.

The Swiss linguist Ferdinand de Saussure (1857–1913) conceptualised the sign as consisting of two separate components: the signifier (*significant*) and the signified (*signifié*). This distinction is usually explained as a dualism of form and concept (e.g. Hall 1997: 30–3; Chandler 2007: 14–16), one based on the assumption that a specific signifier (a spoken or written word, a gesture, a musical sound, etc.) evokes a particular mental concept in an individual's mind. In other words, the signifier stands for the perceptible component of the sign – that is, for what can be perceived through our sensory organs (touched, seen, smelled, etc.) – whereas the signified constitutes the sign's intelligible component. The 'classic' Saussurean example for the dyadic model of the sign is the word 'tree' (written or spoken) which, in an English-speaker's mind, commonly evokes the concept of a green-leaved, wooden plant with an elongated stem, though the concept does, of course, evince individual variation (see Figure 13.1).

On a related note, Saussure stresses the arbitrariness of the sign – he points to the absence of any intrinsic or natural connection between the signifier and the signified. This is indicated by the simple fact that several

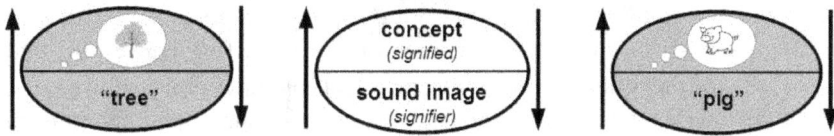

Figure 13.1 Ferdinand de Saussure's dyadic model of the sign; adaptation by the author.

signifiers may relate to one and the same concept while, at the same time, one single signifier may evoke different concepts in different social or historical contexts (polysemy). The words 'pig', '*domuz*', '*khinzīr*' and '*Schwein*' all evoke the image of a pink-skinned, curly-tailed animal, albeit related to different sign systems (English, Turkish, Arabic, German). However, the word 'pig' can also function as a signifier for two very different concepts: though the aforementioned animal represents a symbol of good fortune in a German context, it signifies impurity, sin and apostasy in Islam (see Figure 13.2). However, the principle of the sign's arbitrariness does not mean that 'the relation between a signifier and a signified is a matter of individual choice; if it were, then communication would become impossible' (Chandler 2007: 27). In fact, arbitrariness is limited by conventionality, which leaves us with the task of identifying the dominant and deviant readings of a sign within a particular context.

In his *Course in General Linguistics* Saussure also famously differentiated between *langue* and *parole*. *Langue* in Saussurean linguistic theory encompasses the structural components of language – its grammatical rules and stylistic conventions – whereas *parole* refers to its individual usage. For clarifying this distinction, Saussure resorted to bringing language in comparison to chess. Chess, he argued, relies on a set of rules that have been 'fixed once and for all' (Saussure 2013: 102), wherefore whoever wants to play the game has to conform to these rules. If the number of chess pieces is diminished or increased or if their position on the board is changed, this profoundly affects the 'grammar' of the game (ibid. 25). Language functions accordingly. That is, *parole* operates only upon *langue*. Saussure's opinion that *langue* precedes and thus determines *parole* brings us back to the conventionality of the sign.

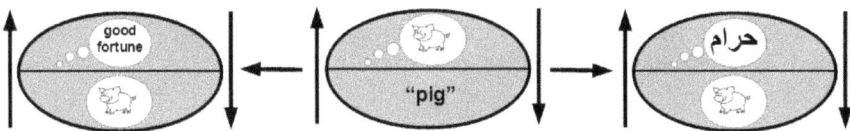

Figure 13.2 First-order and second-order meaning of the sign; adapted by the author from Roland Barthes.

Today, this position is however contested insofar as it ignores the transformative impact everyday practices can have on (pre-)existing conventions and rules. Even the rules of a game can be changed if players agree to do so.

The distinction between *langue* and *parole* has long found its way into various, non-linguistic fields of research. French (post-)structuralism and British cultural studies have equally made use of Saussure's ideas, thereby not only following Saussure's main concern – the study of linguistic rules – but also the question of how 'ordinary people' put these rules into practice. In line with its broadening usage in various semiotic fields, *langue* can thus be defined as the rules and conventions of a semiotic system, whereas *parole* relates to how individuals put these rules and conventions into practice. It is this broader understanding of the Saussurean idea that has importance for Islamic studies. Conceptualising dominant religious norms and conventions as *langue* and as *parole* the way 'ordinary believers' put these rules and norms in everyday life into practice, introduces a fresh perspective to the study of Islam, especially as far as the semiotics of Islam in everyday life are concerned.

'Ordinary believers' generate a variety of signs that are meant to signify an Islamic way of life. These signs manifest in particular gestures, objects, verbal expressions, or behavioural practices, all of which are meant to fulfil a person's religious duties toward God. Since Muslims have always interpreted religious sources differently, different rules and conventions have evolved and circulated, on the basis of which believers conduct (sometimes only slightly) different religious practices. Islamic representations in everyday life, therefore, are by no means coherent. They might indeed point toward different ideological concepts. Although daily prayers are commonly acknowledged to represent a religious duty, Sunni and Shiite practices of prayer differ from one another. Sunni Muslims, for instance, fold their arms during prayer, whereas Shiite Muslims usually position their arms at their sides. Both practices signify Muslimness. Yet, they also represent different ideological concepts and a general lack of consensus among Muslims that is often accompanied by acts of discrimination and mutual stigmatisation. Ideological power struggles often manifest in ordinary signs, which is also what makes semiotic analysis so important. The fact that anything (!) can be seen as a sign makes semiotic analysis applicable to almost any 'thing', which, at first, comes along with a considerable problem of methodological arbitrariness. The semiotic approach proposed in this chapter, therefore, needs to be understood as an approach that brings into focus questions of ideology and power, thereby clarifying the overall research interest.

THE POLITICS OF WINE AND 'BUTTER'

Saussure's dyadic model of the sign was prominently adapted by the French cultural critic and literary theorist Roland Barthes in a theoretical essay entitled 'Myth Today' (Barthes 2009 [1957]). Myth Today was intended to provide an analytical underpinning for a series of monthly essays previously written by Barthes for the French magazine *Les Lettres Nouvelles*. Barthes' stated aim was to uncover the ideological abuse of modern-day myths as represented in post-war French consumer culture (Barthes 2009 [1957]: xix). These myths present themselves as universal, unquestionable, and even timeless, but Barthes exposed their historically specific and ideologically coloured character (Allen 2003: 34). In order to reveal the ideological meaning of myth, Barthes modified Saussure's original model of the sign by differentiating between first-order meanings (denotation) and second-order meanings (connotation). Once again, this can be readily illustrated with reference to the example of the word 'pig'. The first-order, denotative (or 'literal') meaning of the signifier 'pig' evokes the image of a particular species whose living representatives we may have encountered in the physical world. It is the second-order, connotative meaning that Barthes describes as a myth: a 'pig' as signifying 'good fortune' or, conversely, 'sin' and 'impurity' as related to dominant dietary rules that, in Islamic tradition, are based on the dualism of *ḥalāl* ('what is permitted') and *ḥarām* ('what is forbidden') (see Figure 13.2). Both concepts are presented as natural, unquestionable, and timeless, and yet Barthes shows that they assume only a temporary meaning in a particular context.

In his 'mythologies of the month', Barthes addressed such mundane topics as 'The World of Wrestling', 'Soap-powders and Detergents', 'Toys', 'Striptease' or 'The New Citroën'. In 'Wine and Milk', he elaborated on the role of wine in French society. The meaning of wine, as Barthes stressed, 'does not trouble about contradictions' (Barthes 2009 [1957]: 65): wine quenches thirst; it can be sustenance for the worker, a source of virility for the intellectual; in winter it keeps you warm, in summer it refreshes; it makes a weak man strong and a silent one talkative; it even possesses philosophical power. French do not drink to get drunk, their leisurely act of drinking is meant to celebrate the pleasures of life and provide temporary equality among those who have come together to enjoy a good glass of wine. Yet, to believe in wine, in the eyes of Barthes, is also a coercive collective act (ibid. 66). It requires people to conform. To abstain from drinking wine would raise questions. The one who abstains would have to explain him or herself and would finally be perceived as an outsider, whereas 'an award of good integration is given to whoever is a practicing wine-drinker' (ibid. 67). Wine in France is part of the reason of state. Ultimately, it signifies Frenchness, which is also the reason why all the various contradictions associated with it can be sustained. This is the way, in which myth functions in modern society. Myth converts wine into the sign of a universal value; in this case, collective French identity (Allen 2003: 36).

Even sixty years after Barthes wrote his essay, wine is still an inherent part of the reason of the French state. In November 2015, Iran President Hassan Rohani was expected to meet his French counterpart Francois Hollande while on a diplomatic mission through Europe. Rohani's trip was, in fact, the first visit of an Iranian head of state to Europe in a decade and, therefore, of high symbolic importance. The meeting of the presidents at the presidential palace in Paris was finally cancelled by the Iranian side on short notice because the French authorities refused to break with the tradition of serving French wine at official state lunches and dinners. The Iranian delegation had requested a *ḥalāl* menu, which without saying goes without alcohol.

The unwillingness to compromise over what appears to be a purely ceremonial issue may seem surprising. Both sides had considerable interest in the meeting. Rohani's trip represented a landmark visit. Only a few months earlier, Iran and the leading world powers, including France, had reached an agreement on Iran's nuclear program. Economic sanctions were about to be lifted and both presidents were hoping to re-establish business relations between their countries. Why would both statesmen risk tensions over the presence or absence of a glass of wine? A closer look reveals the ideological dimension of the situation. Neither Hollande nor Rohani would have been able to ignore the significance of this 'wine-related' incident without putting their Frenchness or respectively Muslimness publicly at risk. Banning wine from the dinner table, from a French perspective, would have meant to symbolically concede that wine is potentially harm- or even sinful. By the same token, the Iranian delegation's acceptance of wine would have forced them to symbolically acknowledge the social and cultural value of wine and implicitly put into question the universality of religious doctrines in Islam. Concessions to the cultural demands of the other may have furthermore be read as a sign of weakness, the admittance to the moral superiority of the other, and a personal lack of ideological commitment. Wine is a modern day myth insofar as it represents purportedly universal, timeless values that turn out to be rather volatile in nature or, at least, valid only in a specific historical environment.

Wine and Frenchness were also subject of French band Zebda's music video 'Je Crois Que Ça Va Pas Être Possible' ('I don't think that will be possible') released in 1998. Zebda, which means 'butter' in Arabic, is a reappropriated derogatory term that goes back to the word *beur*, an allegory of the French word for butter (*beurre*). *Beur* is a reversal of the syllables of the word *Arabe* and used to designate French citizens of Arab descent. Zebda vocalists Mouss Amokrane, Akim Amokrane, and Majyd Cherfi are all French citizens of Maghrebian descent. They are well known for their political activism and public criticism of French politicians, especially as far as everyday racism and the unequal treatment of immigrants is concerned. In their song 'Le Bruit et L'Odeur' ('The Noise and the Smell') they prominently criticised later French president Jaques Chirac for his racist remarks on immigrants while he was still the mayor of Paris. 'Je Crois Que Ça Va Pas Être Possible' also complains about everyday discrimination and the feeling of being rejected by French society. The song's angry undertone can be interpreted as a direct reference to the founding principles of the French nation: *liberté, égalité, fraternité*. Zebda apparently seeks to reveal these as a myth because not all Frenchmen and – women are being treated equally in a brotherly (or sisterly) manner.

Semiotic analysis, at least as far as wine and Frenchness in this example is concerned, has to focus on visual aspects rather than words. Zebda's video clip is replete with visual representations of Frenchness. It appears as though the artistic director(s) of the video intended to represent all mythologies of French identity at one and the same time. The scenery depicts an ethnically mixed group of different age (including the members of Zebda) gathered around a long table overflowing with food and situated in front of a beautiful, old country house. The summer sun is shining and red wine is served and consumed throughout the entire clip. The French ideal of joyful country life finds expression in the mythical theme of everyone coming together over food and a bottle of red wine, enjoying themselves and each other's company. This image of French authenticity is further added by the figure of an old man wearing a *casquette*, a little blond girl hugging a piglet, and a group of children playing in and around an old Renault 4L (the French counterpart to Germany's Volkswagen Beetle), which is another symbolic icon of post-World War II Frenchness. Detached from the song's lyrics, the message of *liberté, égalité, fraternité* would certainly go unchallenged. It is only the contradictory message of the visual and the verbal that reveals the ideological abuse inherent to these concepts. Even those who conform to the requirements of French authenticity are still denied to participate and benefit from the nation's exalted ideals.

Although we do not learn anything about the religious identities of the protagonists of the music video, the viewer might assume that, at least, some of them are to be considered Muslim because of their Maghrebian descent, which commonly signifies Muslimness in French society. This change of perspective makes us move from reflecting about mythologies of Frenchness to thinking about mythologies of Islam. What does it mean to see a Muslim drinking wine in a pre-arranged music video? Does it say that even a Muslim who concedes to drinking wine is not accepted as an equal French citizen? Would a Muslim viewer decode the message of the video clip as suggested above or would he or she read it as a deviant act of un-Islamic behaviour and an unnecessary concession to French lifestyle practices that goes against the rules laid out by God? And why does a supposedly Muslim band present a little piglet in such a positive, socially acceptable way? We might spin these thoughts further and further without making much of a point. What appears necessary to demonstrate here is that particular, supposedly inconspicuous signs – i.e. their signifiers and the abstract concepts they imply (signified) – deliver ideological messages that might function as a source of conflict or power struggle. Semiotics may be the most suitable tool to uncover the various layers of ideological meaning that otherwise might go unnoticed.

THE SEMIOTICS OF THE KORAN

The Koran is Islam's sacred book. According to Islamic belief, it holds the divine revelation sent to mankind through God's own messenger, the Prophet Mohamed. The Koran, in the Islamic faith, thus represents the unaltered word of God delivered in Arabic and conveyed into a written text shortly after Mohamed's death in 632 CE. The Muslim believer, at all times and in all places, faces the task to read and interpret the Koranic text and align his or her life with God's will accordingly. Islamic scholars commonly agree, however, that the divine message as represented in the Koran is, by no means, always explicitly clear. For this reason, the question of how to extract the true meaning of God's words has pre-occupied Islamic scholars ever since the Koran was revealed. Theological attempts to define universally valid principles of Koranic exegesis have yielded a set of dominant, though not uncontested, rules and conventions as to how the Koranic text should be interpreted. Despite these attempts, Koranic exegesis has seen considerable variation and change (Abdullah 2008: 194; Berger 2010: 9).

Speaking in semiotic terms, the Koran can be seen as a system of signs that operates on the basis of common semiotic concepts (signifier/signified, *langue/parole*, etc.). Applying the principles of semiotics to the Koran undoubtedly poses a certain challenge to religious belief. A religious position that assumes the existence of divine truth must also assume that meaning lies in the Koran itself. 'Truth', in this line of argument, is not constructed through human intervention as the result of a process of decoding, but directly inserted by God himself. The Koran thus only needs to be read in the right way to reveal God's intended message to mankind. From a perspective of faith, the meaning of the Koran thus cannot be arbitrary. If the Koran is the genuine, unaltered word of God, then all signs in the Koran are God-given as well. The believer necessarily needs to assume an intrinsic, inevitable relationship between the signifier (a single word or sequence of words in the Koran) and the signified (God's message). This idea of predetermined, divine meaning or, differently speaking, of a divine connection between the signifier and the signified runs contrary to Saussure's argument of the arbitrariness of the sign, which precludes the existence of intrinsic, universal meaning. A semiotic perspective on the Koran must, therefore, assume that it is human beings who create and attach meaning to the Koran and the written signs it consists of. It is the process of decoding which is of main interest here because it determines how particular meanings evolve, change and take effect on people's daily lives.

The process of decoding, as commonly agreed on in semiotics, is determined by conventionality. Conventionality constrains the arbitrary nature of the sign given that communication necessarily follows certain conventions that have been agreed upon or learned beforehand. If the relation between a signifier and a signified were a matter of individual choice, communication would be impossible (Chandler 2007: 27). The intelligibility of a sign system is thus based on shared conventionality (Fry 2012: 106). In a similar way, the believer cannot arbitrarily attach meaning to a given signifier in the Koran. The reading of the Koran is conventional as well. It depends upon certain rules and conventions that Islamic scholars have developed and sought to standardise in a long process of theological negotiation. Over time, different schools of Koranic exegesis (*tafsīr*) have evolved out of a myriad of theological schools and traditions. Exegetical variation is not only characterised by the general Sunni-Shia divide but also linked to different schools of theological thought within Islam's two major denominations as well as the intellectual ways of rather small denominational groups such as, for instance, the Ahmadiyya Muslim Jamaat or the so-called Fethullah Gülen movement which follow their own line of exegesis (see Albayrak 2010). Sectarian incoherences have certainly contributed to making the field of Koranic exegesis a source of theological and political conflict (Abdul-Raof 2010: 13–14). The question of how to authoritatively interpret the Koran is therefore not only a matter of complex theological debate but also of ideological contestation as related to the political situation an Islamic scholar lives in.

For the purpose of exemplifying the relevance of theological conventions for the interpretation of the Koran, this chapter mainly draws on Abdullah Saeed's writings on individual reasoning and contextual interpretation of the Koran (2006, 2008) and Hussein Abdul-Raof's comprehensive work on *Schools of Qur'anic Exegesis* (2010). Broadly speaking, the exegesis of the Koran (*tafsīr*) is structured by the overriding polarity of tradition-based and reason-based exegesis. Tradition-based exegesis (*tafsīr bi-l-ma'thūr*), which represents today's dominant approach to the interpretation of the Koran, interprets the text either by referencing to the Koran itself, the tradition of the life of the Prophet Mohamed (*hadīth*), or the eyewitness reports of the Prophet's 'companions' (*ṣaḥāba*) that provides information on what the prophet said and did. Tradition-based approaches thereby clearly restrict independent reasoning. Reason-based exegesis (*tafsīr bi-l-ra'y*), in contrast, does not only consider the aforementioned sources of tradition-based exegesis, but also allows independent rational reasoning as based on linguistic analysis, metaphorical reading, allegorical interpretation, and the opinion of other Islamic scholars (Saeed 2008: 178–82). It is this reason-based approach to exegesis, which comes closest to a (Barthean) semiotic perspective.

One of the many principles commonly mentioned when it comes to the exegesis of the Koran is the dichotomy between literal (*ḥaqīqī*) and metaphorical (*majāzī*) meaning. While dominant, tradition-based exegesis gives priority to a non-allegorical, literal, denotative *ḥaqīqī* meaning, reason-based exegesis preferably adopts an allegorical, non-literal, connotative stance of interpretation (Saeed 2008: 184, Abdul-Raof 2010: 71, 77). The *ḥaqīqī–majāzī* dichotomy reveals an ideological rift between Islamic scholars who claim that the literal meaning of Koranic signifiers is always clear and those who argue that some texts can only be understood by exposing the metaphorical meaning of God's will. Abdullah Saeed, in this connection, refers to the example of God's 'hands' in the Koran. He argues that most theologians find it inappropriate to attach human attributes ('hands') to God, wherefore a non-literal, metaphorical meaning – 'hands' as signifying the 'power' of God – appears preferable (Saeed 2008: 184). This exegetical distinction between literal and non-literal, metaphorical meaning of the Koran at first appears to correspond to Barthes' idea of first-order meaning (denotation) and second-order meaning (connotation). What distinguishes these exegetical approaches from Barthean semiotics, however, is the absence of what Barthes has described as 'myth.' Myths, according to Barthes, are second-order meanings that shape our perception of reality, evoke further images and narratives in our minds, and impose upon us the belief that something goes-without-saying. For the purpose of better understanding the difference between both approaches, the following section of this chapter will draw on the example of female veiling in Islam. The practice of Islamic veiling will then be related to the semiotics of Islamic fashion in order to point out the volatility of religious interpretations.

MAKING SENSE OF ISLAMIC VEILING

The practice of women's veiling in Islam commonly draws on sura 24, verse 31. Mohammad Abdel Haleem's translation of the respective verse reads as follows:

> And tell the believing women that they should lower their eyes, guard their private parts [*furūj*], and not display their charms [*zinā'*] beyond what (it is acceptable) to reveal; they should draw their coverings [khumur] over their necklines [*juyūb*] and not reveal their charms [*zinā'*] except to their husbands, or their fathers, or ...

The dominant reading among Islamic scholars sees these words as a command from God to the believing women to veil themselves in public. From a semiotic perspective, this assertion necessarily triggers a search for signifiers in the text or, differently speaking, the question: What are the signifiers Islamic scholars assume to command veiling in Islam (signified)? Looking at which words are comprehensively discussed among Islam's most respected commentators, four signifiers – the Arabic words *furūj*, *khumur*, *juyūb* and *zinā'* – appear to be most relevant in this regard. Islamic exegetes seek to attach the precise meaning to these terms by drawing on the aforementioned principles of Koranic exegesis (the traditions of the Prophet, the reports of the Prophet's companions, etc.). In doing so, they also address a series of questions that need to be answered when it comes to the practice of veiling in everyday life: What are the 'private parts' (*furūj*) of the female body that God commands to be concealed in public? What type of clothing is a *khimār* (singular of *khumur*)? What are a woman's *jayb* (singular of *juyūb*) and *zinā'*? In other words, what is the 'literal', first-order meaning of God's words here? Furthermore, the exact meanings of 'to guard' or 'to reveal' need to be explored before God's command can be put into practice.

On the one hand, *zinā'* is commonly interpreted as a woman's adornment in terms of jewellery, necklaces, rings and other decorative items meant to adorn the female body; on the other hand, it is decoded in metaphorical terms as female charms in general. The signified therefore either takes a literal, denotative meaning that refers to physical objects of adornment or a non-literal, metaphorical meaning that evokes a completely abstract concept of male-female relationship. In reference to the aforequoted verse, Muhammad ibn Jarīr al-Tabarī (839–923 CE), one of the most influential exegetes of the Koran, distinguishes two categories of *zinā'*: 'apparent adornment', which is what is appropriate to reveal, and 'hidden adornment', which refers to what has to be concealed. In al-Tabarī's opinion, 'hidden adornment' comprises anklets, bracelets, earrings, and necklaces, meaning that those parts of the female body upon which these items are worn have to be concealed; 'apparent adornment' is an exemption that only relates to a woman's face and hands and the decorations worn upon them (jewellery, rings, henna, etc.). Prominent Shiite exegete Muhammad Husayn ('Allameh') Tabataba'i (1903–81 CE) agrees with al-Tabarī not only on the face-and-hands opinion but also on the conclusion that *zinā'* refers to those parts of the female body on which jewellery is commonly worn; a woman is therefore permitted to wear jewellery, she has yet to conceal the respective parts of her body in public. Only a minority view among Islamic scholars comes to the conclusion that even the face and the hands have to be concealed, in case a woman wears adornment on these parts of her body (Hasan 2013: 67). What appears yet to be widely common is the use of analogy in terms of understanding *zinā'* as female charms, wherefore the concept thus has to be applied to whatever has a charming effect on men.

Even the allegedly easy to decode term *khimār* causes dissent among Islamic scholars and believers. *Khimār* apparently stands for a particular form of garment that ought to be drawn over a woman's *jayb* – another critical term, which in the commentaries, is either explained as the neckline of a woman's dress, cleavage, or chest and ribs. From a historical perspective, it is impossible to determine what a particular form of garment, which in seventh-century Western-Arabia was commonly called '*khimār*', typically looked like. What type(s) of garment did Muhammad's contemporaries refer to when they spoke of '*khimār*'? What kind of fabric was it made of? What was its exact form and colour? Which parts of the (female) body did it actually cover? Did it cover a woman's head, face, and eyes?

This demonstrates that even a mundane piece of clothing such as the *khimār* cannot simply be reproduced in everyday life in an allegedly 'literal', denotative way. Even in this case, it is the process of decoding grounded in particular rules and conventions that attaches meaning to a single signifier in the Koran. Based on the predominant face-and-hands opinion, form and colour of the *khimār* apparently do not have key priority for Islamic scholars. The question of which parts of the body ought to be concealed dominates the discussion. Accordingly, Ismail Ibn Kathīr's (1300–73 CE) exegesis of the Koran states that the *khimār* is a garment that covers a woman's head, neck, ear, and chest. The dominance of this opinion goes so far that Al-Azhar University's official translation of the Koran translates *khimār* with 'headscarf', even though 'head' is not explicitly mentioned in the text itself. This stands in sharp contrast to some contemporary interpretations that seek to contest the hegemony of exegetical tradition. Some scholars hold the opinion that veiling should be seen as an interpretation of the Koran (by predominantly male exegetes of the past) rather than a command by God, thereby denying the existence of a specific dress code for women in Islam. The question of veiling, in this sense, represents a site of ideological struggle among Muslim believers.

A semiotic reading of the Koran cannot stop at the point of theological exegesis. The process of decoding needs to also examine the complex array of symbolic meanings that emerge when the conventions laid out by Islamic scholars operate in real-life societal contexts. The practice of veiling, for instance, does not simply hold meaning because the Koran prescribes it. It holds meaning because it is an act of communication in everyday life. The veiling of the female body sends a message that is defined in relation to the social environment it operates in. The veiled female body thus becomes a symbol for completely abstract concepts such as chastity (as not to stir sexual desire in men and prevent acts of sin), difference (as to distinguish believing women from non-believing, pagan women), or exceptionalism (as to emphasise the ownership of divine truth). In this sense, veiling operates as a symbolic code that carries connotative meaning. Veiling turns into a myth insofar as it seeks to establish a particular worldview as the dominant norm that goes-without-saying. By claiming the moral superiority of the believing woman over the non-believing woman, by establishing control over gender relations, or by strengthening the collective identity of the believers, veiling signifies dominance and power.

In the meantime, it must not be forgotten that the myth of veiling also comes with a behavioural directive for the believer in everyday life. The principles of veiling as laid out in the exegeses function as a reference point for the believing women who seek to conform to the will of God. Differently speaking, the rules and conventions of veiling as laid out in the *tafsīr* form the 'grammar' of veiling (*langue*) that structures the practice of veiling in everyday life (*parole*). The myth of veiling eventually takes a purely cultural and historical piece of garment (*khimār*) and converts it into a sign of divine value that not only holds symbolic meaning but also affects women's daily routines and choices of clothing. The desire to conform to the divine precepts revealed in the Koran, therefore, has a considerable impact on 'Islamic fashion'.

THE POLITICS OF ISLAMIC FASHION[1]

The semiotics of Islamic fashion are mutable. They change over space and time. In the same way, as individual fashion choices are subject to considerations of whether or not they signify an Islamic way of life, the pertinent question for the fashion designer, who wants to market self-designed products to a pious consumer audience, is whether or not a particular style signifies the divine precepts sufficiently. This challenge requires him or her to ask: what are the signifiers that represent Islam, what is required in order for a female customer to be recognised as 'Muslim', or, conversely, what might make a believing woman appear un-Islamic? It goes without saying that the signifiers for an Islamic way of life are socially and historically determined and lack universal validity: what is considered Islamic or un-Islamic today may not be considered Islamic or un-Islamic tomorrow.

The semiotics of Islamic fashion will be briefly illustrated on the basis of two fashion photographs from the 2013 winter collection of the Turkish textile companies Armine and Aker. Both companies are well known for being part of Turkey's modest fashion industry and frequently place full-page advertisements in Islamic fashion and lifestyle magazines. The photographs (see Figures 13.3 and 13.4) were taken by the author in Istanbul in autumn 2012 – that is, they are drawn from two separate advertisement campaigns in the streets of Istanbul at around the same time. It is important to note that these photographic images are not snapshots of coincidental, real-life encounters with two separate women: the fact that they are part of a fashion advertising campaign has several implications for the semiotic analysis because fashion photographs are staged. They are usually aimed at a previously identified group of consumers and are therefore intended to communicate a particular message that can be easily decoded by this group. For this reason, it can be assumed that the signifiers placed in fashion photography are the result of a conscious decision-making process. In the present case, it can be further assumed that the relevant companies aim to sell their products to a pious consumer audience. The photos reproduced here must, therefore, be seen as depictions of two young fashion models who are intended to represent modest fashion to a particular consumer audience. And the question of how to communicate modesty has, it seems, been answered in slightly different ways by the two companies. Armine and Aker use different signifiers, wherefore it could be argued that the companies aim to communicate different concepts of modesty targeted at different audiences.

The photographic image in the Armine advertisement contains a variety of visual signifiers. Except for her face and hands, the model's body is covered. Her headscarf consists of two layers of cloth, one of which is apparently meant to completely cover the hairline. The slim-cut, long blue coat fits the model tightly without, however, revealing her bodily features too starkly. The decently coloured headscarf is tied under her chin with a specific knot (one that was once popular among followers of the Süleymancı order). Moreover, the model seems to be wearing makeup (eyeliner, lipstick, blusher). Her head is slightly bowed and her gaze is directed not toward the camera, but rather toward a spot that is not perceptible to the observer. The producers of the photograph, it seems, intended to communicate the concepts of innocence and purity through the model's posture.

The fashion model in the Aker advertisement also wears a headscarf. The loosely tied scarf, however, reveals the model's hair and part of her neck, functioning more as a colourful accessory rather than a marker of religious identity and modesty. Since the photograph only depicts the upper body, not much can be said about the model's overgarments. Although she might wear less makeup than the Armine model, however, it is the Aker model's bodily posture and facial expression that might be perceived as highly provocative from a *tesettür* perspective. In an upright posture, the model looks straight toward the camera. Her red lips are slightly parted, while she holds a dark red handbag in her left hand. The level gaze and parted lips signify interaction with the observer and might be even read as an erotic or seductive overture. This impression is further buttressed by the golden ring on the middle finger of the model's left hand. The very fact that she does not wear a ring on the ring finger of the left hand signifies that she is not married, which renders

Figure 13.3 Outdoor advertising for the Armine 2013 Winter Collection; photographed by the author in Eminönü, Istanbul.

her general posture even more deviant. There are certainly more signifiers to be found and discussed here but, for the purpose of this very brief analysis, it is sufficient to highlight the various differences in modest fashion and to highlight the subversive potential regarding the traditional concepts of veiling.

Figure 13.4 Outdoor advertising for the Aker 2013 Winter Collection; photographed by the author in Kabataş, Istanbul.

The photographic images reproduced here do not provide any information on whether the fashion designers, photographers, and marketing managers involved in the Armine and Aker campaigns had been fully (or even partly) aware of the theological debate on Islamic veiling when arranging the specific fashion ensembles. There is also no information on whether they attempted to exactly reproduce the Koranic *khimār* and implement the 'literal', first-order meaning of the divine text or whether they were rather committed to conform to the abstract concepts (second-order meanings) commonly associated with the debate, such as, for instance, female chastity. Turkey's modest fashion industry most likely models its designs on the lived experience and expectations of its customers more than theological discourse. The ideological meaning of Islamic fashion or, differently speaking, the politics of veiling as represented in the aforementioned fashion photographs, only fully comes to light when related to the socio-political context of its production. Turkish Islamist groups, for instance, commonly associate Islamic fashion with the act of 'unveiling', which ultimately implies a loss of faith and religion (see Hecker 2018). Furthermore, Islamic fashion is being associated with a general tendency towards secularisation and the trivialisation of religion in connection with religiously inspired consumption habits. Semiotics, in this sense, enables us to identify Islamic fashion as a site of ideological struggle in which the meaning of Islam is being (re)negotiated.

CONCLUSION

The main purpose of this chapter was to make use of semiotics in Islamic studies and, on a related note, encourage greater awareness for questions of ideology and power. Islamic studies is by no means an essentially descriptive science as often claimed by its critics; even though, as a university discipline, it has not done much to overcome its methodological weaknesses in recent years. In this sense, the present chapter also intends to encourage the usage of 'new' research methods in Islamic studies, especially from the field of social sciences and cultural studies. This appears to be particularly important if Islamic studies seeks further emancipation from other academic disciplines such as Islamic theology, historiography or linguistics.

Semiotics appears to be the most suitable method to uncover the various layers of ideological meaning that often go unnoticed and to better understand how particular meanings happen to become dominant while others don't. Having said this, various power-related questions need to be addressed here as well. We might ask, for instance, how does a particular reading of the Koran emerge and become dominant while others seem to loose importance or disappear? Who has the power to establish a particular reading of the Koran as the commonly accepted norm? And what are the distinct signifiers that mark a particular person, practice, concept or agenda Islamic? These questions are just a few examples in order to illustrate how the semiotic lens has the potential to influence the way we do research in the field of Islamic studies.

NOTE

1. In part, the following paragraphs have been published in an article by the author for *Sociology of Islam* 6 (2018). 'Islam. The Meaning of Style' is a direct reference to Dick Hebdige's famous book *Subculture. The Meaning of Style* and studies the subversive implications of Turkey's modest fashion industry.

BIBLIOGRAPHY

Abdel Haleem, M. A. S., *The Qur'an*, English translation and parallel Arabic text (Oxford: Oxford University Press, 2010).

Abdullah, Saeed, *The Qur'an. An Introduction* (London and New York: Routledge, 2008).

Abdul-Raof, Hussein *Schools of Qur'anic Exegesis. Genesis and Development* (London and New York: Routledge, 2010).

Albayrak, Ismail, *Fethullah Gülen Hocaefendi'nin Tefsir Anlayışı* (Istanbul: Nil Yayınları, 2010).

Allen, Graham, *Roland Barthes* (London and New York: Routledge, 2004).

Barthes, Roland, *Image, Music, Text* (London: Fontana Press, 1977).

Barthes, Roland, *Mythologies* (London: Vintage Books, 2009 [1957].

Berger, Lutz, *Islamische Theologie* (Vienna: Facultas.wuv, 2010).

Chandler, Daniel, *Semiotics* (London and New York: Routledge, 2007).

Fry, Paul H., *Theory of Literature* (New Haven: Yale University Press, 2012).

Hall, Stuart, 'The Work of Representation', in *Representation. Cultural Representations and Signifying Practices*, Stuart Hall (ed.) (London: SAGE Publications, 1997), pp. 15–74.

Hasan, Usama, 'The Veil: Between Tradition and Reason, Culture and Context', in *Islam and the Veil. Theoretical and Regional Contexts*, Gabriel, Theodore and Rabiha Hannan (eds) (London and New York: Bloomsbury, 2013), pp. 65–80.

Hecker, Pierre, 'Islam: The Meaning of Style', *Sociology of Islam*, 6 (Leiden: Brill, 2018), pp. 7–28.

Saussure, Ferdinand de, *Course in General Linguistics* (trans. and annotated by Roy Harris) (London and New York: Bloomsbury, 2013).

Notes on Contributors

İdil Akıncı is a Teaching and Research Fellow at the University of Edinburgh, Department of Islamic and Middle Eastern Studies and Sociology. Her research expertise centres on migration and citizenship, with a focus on the Arab Gulf States. She holds a PhD in Migration Studies from the University of Sussex, where she explored the everyday experiences of national identity and citizenship of young Arab communities and Emirati citizens in Dubai. She has published her work in journals on migration studies such as *Journal of Ethnic and Migration Studies*, and *Journal of Ethnic and Racial Studies*. She is currently working on her post-doctoral research, where she investigates how Syrians born and raised in the Arabian Gulf States develop new strategies to acquire alternative citizenship from Western European countries, taking into consideration the ripple effects of the political situation present in Syria and the ramifications of such upon their relationship to citizenship and future plans, within the Gulf and Europe.

Ana Almuedo-Castillo holds a PhD in Political Sciences at the Institute of Arab and Islamic Studies at the University of Exeter, United Kingdom. She is currently working as the Coordinator of the Department of Social Inclusion at the Spanish Commission for the Aid of Refugees (CEAR) in Seville, Spain. Dr Almuedo-Castillo has worked and researched in the Middle East, especially in Lebanon. Her PhD thesis investigates the issue of civil marriage in Lebanon, social movements and the construction of political identities.

Veronica Buffon is a social and medical anthropologist (Milan-Bicocca University, Doha Institute for Graduate Studies and, currently, University of Exeter), and member of the ANPIA (Associazione Nazionale Professionale

Italiana di Antropologia). Her most recent postdoctoral research examines Syrian asylum seekers' reception in the European periphery (Italy and Greece) and the reconfiguration of Syrian families. She has been conducting ethnographic research in Morocco, Italy, Turkey and in the Kurdish regions. She has published on Kurdish women, refugees and asylum seekers in Italy.

Lorraine Charles is a Research Associate at the Centre for Business Research, University of Cambridge and Co-Lead of the Digital Skills and Digital Work Programme at the Centre for the Study of Global Human Movement, University of Cambridge. She is also Project Affiliate for Refugeework.net, a research project at the University of Edinburgh. She is a social entrepreneur, Co-Founder, and Executive Director of Na'amal, which provides support for refugees and other vulnerable populations to access dignified livelihoods, particularly remote work, via soft skills training, mentorship, and links to the private sector. She has worked as a consultant with NGOs, INGOs, UN agencies, and government entities as well as in academia and the private sector. Her research focuses on migration and refugees, education, and livelihoods in the Middle East with a particular focus on digital livelihoods. She has also worked on issues related to the Syrian crisis since 2011.

Irene Costantini is adjunct professor at the University of Bologna (Department of Political and Social Sciences) and post-doctoral fellow at the University of Naples, l'Orientale (Department of Human and Social Science). She holds a PhD from the University of Trento (School of International Studies). Prior to her current position, she worked as a Research Fellow at the University of York (UK) and at the Middle East Research Institute (Erbil, Iraq). Her research interests include the politics of international interventions in conflict-affected contexts and post-conflict transition, focusing on the Middle East and North Africa region. She has been published in various academic journals, including *International Peacekeeping*, *Ethnicities*, *Ethnopolitics*, and *International Spectator*. She is the author of *Statebuilding in the Middle East and North Africa: The Aftermath of Regime Change* (2018).

Hannah Scott Deuchar is a doctoral candidate in Arabic Literature at New York University. Her work has been published in *Alif: Journal of Comparative Poetics and Comparative Literature Studies*, and her dissertation asks how nineteenth-century Arabic language and literary 'reform' movements in Egypt were shaped by the legal and economic transformations that accompanied the expansion of imperial capitalism.

Giorgia Ferrari is a lecturer in Arabic at the Institute of Arabic and Islamic Studies (IAIS) at the University of Exeter, where she teaches Arabic at all language levels and she is currently leading the restructuring of the teaching materials and syllabi for beginner levels. Giorgia is the Year Abroad Coordinator, setting the curricula for IAIS students who spend a year in Jordan. Giorgia holds a PhD in Arabic Applied Linguistics and her research focuses on vocabulary acquisition, language awareness and on the development of language skills in multiple Arabic language varieties. She also supervises undergraduate research projects carried out by IAIS students in the Middle East.

Pierre Hecker is a senior researcher and lecturer at the Centre for Near and Middle Eastern Studies at Philipps-University Marburg, Germany. He is the author of the book *Turkish Metal. Music, Meaning, and Morality in a Muslim Society* (2012; 2016). His recent publications include 'Islam. The Meaning of Style' (*Sociology of Islam* 2018) and 'The "Arab Spring" and the End of Turkish Democracy' (2019). He is the head of the research group '"Ne mutlu ateistim diyene" Atheism and the Politics of Culture in Contemporary Turkey' funded by Stiftung Mercator and co-editor of the forthcoming volume *The Politics of Culture in 'New Turkey'*.

Richard McNeil-Willson is a Research Associate at the Robert Schuman Centre for Advanced Studies, European University Institute, in Florence. He works primarily on the BRaVE Project, a European Commission project which explores issues of polarisation and counter-extremism in Europe. He also works directly with the EU Commission, advising on the development of European Union Member State policy towards the Far Right, and is an International Advisor for the CHAMPIONs project on polarisation in Central and Eastern Europe, at the Peace Action Training and Research Institute of Romania (PATRIR), Cluj-Napoca, Romania. Richard has a PhD from the Institute of Arab and Islamic Studies, University of Exeter, as an Economic and Social Research Council (ESRC) scholar, exploring the impact of counter-extremism on Islamic activism. He holds additional degrees from the universities of Edinburgh, Durham and Exeter (UK) and visiting fellowships at the University of Aarhus (Denmark) and Scuola Normale Superiore (Italy).

Alex Mahoudeau is a Postdoctoral Fellow at the Urban Futures Laboratory at Eastern Paris Federal University where he has been working alongside the Justice, Space, Discriminations, Inequalities (JEDI) project since 2018. His work focuses primarily on the geographies of social movements and processes of ambiguous politicisation. He has been a fellow researcher with the French Institute of the Near East (Ifpo), and holds a PhD in Political Science from King's College London's Department of Middle Eastern Studies. Between 2013 and 2017, Alex was a PhD student, working on the spatial dimension of mobilisations in the Palestinian camps of Beirut. Since then, he has been working on the appropriation of space in processes of remobilisation of Syrian refugees in Paris and been a coordinator of the French Sociological Association's thematic network on social movements.

Sansom Milton is a Senior Research Fellow at the Center for Conflict and Humanitarian Studies (Doha, Qatar). He holds a PhD in Post-war Recovery Studies from the University of York. Prior to his current position, he worked as a Research Fellow at the Post-war Reconstruction and Development Unit at the University of York. His research interests lie in post-conflict recovery, humanitarian policy, conflict analysis, conflict mediation and in particular the role of higher education in conflict-affected societies. His research has been published in journals including *Disasters*, *Journal of Intervention and Statebuilding*, *Higher Education*, and *International Journal of Educational Development*. His book *Higher Education and Post-Conflict Recovery* was published in 2018.

Yves Mirman is a research associate at Sciences Po Aix-en-Provence (France), teaching general political sociology. He has a PhD from Aix-Marseille University (research centre CHERPA), and was fellow researcher with the French Institute for Near East (IFPO), at Beirut (Lebanon), with a teaching position at University Lumière Lyon 2. He worked on a comparison between the cause of the political detainees in contemporary Jordan society (2012–13) and the cause of the missing persons of Lebanese civil war and occupations (2011–18) based on various long term fieldwork with qualitative investigations. His thesis is entitled 'Commitments shaped by the test of time. The cause of the disappeared in Lebanon (2011–2018)'. He is currently publishing on issues such as post-conflict memory studies, the sociology of collective action, and the judicialisation of politics in Middle-East societies.

Ilan Pappé is a professor with the Institute of Arab and Islamic Studies at the University of Exeter. He founded and directed the Academic Institute for Peace in Givat Haviva, Israel, between 1992 and 2000 and was the Chair of the Emil Tuma Institute for Palestine Studies in Haifa between 2000 and 2006. Professor Pappé was a senior lecturer in the department of Middle Eastern History and the Department of Political Science in Haifa University, Israel, between 1984 and 2006. He was appointed as Chair in the Department of History in the Cornwall Campus, 2007–9. His research focuses on the modern Middle East and in particular the history of Israel and Palestine. He has also written on multiculturalism, critical discourse analysis, and on power and knowledge in general.

Sophie Richter-Devroe is Associate Professor in the Women, Society and Development Programme at Hamad Bin Khalifa University, Qatar, and an Honorary Fellow at the European Centre for Palestine Studies at the University of Exeter, UK. Sophie's broad research interests are in the field of everyday politics and women's activism in the Middle East. Her research is based on long-term ethnographic fieldwork in Palestine, Lebanon, Jordan and Greece. She has done research and published work on Palestinian and Iranian women's activism, Palestinian refugees, Palestinian cultural production, Syrian refugees, and the Naqab Bedouin. She is the author of *Women's Political Activism in Palestine: Peacebuilding, Resistance and Survival* (2018).

Monica Ronchi is a graduate of the Università Cattolica del Sacro Cuore in Milan, Italy, where she obtained a BA in Languages for International Relations. She then obtained an MA in Middle East and Islamic Studies from the University of Exeter with a dissertation on the political institutionalisation of Sheikh Abdessalam Yassine, founder and former leader of the Moroccan al-Adl wa al-Ihsan movement. She was recently awarded a PhD in Middle East Politics with a thesis titled 'Through the Settler's Eye: A Visual History of Indigeneity in French Algeria and Israel/Palestine'. Her research interests include the effects of colonialism in the MENA region and theories related to state-led repression and anti-psychiatry. She was awarded the best postgraduate teacher award from the Students' Guild for the 2014/15 academic year. She is now a social entrepreneur working in the education sector in Europe and the Middle East.

Kenneth H. Schmitt is Visiting Assistant Professor in the Department of Urban Studies and Spatial Practices at Al-Quds Bard College in Abu Dis, Jerusalem. His research interests lie at the intersection of Muslim religious practices and contentious political spaces in addition to the social history of the Middle East and Muslim–Christian relations. He earned his PhD in Arab and Islamic Studies from Exeter University in 2018. His dissertation, titled 'Living Islam in Jerusalem: Faith, Conflict, and the Disruption of Religious Practice', is based on five years of ethnographic research in East Jerusalem (2011–16). His current project, titled 'Gazan Christians: The Social History of a Community on the Precipice', is funded by the Palestinian American Research Center (PARC) and the National Endowment for the Humanities (NEH). He has published in *Jerusalem Quarterly*, *Contemporary Islam*, *Exchange – the Journal of Contemporary Christianities in Context*, as well as contributed chapters with Routledge and Cognella. Schmitt has held visiting fellowships at the Hebrew University of Jerusalem (2015–16) and Yale University (2016–17).

Bethany Shockley is a political scientist who studies public opinion, women in politics, and research methods. She is particularly interested in capturing public opinion related to identity politics and economic reform, often using survey experiments. Her work on the Arab Gulf has been published in Comparative Politics, Electoral Studies, and Governance, among others. Currently, she is an Assistant Professor of Political Science at the American University of Sharjah where she teaches courses in comparative politics and research methods.

Index

EU representative:
Easy Access System Europe
Mustamäe tee 50, 10621 Tallinn, Estonia
Gpsr.requests@easproject.com